the watcher and the watched

Bruno M. Cormier M.D.

the watcher
and the watched

 Tundra Books

Cover by Molly Pulver
Printed in the United States.

Published simultaneously in Canada by

Tundra Books of Montreal,
Montreal, Quebec.   H3G 1J6
ISBN 88776-053-8

And in the United States by

Tundra Books of Northern New York
Plattsburgh, N.Y. 12901
ISBN 0-912766-13-1
Library of Congress Card No. 75-2791

To our colleagues at McGill University in Montreal, Canada.

To our colleagues in New York State who worked with us.

To the guards and prisoners at Dannemora who taught us so much.

Table of Contents

Preface

This book is based on papers written about the work of the McGill Clinic in Forensic Psychiatry at the Dannemora State Hospital's Diagnostic and Treatment Center at Clinton Prison between October 1966 and June 1972. The New York staff took over the program when the McGill contract expired.

The McGill Clinic, because of its past work with prisoners, had been invited to submit a program to the New York State Department of Correctional Services. We did this and were then contracted to put it into effect in cooperation with that office. The aim of the program was "to promote the greatest benefits to the interests of science, correction, education and the general public ..." The six-year contract is probably the only one where a state correctional service and a university have worked so closely together.

The McGill Clinic thanks Paul D. McGinnis, formerly Commissioner of Correction of New York State; John Cain, formerly Deputy Commissioner of Correction; Russell G. Oswald, formerly Chairman of the State Board of Parole and later Commissioner of Correction (now retired); and Peter Preiser, then Executive Director of the Governor's Special Committee, later Commissioner of Probation and until recently Commissioner of Correctional Services, for having invited McGill University to open this Center in cooperation with New York State.

The Clinic also thanks Dr. Ludwig Fink, first Director of the Center, who was present at all of the discussions prior to opening the Center in October, 1966; Dr. Paul Agnew, Director of Dannemora State Hospital; Merle F. Cooper, Administrator of the Center; and Dr. Carlton D. Marshall, Clinical Coordinator, who held office while we were associated with the Center.

Gratitude must also be expressed to the Donner Canadian Foundation whose generous financial support to the Clinic during the three-year period from 1972-1974 made it possible for us to put together much of our writing. This support also provided the Clinic with an opportunity to broaden its horizons.

These papers, several of which have been published, were written by members of the McGill staff working in the program, though one paper was written by Professor John T. Goldthwait of New York University College of Arts & Science at Plattsburgh. We are pleased that Professor Goldthwait agreed to have his paper included in this book. The papers were edited in an attempt to remove repetition but some, inevitably, remains. Pseudonyms (in italics) are used to designate the inmates; behind each name is an emotional reality lived not only by one man but by many.

A list of titles with authors and places of publication, where applicable, is added for those readers who may wish to consult original texts. We gratefully acknowledge the participation of the different authors: Colin C.J. Angliker, Paul Boulanger, Ingrid Cooper, Bruno M. Cormier, Abraham Ferstman, Harold Finkler, Lydia Keitner, Miriam Kennedy, Betty Malamud, Guyon Mersereau, Susan M. Waters, Paul J. Williams and Joshua Zambrowsky. We also wish to thank Lorna Graham for her assistance in preparing this book for publication.

It is hoped that the stylistic shortcomings arising from the attempt to co-ordinate writings from so many sources into a cohesive book will be offset by the information reported.

Montreal, Quebec, Canada   Bruno M. Cormier, M.D.
August 15, 1975

Introduction—
The Watcher and the Watched

When freedom is lost, everybody watches everybody.

  Persistent offenders are men in search of good objects. The under privileged state in which they developed openly invites them to seize what they have been denied. Immersed from childhood in a depressed and depressing environment, they are fated to encounter bad objects. The absence of good objects elicits a response, and persistent offenders elect not to withdraw, but to fight. This fight, in the early stages, is not considered to be retaliation but simply the means to obtain denied objects.

  When society imprisons a persistent offender it rightly protects itself, but it also closes a door. The persistent offender is shut away from his battleground, society, the source of good objects. Tormented by bad objects inside, unable to obtain good objects outside, he feels persecuted. In return his solution is to persecute.

  Imprisonment is more than a punishment. It creates a new society, the society of the captive. Whereas liberty engenders democratic thinking, captivity produces paranoid thinking. In prison the persistent offender comes to believe that society is his enemy. Although at times he blames specific individuals in his early or pre-prison life, he generally blames "society" and "the whole world ." Consequently the persistent offender will treat any person representing society as a persecutor. The immediate target is, of course, his guards.

  Exposure to paranoid thinking presents the danger of being drawn into it, and this danger becomes very great where groups of men interact. In severe psychotic illness the world

10

can be interpreted through *paranoid thinking*. A paranoid
patient may perceive the world as being malevolent or benevolent;
he may find it hostile and feel justified in retaliating or find it so
kind it has given him special gifts he would like to share with
others. In present psychiatry this latter aspect of paranoid
thinking is not given the emphasis it previously held. The
persécuté-persécuteur is a classic example in textbooks of
psychiatry, but is rarely used today.

Paranoid thinking works two ways. The person is
irrational not only about himself, but also about others. He
changes himself and wants to change others. He "acts out" in
self-defense. He wants to change the world because of either
pathological hostility or kindness. Thus in treating him it is
necessary to think not only of his protection but of protecting
those in contact with him.

In order to protect himself, the therapist sometimes uses
the same mechanism used by the paranoid patient. In not
allowing himself to be irrationally persecuted, the therapist
becomes what may be called the "rational persecutor." The
very treatment of a paranoid patient often implies that some
action is in fact taken which reinforces his feeling that he is
being persecuted. By being put in a position where he is seen
as the persecutor, the therapist is given an experience of what
the patient himself feels.

The treatment of the paranoid, more than other types of
patient, gives the therapist an experience comparable, but not
similar in quality, to that of the patient himself. It can even
become similar if the therapist fails to assess properly the
patient's irrational thinking. If this takes place, the therapist
himself becomes entangled. As long as the therapist fails to
recognize that he is taking part in an irrational system of
thought, progress is impossible and the relationship can become
dangerous to both.

From our many years of work in maximum security
institutions, we have observed that a mutual distrust exists
between the guarded and the guards. Persistent offenders may
respect individual guards, yet in general, they are affected by
the paranoid thinking pervading the prison and this supersedes
individual liking. The guard is the "screw," the "hack," the
"dog" (needless to say he is the "dirty"dog, not the friend of
man). In the relationship between the guard and the "con,"
the paranoid aggression that is easily observed erupts frequently.

As already noted, the danger in being exposed to paranoid thinking is that one becomes involved in it. Nowhere is it more necessary to be aware of this danger than in the correctional field. Few individuals in a democratic society are exposed, day after day, year after year, to so much paranoid thinking as are prison guards. They are constantly exposed to persecution. Theirs is perhaps the only profession where the basic challenge is to resist the ever-present temptation to become persecutors. Guards themselves are seldom aware of the danger, and a persecutory response can easily be disguised in the name of authority.

At Dannemora we intended that the forty correctional officers we trained would work in a therapeutic community for the treatment of persistent offenders. In milieu therapy all participants relate to one another and gain insight into their relationships. We felt that the usual teaching methods with lectures, seminars, audio-visual techniques and socio-drama did not promote direct contact between the guard and the offender. We therefore augmented it by following the system used in medical training, where the student learns directly from the patient. We decided that the guards should learn in a similar way from organized interviews with groups of offenders.

Articulate persistent offenders who knew how to express their persecutory feelings were selected. In the past, two of these had taken hostages and attacked prison guards, not in an attempt to escape but merely to retaliate. It was agreed that in interviews both guards and inmates would be permitted to express their feelings fully and freely.

An officer brought up this point: "If some of you are friendly with me, the rest of you feel that we are 'ratting'." This was acknowledged to be true. It was implied however that in such a situation some offenders as well as officers were "rats." Prisoners were watching prisoners as well as guards, and guards were watching guards as well as prisoners.

This became clearer when the second point was brought up, this time by a prisoner. "When an officer is friendly with us most of you feel that he is a softy and a dope." The officers admitted that this too was true. In discussion it became clear that the relationship between guards and prisoners went far beyond mere hostility. In these two solitudes there is, as well as mistrust, a fear of identifying with one another. When a link becomes possible the reaction is to prevent it so as to avoid the danger of attachment to a bad object. It was easy to identify the paranoid retaliation in those who were watched but paranoid feelings in the watchers were covered up and had to be unearthed.

In a community where the guards are required to take a therapeutic role as well as to maintain some minimum security, this basic conflict must be understood and dealt with. If the guards fail to recognize the conflict they are no more able to enter a therapeutic relationship than a psychiatrist or other professional who fails to recognize paranoid thinking and falls victim to it.

When the training period was over and the therapeutic community began to function, the basic conflict between guard and inmate revealed itself. We recognized that this conflict was crucial to understanding prison life and that it needed to be analyzed and re-analyzed. Offenders leave prison but guards remain.

When man loses his liberty he suddenly feels that he was living in paradise when he was free. To be free is not an easy way of life, and it is not experienced as blissful when one is struggling with it; only when freedom is lost is it thought to have been paradise. The other and better side of this coin should be noted too. It means that when freedom is surrendered through passivity and neglect, the impact of the loss may mobilize the forces required to regain it.

Freedom was gained by western civilization only through intellectual effort and physical struggle. When man is free concern for freedom is pushed into the background, but when free men find themselves deprived of freedom, they fight back, and also become, in a sense, persecutors. They feel no alternative but to fight. They may use paranoid energy with the same violence as the aggressor to win. This can be a healthy and useful reaction. For instance, when a country is invaded and conquered, a dictator can establish a regime which might be passively accepted by the majority. But once such a persecutor takes over, he must become the watcher of those he keeps under control. Then an underground resistance develops among those who do not accept persecution so that they in turn become watchers, or persecutors.

Psychopathological formations, especially of a social nature, cannot be studied experimentally. No human individual would wish to establish a dictatorship in order to carry out experiments

13

on the effects of various types of deprivation of liberty. The paranoid thinking vis-à-vis each other of the watcher and the watched must nevertheless be studied.

A penal institution is the only legal institution in a democratic society that deprives man of his liberty. Its legality, however, does not prevent the ill effects on the keepers and the kept. From this reality emerges our duty and responsibility to look closely at what society may regard as a mild punishment (seen in the history of crime and punishment), but which is in fact a dangerous way of life.

Ideally, the specific reaction to deprivation of liberty should be the establishment of a social order in which paranoid thinking is not only prevalent in the sick mind of the dictator and his followers, but becomes a healthy reaction of those who refuse to be persecuted.

Once a persecutor takes over, he must become the watcher of those he keeps under control. What he does not sufficiently realize, in his rather naive omnipotence, is that because of his watching, people in turn become watchers, though concealed and underground. In the loss of freedom, everybody watches everybody.

PART I:
THE THERAPEUTIC COMMUNITY

1.   Little Siberia: The Search for a Better Way

*Loss of freedom is a trauma which leaves no one
untouched though it is differently experienced by
persistent criminals, political prisoners, prisoners
of war, mental patients and "ordinary" citizens.*

Since deprivation of liberty is now considered a punishment
in itself, there is some question as to whether any form of
treatment besides humane custody is possible in penal
institutions.   It is therefore relevant to trace the history of
such deprivation as a form of punishment, the meaning of
liberty in present society, and the psychological effect of its
loss.

Before the deprivation of liberty could become a punishment, it was necessary that freedom be not just a philosophical
or theological concept, but a way of life.   In the eighteenth
century, social and political philosophers such as Rousseau and
Montesquieu contributed much to the liberating ideas that
inspired states to establish regimes where freedom would
become a way of life, a political, social and individual right with
corresponding responsibilities.   First in the eighteenth century,
and then very rapidly afterward, deprivation of liberty came to
replace capital and corporal punishment to the point where
today total or partial deprivation of liberty may soon be the
only form of punishment and now we are searching for alternatives to deprivation of liberty for most offenders.

Passionate debates, like those over the merits of the
Auburn and Pennsylvania systems, are unlikely to occur again.
(39, 40)   Yet neither New York State nor Pennsylvania could
claim full originality for the penal treatment each defended so
strongly, since the ideas and the practices in both systems could
be traced to England and continental Europe.   What was original
in both systems — silent association between several inmates in

one cell during the day and solitude at night, under the Auburn regime; complete isolation and solitude with or without work, under the Quaker Pennsylvania system — was that probably for the first time deprivation of liberty was thought to be reformative in itself, provided certain conditions were met. In 1818, lawmakers were urged to set up a penal system calling for the separation of prisoners and for proof of "the efficacy of solitude on the morals of these unhappy objects." (3)

In 1835, when such a system was considered operative, McElwee described the admission routine of a Pennsylvania institution and added, "In about two weeks they begin to feel all the horrors of solitude . . . Existence has no charms unless witnessed by, or enjoyed with, our fellow men. The convicts *feel* it so. Ennui seizes them, every hour is irksome, and they supplicate for the means of employment with the most abject humility . . . They are also furnished with a Bible, some religious tracts, and occasionally other words, calculated to imbue their minds with moral and religious ideas." (41)

Behind the religious ideas that inspired both systems, the disciplinary regime was harsh, although it is generally acknowledged that Auburn was the harsher of the two. These two systems eventually failed, not because the punishments were cruel but because they were based on the idea that deprivation of liberty was reformative in and by itself. This illusion was soon dispelled despite the fact that the ill effects of extreme deprivation of liberty became apparent at a time when very little was known about mental health and isolation. If the Auburn and Pennsylvania systems were the first to imply that penal treatment could be based on imprisonment by itself, they were also the last. Gradually the problem became one of how *treatment* could be carried out within the framework of the deprivation of liberty.

At first sight it is tempting to compare what has been called "self-government" in the prison system to what is today referred to as *therapeutic community* or *milieu therapy*. The differences are great, but there are a few similarities. Edwin Sutherland gives a sound analysis of the experience of self-government, a system abandoned by 1900. (56) Some attempts at self-government in prison began as early as 1793. However, it was the well-known New York State warden, T.M. Osborne (1859-1926) who shaped the concept and developed the practice which ended with him. (44)

17

W. D. Lane, in an article entitled "Democracy of Law-Breakers" describes self-government in prisons as "simply an application of the educational principle that people learn by doing . . . Its method is to establish on a small scale a society in which he [the prisoner] can form the habits, accustom himself to the responsibilities and gradually acquire the whole-some mental attitudes that make normal life attainable . . . It is an effort to train persons in the art of living in concert . . . The traditional fealty of the lawbreaker is first to himself, and then to his 'pal.' Often this fealty is loyalty to the whole body of prisoners. By its very operation, self-government identifies each inmate with all of his fellow inmates." (37)

This statement clarifies both what self-government and the therapeutic community have in common and how they differ. Loyalty to one's peer group is certainly a basic concept of the therapeutic community. However, the exclusion of a custodial staff, as practiced in Osborne's system of self-government, is a fundamental difference. In their comment on this difference, Barnes and Teeters state: "No keeper or guards were allowed in the shop where discipline was wholly in the hands of the prisoners." Disciplinary measures were decided on by the prisoners themselves "and carried out by the officers of the "prison." (3) Sutherland mentions a number of institutions where self-government was terminated at the request of the prisoners themselves or, as was sometimes the case, "it was voted out unanimously." (56) The weakest point in self-government lies in this last fact. Today it would be unthinkable to establish a therapeutic regime which could be abolished on the whim of the very ones who need it. If a therapeutic community could vote itself out of existence, it would, like self-government, be destroying its own technique of reeducation.

Self-government may have in common with the therapeutic community "loyalty to the whole body of prisoners," but it differs from the concept which requires that prisoners and guards form a living group and all interactions taking place inside the community are exposed and analyzed. If inmate relationships are important, so are relationships among correctional officers and *between* inmates and correctional officers.

The officer in the therapeutic community represents the society which has confined the inmate as well as that part of society which has goodwill toward him. In the name of a liberal and liberating system, the Osborne experience of self-government perpetuated the antagonism between guards and prisoners. Despite the glowing accounts of success where prisoners lived up to their responsibilities, the system was bound to fail. In the self-government experiment it was illusory to believe that persistent offenders could be helped without the participation of society through its agents: administrators, professionals and correctional officers.

The next meaningful step in penal reform came when sociological studies of prisons made us realize that in depriving offenders of their liberty we were not only intentionally punishing them, but were actually promoting a parallel society to our own, a penal society that was a continuation of the criminal milieu outside the prison.

The "prison community" (8) or the "society of captives" (57) as they have been referred to in studies, is the challenge that we must meet if prisons are to become effective treatment centers. Our knowledge of the sources of human behavior and our understanding of the conflicts experienced by persistent offenders are constantly growing. Left to themselves in prison, persistent offenders rapidly reestablish the kind of life they lived on the outside. They organize cliques and in-groups, and soon rebuild a structure in which they reinstate the very emotional states which brought them to prison in the first place.

A fundamental principle of psychotherapy is that people in conflict will reproduce their conflicts in a therapeutic situation, or, for that matter, in any setting. In a therapeutic milieu, however, the difference is that the repetition of conflicts is checked, analyzed, and where possible, undone. This is a basic principle made use of in a therapeutic community: it allows conflicts, symptoms, acting out and affects to show themselves. Treatment, control and security consist in analyzing the components of the symptoms rather than in resorting to punishment to repress behavior and other manifestations which need to be known if treatment is to be attempted. We have reached the stage in prison reform and psychology where we can envisage that treatment can be rationally established provided we take into account the psychology and psychopathology which affect both the prisoner and the staff, that is, "the watched and the watcher."

A persistent offender, punished and repunished by

successive sentences, whether justly or not, continues to confront society with the fact that he has failed to reform. This
is only a minor part of the larger problem for deprivation of
liberty affects the non-criminal and the criminal. Here we
enter into a new field of investigation: the psychology and
psychopathology of freedom and its loss. (11, 1) Not to be
free is to live in a pathological state. Without freedom the
danger of individual and social pathology is great. (19, 21)
Loss of freedom is a trauma which leaves no one untouched
though it is differently experienced by persistent criminals,
political prisoners, prisoners of war, mental patients, and
ordinary citizens.

Deprivation of liberty as a form of punishment is usually
accompanied by depression and regression, the extent of which
is predetermined by the offender's personality. All criminals
do not react in the same way. At the two extremes, the
incidental offender at one end and the persistent criminal at
the other, we notice markedly different responses.

The incidental offender's first reactions to prison are shock
and depression along with psychological regression. As time
goes on he reaches an equilibrium but it is different from that
of the persistent offender's. The incidental offender's reaction
to imprisonment has been compared to that of political
prisoners. The two are similar in not being basically anti-social,
though they differ in how they see themselves. One has failed
society at least once, while the other believes he has fought for
a specific cause. Despite this difference, both feel themselves
to be members of a community to which they long to return. (33)

The reaction of persistent offenders is entirely different.
These are men who, no matter what the stage of their criminal
career, are unable to conform to the life around them, either in
or out of prison. If the incidental offender suffers a temporary
psychological regression, the persistent offender's regression is
far deeper. Imprisonment confirms his feeling that he never
was and never will be part of the world at large. This attitude
is changed with great difficulty as his sense of being unwanted
and unwelcome is at least partly confirmed by the attitudes of
the law abiding. Imprisonment, even when just, may defeat its
purpose because the experience itself reinforces his antagonism
against society. While we accept that prison is necessary for
most persistent offenders, we must face the consequence that
it aggravates already existing conflicts.

20

Our present penal system gives rise to these problems, among others:

1)   Though intended as a means of reform as well as punishment, prison eventually becomes a way of life. It forces an artificial milieu on an individual, negating the one of which he should be part.

2)   Imprisonment is accompanied by a great loss of the responsibility which the persistent offender most lacks.

3)   Prison itself is a means of establishing and reinforcing ties between the inmate and criminal society.

4)   With the serving of many sentences a pattern of imprisonment often sets in. Men become not so much habitual offenders as habitual prisoners. Though no longer antisocial, some continue to commit offenses because they have lost whatever potential they may have had to live in freedom.
(One great defect of imprisonment is its effect on the thinking of the watchers as well as of the watched. In any setting where freedom is cut off or severely limited, paranoid thinking becomes a specific response. This paranoid thinking affects both guards and inmates.)
Our attempt to treat persistent offenders in a penal therapeutic milieu took into account from the start the barriers in the way of forming therapeutic relationships. The next step is to gain insight into what prevented earlier penal programs from using therapeutic relationships as a tool. To understand the psychology and psychopathology of deprivation of liberty is to break down the barrier. But even when this has been overcome it is only the beginning of the long journey.

Dannemora is reached by a long winding road that sharply curves just before it enters the town. A sign proclaims that one is about to arrive in "Little Siberia." Indeed, that is the accepted nickname. When the guards and town elders were asked about its origin, nobody seemed to know, nor is anyone offended by the term.
Dannemora is situated in Clinton County, upper New York State, close to the Canadian border. It is surrounded by farmland that has known more prosperous times; the many abandoned

farms attest to those who have given up the struggle against the difficult mountain soil and the long winters. The closest large center is Plattsburgh, twelve miles to the east, a small quietly charming city on the shores of Lake Champlain with a progressive university that was to play an important role in the rehabilitation program of Clinton Prison. Montreal is only sixty-five miles north of Plattsburgh, whereas New York is three hundred miles away.

Often, as one arrives in a prison town, one wonders which came first, the prison or the town. In the case of Dannemora, it was the prison or, more precisely, the prisons. Not only does the high, armed tower-wall of Clinton Prison rise from the very middle of the town, but right beside it an impressive red stone building looks like another prison or a mental hospital. It is both. Dannemora State Hospital was opened in 1900 for the treatment of prisoners declared insane while serving a sentence. These two institutions make Dannemora the most important penal town in New York State.

The project described in this book took place within Dannemora State Hospital, but a brief history of both institutions is given here as background.

In the early 1800s, small artisans began protesting the competition given them by the goods being produced by prison labor. Later organized labor joined the protests, and the conflict reached such intensity by mid-century that New York State enacted policies restricting prison labor to activities and products that would not be in competition with the free market. The principle forbidding the outside sale of prison-made articles and restricting them to state use was formulated soon after. (This practice, known as the "State Use System," remains to this day.)

Many suggestions were put forth to provide convicts with work which would not compete with free labor. One such plan recommended iron-ore mining and the manufacture of ironware. Few artisans in the state were so engaged. Such an enterprise had already been proposed for Clinton County. Ransom Cook, who was to become the first warden of Clinton Prison, reported that he had found a tract of land seventeen miles west of Plattsburgh which could be mined for years to come. In 1844 a law was enacted establishing a new state prison to be located north of Albany; the site was the one proposed by Cook.(39)

22

Labor groups and small artisans were pleased about the project and a contemporary legislative document states that such a project would remove prisoners from competition with free workers "as effectively as if they were transported to Russia or Sweden." (40)

In his study on pentitentiary growth in New York, *From Newgate to Dannemora*, W. David Lewis gives much information on the early days of Dannemora. "In anticipation of the institution's success, citizens named the agglomeration of dwelling houses and log shanties which came to be scattered throughout the woods near the prison 'Dannemora' after the well-known Swedish iron center." (40) The allusions to both Russia and Sweden anticipated that future citizens of Clinton County would adopt the names Dannemora and Little Siberia.

The mining project was a short-lived success. The iron ore, initially thought to be unlimited, was practically exhausted by 1851. By the 1860s it was proving to be a costly enterprise and the location was looked on as a mistake. There was even some talk of closing the new institution. However, penitentiaries in the southern part of the state were so overcrowded that, to relieve the situation, inmates were transferred to Clinton and it soon became the largest penitentiary in New York State. To this day, most of the inmates come from southern New York State, and Dannemora remains very much a penitentiary town.

Its status was even more firmly confirmed when the Dannemora State Hospital opened in 1900.

The problem of caring for mentally ill convicts has always been a major one. Deutsch devotes a special chapter to this question in his book, *The Mentally Ill in America*. In New York State, as in the rest of America, the criminally insane were often incarcerated with common felons, or locked up in special rooms in almshouses. With the opening of mental hospitals, several states, including New York, passed laws that forbade any mentally ill patient being confined in a prison. As Deutsch points out, "The state hospitals and almshouses became the only legal places of confinement for the criminal insane, although the laws were never strictly observed and this class continued to be frequently incarcerated in prisons and jails." (23)

In New York State the Utica State Asylum was opened in 1843 and the criminally insane were sent there. In 1859, a state lunatic asylum for insane convicts was established at

Auburn; this was the forerunner of the Dannemora State Hospital. Although Auburn was at first only for convicts who became insane after incarceration, it soon began to receive criminally insane prisoners from the courts as well. As a result it became overcrowded and was moved to Matteawan. Dannemora State Hospital was opened some eight years later, and limited itself to prisoners declared mentally ill while confined in a penal institution for felony. Until recently these remained New York State's two mental hospitals for prisoners: Matteawan for the criminally insane, and Dannemora State Hospital for convicts who became mentally ill while serving their sentences.

The creation of Matteawan and Dannemora State Hospitals could have been a step in the right direction in prisoner rehabilitation. Unfortunately they were conceived when the relationship between law and psychiatry was even less clearly defined than it is now. Only in recent years have criminally insane and mentally ill convicts been recognized as having human rights equal to those of the overall population.

2. The Theory and Practice of the Therapeutic Community

The therapeutic community's techniques and dynamics contain the seeds of self-destruction.

Is the therapeutic approach viable no matter what the setting ?   If one judges by the literature on the subject, one realizes many therapeutic communities have been started since Jones outlined the technique in the late 1940's.   Most were short-lived, and two factors would seem to have contributed to this: (1) the role of the leading figure and (2) the therapeutic community's techniques and dynamics which contain the seeds of self-destruction.   Many programs with some patient participation have been called therapeutic communities when in fact they were nothing more than hospital improvements in treatment and management.   The number of bona fide therapeutic communities, therefore, is not as large as the literature would suggest.

When a therapeutic community flourishes it is usually because a "leading figure" took the initiative in the venture's development.   It seems obvious that a therapeutic community needs a dominating figure.   By dominating, we do not mean authoritarian, but rather one for whom most of the people in the community will, most of the time, have positive feelings. When such a person leaves, it seems that the community itself generally folds up.   The number of communities that have failed to survive such a loss would appear to bear this out.   It must therefore be assumed that so much of the program and the climate were determined by the leader that a vacuum was created when he left.   This is not to say that the community existed solely as the result of his presence, but that his personality engendered staff and patient participation to such a point that his departure critically weakened the links.

Is such a dominating figure absolutely necessary, or even desirable, in the running of a therapeutic community? There is no pat answer. Those communities which have had the longest life seem to have been led by strong figures, but this kind of leadership poses ethical problems as much as practical considerations. Ethically, both the leader and the institution must ask themselves whether the leader will remain long enough both to launch the program and to continue it. On the practical side they must ask whether the program is even worth starting if it is to be short-lived.

Although we would like to conclude that a leading figure is not necessary, either in theory or in practice, we cannot do so. In one-to-one therapy, transference is an essential feature of the overall process. The problem of shared transference exists in group therapy, but it is less complex than in community therapy. It can be argued that since there are many persons on whom one can transfer feelings (there are as many therapists as members in the community) is it really necessary to have *any* communal or shared transference to one person? Our experience suggests that such transference is necessary to hold together, even if loosely, the many positive and negative relationships that community participants entertain. It is the task of the person in control to be responsible for the community's working out of critical points — whether of depression or of elation. He also prevents anarchic situations from building up. The many feelings encouraged to emerge in community experience would be in danger of exploding into chaos without the support of a leading figure who can restore confidence, and to whom the community can turn in moments of crisis.

Most members of a therapeutic community, those precisely for whom it is intended, spend a relatively short time together — especially where short, intensive therapy is the policy. Not only the patients, but also the staff move on, particularly when the center has a good reputation. Such centers attract people who come to learn and then go on to other places. It is necessary to have a leader who assures continuity.

We have observed that when a therapeutic community has been led by a strong, confidence-inspiring director — even if his expertise leaves with him, and even if his community ceases to exist — the center itself has generally benefitted. There have been improved atmosphere and management, and what remains is often a better relationship between staff and patients. A therapeutic community started and directed by a weak leader or by a clinician temporarily interested in this technique is usually short-lived. Consequently little benefit is derived in its lifetime and little remains thereafter. More therapeutic communities have died because of a weak or basically uninvolved leader than through the departure of a strong and dedicated one.

Although our temporary conclusion is that a communal transference is needed, we should stress that the personality, attitude and wisdom of the leading figure should not be so overpowering as to make it impossible for another person to assume his role. A new leader ought to give the community a new flavor, while retaining basic techniques. A therapeutic community that passes through the experience of having a new transference figure is possibly comparable to a patient who has to change analysts.

Another potential for self-destruction exists in the dynamics of the therapeutic community and this shows itself in many forms. For example, permissiveness beyond that generally accepted outside is necessary in order to expose fully symptoms in the individual and the group, but aggressive behavior arising from these symptoms can by no means be condoned. It should, on the contrary, be under constant discussion until such time as the symptoms recede. As in individual therapy, such disappearance does not necessarily indicate the resolution of the symptoms. It may be a temporary suppression, a defense against the discomfort of dealing openly with the problem. When this is the case, the symptom will soon bounce back.

One of the challenges and difficulties in maintaining a community at a therapeutic level lies in the tension created by non-acceptance of some symptomatic behavior, yet at the same time repeatedly confronting the community with the problem. The need for constant confrontation becomes exceedingly taxing for all who participate. Some communities fail because, after an enthusiastic beginning, resistance sets in and interest tends to lessen in the face of the daily repeated demands of the therapeutic setting. A tendency develops which, for lack of another term, we have called "self-destructive mechanisms." These operate for both inmates and staff. In the Clinton Project there was required participation in organized forms of therapy for ten to eleven hours a week. This was exclusive of actual working time: five community meetings, a group therapy session, individual interviews, participation in committees and in adult education programs. It was a heavy program for all concerned, especially for the correctional staff who spent thirty-five to forty hours a week with the inmates.

In the face of this pressure, there was a temptation on both sides to relieve the strain, and this showed itself in both overt and insidious ways. One overt way is the request, which may seem reasonable and justified, for changes in the program. At Clinton, for example, the inmates complained after some months that five community meetings a week were too many. The argument that the meetings were becoming a bore, that there was not enough material for discussion, and so on, were obvious rationalizations. It was hard to believe that people with lifelong problems of such magnitude, trying to work them out in living together, would not have plenty to discuss. The boredom was a form of resistance to painful exploration.

More noteworthy, however, was that such requests also came from the staff, with apparently equal logic. They would, for example, point out that much more could be accomplished in fewer and more concentrated meetings — as if fewer meetings would in themselves bring them more concentration. Thus, through similar rationalization, inmates and staff can work together to dilute the program.

In such a setting, however, compromise must be negotiated among the inmates themselves, among the staff, and between staff and inmates. The staff must also negotiate and come to agreement with the Department of Correction.

During the first year at Dannemora, the staff frequently had to admit that they, too, were required to accept restrictions which they often found binding and irksome. Exchanges between inmates and professional staff frequently occurred particularly when the staff could not answer the inmates' questions and when there were no answers or solutions to problems. The staff's frank admission that they had no answer, even the admission that there were things about which they could or would do nothing, became a valuable therapeutic experience.

Questions which could not be answered, or which were answered negatively, were met by a "Well, there's no use discussing this anyway" reply from the prisoners. This type of response is not adequate. The "let's forget it" attitude which assumes that discussion is permanently closed, bypasses the problem. When one does not get what one wishes, then anger, frustration and sadness are normal reactions.

We paid great heed to this, because outside prison persistent offenders do not accept frustration easily. It was often quite difficult to induce these men to express their feelings openly when faced with a situation they had to accept and could do nothing about, and at the same time convince them that there was something to discuss. The difficulty was to make them understand that, when confronted with a frustration which cannot simply be put aside, a real problem exists: the problem of working it out and learning to live without something one wants. This is an experience everyone has in daily life, but it is more marked in the persistent offender who can vent as much or more anger on a small frustration as a "normal" person can on a big one.

The ways we dealt with not being able to answer a legitimate question or of having no solution to a problem may throw some light on one technique of the therapeutic community. In many cases, the staff did not hide their own sense of frustration when they had reason to feel it, such as, for example, when they could not act because of the administration's indecision. When the staff admitted their frustration and worked it through in the community meeting itself, coping with their own annoyance and disappointment, it was found that the inmates respected these feelings. The staff showed clearly that there were problems and that denying them was no solution. The "acting out" of the staff, to be sure, had limits. They had to "act out" while at the same time maintaining their authority and that of their superiors. In some situations, it was a clear-cut case of disagreeing with a decision but nevertheless accepting authority, even under protest. Our impression is that it was precisely on such occasions that many inmates learned to deal with frustration without undue acting out, thus initiating a genuine learning process.

Perhaps the best example is that of the second Christmas party, fifteen months after the Center had opened. The party was planned as a therapeutic experience as well as entertainment. Many of the men had lived in foster homes, institutions and reform schools in their childhood. From personal experience they were keenly aware of what it is like from both an economic and an emotional point of view to be neglected, unloved and impoverished. It was thought they would enjoy making toys for the children, and they did. The idea of holding a party for the young children from the local orphanage was accepted and plans went forward. But some of the correctional staff began to think that the party was inadvisable. To us these doubts were unwarranted, but finally the party became so diluted and meaningless that the project was abandoned on the pretext that the orphans might be emotionally damaged by a visit to a prison. The professional staff, which actively promoted the party, was perhaps more frustrated and disappointed at the final decision than the inmates, who took the rebuff with relative calm, even though their life pattern had been to react sharply, either verbally or physically, when frustrated. In this case their reaction was simply, "It's no use discussing this any more." Whenever a subject is dropped in this way, it is bound to reappear in another form.

The incident points up some aspects of therapeutic community technique in contrast to individual therapy, especially the psychoanalytic type where "acting out" on the part of the therapist is to be avoided. When this occurs, the therapist must seriously question his counter-transference to the patient. Even in the therapeutic community severe acting out on the part of the therapist is not desirable, but there is a normal acting out incidental to the daily life of the community, and this is another matter. Here a therapist cannot and should not be expected to be the "fifty minute hour" type. He should not attempt to hide the fact that he is himself, that he acts and reacts for better or worse, and that he is an active participant likely on occasion to make statements that might hurt members of the community, as he himself can be hurt.

In individual therapy, the patient generally knows little about his therapist other than some superficial facts. Furthermore, the therapist has to be constantly aware of not bringing his own problems, convictions or beliefs into the therapeutic situation. Such restraint is impossible in a therapeutic community. While the staff should not *deliberately* bring their own personal history and problems into a community not designed for their benefit, this cannot be entirely avoided. Living in such close association, no one can help interjecting his total personality. If the staff are trained to recognize the inmates' problems, the inmates are no less keen in recognizing

30

those of the staff, and this is a healthy process. In such a
situation, it is not unknown for the staff to receive interpretations rather than give them. These can be considered as therapeutic interpretations in so far as they give the staff new insights that may induce a change in behavior. At this point we
may well wonder who is treating whom.

That the inmates learned from this social process in the
community is shown by the fact that in the first year of
operation only four or five incidents required punitive measures.
To put it in the words of one inmate (as stated in a therapeutic
community meeting), "I never apologized in all my life as much
as I have during the first few months I've been here." This
was true for the staff as well as for the inmates. It was a
gratifying experience to see both professional and correctional
officers apologizing to the inmates when necessary. In doing
this the staff's authority was not diminished. On the contrary,
an increasing respect developed.

Another important self-destructive mechanism was the
repetitive demand of inmates for more individual therapy,
which they claimed was better for them than group or
community therapy. On occasion this too was echoed by the
professional staff. Without being aware of it they allowed
themselves to regard their personal caseloads as "private
property," or to believe that their cases were the ones which
required special attention. Here again, staff and inmates, in
contradicting the priorities which they had accepted, were
weakening or destroying the community. It was well understood by all that individual therapy was at the service of
group therapy which in turn fostered community therapy and
not the other way around. Although seemingly rational, such
attempts to modify the program become insidious and, in the
end, self-destructive. Here the leader has a key role as he is
the one who must always be aware of the changing climate of
the community, discover from what sources the changes stem
and in what direction they are going.

Some authors have held that there is no place in the
therapeutic community for individual therapy at all unless
something exceptional turns up. They believe that individual
and community therapy are not compatible because they
negate themselves. We do not share this view. Even in
therapeutic communities which operate without individual
therapy, a drive toward it nonetheless exists. The tendency

always remains to revert to a one-to-one relationship. If no therapist is available, two community members might pair off, or four or five might form a clique. Even though a one-to-one therapeutic relationship is openly discouraged, it will take place in a concealed way that is not therapeutic. Most dangerous of all is the forming of small cliques living as islands in the community; *these* can be very disruptive. Whatever the merits of individual therapy, the health of a therapeutic community can be measured by how much value the members themselves place on social therapy as against individual therapy. When the demand grows for more individual therapy or, if this is not available, when small separate groups begin to form, then the therapeutic community is not healthy.

A therapeutic community is a two-way process. For a staff member whose problems are within "normal" limits, a therapeutic community is an enriching experience. For those whose problems are such that participation in the community is also "therapeutic," the therapy must be rapid as the object is to treat the inmates, not the staff. The difference between therapeutic communities and other settings is that these crises must not be hidden. The question of who is treating whom must always be considered relevant.

After fifteen months of operation we realized that eventually the psychopathology of the staff as a group and as individuals would become as important as that of the treated subjects. Patients leave, but the basic staff remain. The staff tend in time to become less alert and less mindful of the recurring problems inherent in the setting. This is another defense mechanism which must never be overlooked. We had an inkling of it early in the project and as the program advanced, the problem became more serious.

In assessing the Clinton experiment, we feel it is significant to note the change which took place in the reaction of the correctional officers to the inmates and the changing response of the inmates to the officers.

The officers at Clinton began with great optimism. They already had experience with psychiatric patients when they approached their new venture. A two-week intensive training program acquainted them with the philosophy and working methods of the therapeutic community. The experiment commenced and the first few weeks were very rewarding for all concerned. The inmates reacted strongly to the new atmos-

phere and mutual goodwill developed. This made the
correctional personnel perhaps overoptimistic. But persistent
offenders, and for that matter staff and officers, do not change
easily. The men began to turn on the officers and revert to
former practices, testing them out. They also discovered that
the very lack of coercion and restriction presented difficulties.
This latitude forced them to take unaccustomed responsibility,
it offered them choices, it created conflict. They were used
to being ordered and restrained within the prison setting. In
an atmosphere of permissiveness they started to live as they
had on the outside, keeping as few rules as possible and
reverting to "acting out."

In the face of what seemed a poor return for the effort
expended, the officers reacted. Some officers, though tense
and anxious, continued on the whole to be confident. Others
were indulgent and permissive, excusing conduct which should
not have been overlooked in the belief that this was the
spirit of the therapeutic community. They were bound to
conclude eventually that this setting failed to control
difficult behavior and that the old regime should be restored.
This was a kind of retaliatory gesture.

Another officer reaction was discouragement and a sense
of failure. But a good community meeting where feelings
could be aired and situations resolved usually helped.

One belief long and stubbornly retained by the
correctional officers, despite emphasis to the contrary, was
that they were not an integral part of the treatment program,
that therapy was the function of the professional staff. It
was hard for them to acknowledge how important their work
was, and constant reassuring was required. A number became
thoroughly integrated in the program, however, and could
openly discuss their relationship with the inmates and the
problems they came upon with considerable good humor and
wisdom, and at times — like the inmates — with irritation
and anger. In these exchanges the inmates found that the
correctional officers were human, that they had their share
of personal difficulties and that they, too, "acted out" in some
fashion. One inmate remarked after a long discussion with
one of the officers about the latter's home and family situation,
"I think I have problems. Joe has worse."

Significantly, in a blind questionnaire given at the end of
the first year of the program, a large number of the inmates

33

stated that they had found the correctional officers the most therapeutic of all personnel, a far cry indeed from what they normally would say in a maximum security prison. In spite of the great freedom of movement within the community itself disciplinary problems were rare and minor in character.

This says something for both guards and prisoners: for the capacity of correctional officers to learn new techniques and practices and for the capacity of prisoners whose mode of life had been undisciplined, who had endless trouble in getting on with others, and for whom it was believed that only great personal restrictions could avoid violence and disorder. The Center was opened with no punitive cells. We were confident that the technique of the therapeutic community would provide sufficient social control, and it did.

3.   The Natural History of Persistent Offenders

*Depression permits a criminal to make a true,
though painful, contact with the real world.*

To learn the different ways in which criminality comes
into being and develops, we must trace the natural history of
criminal processes, their beginnings, evolutions and ends. The
intricate changes in the criminal psyche are reflected in the
outward patterns of criminality.   The history of criminal
processes may help us prevent as well as treat and abbreviate
delinquency. (15, 16, 9)
Persistent criminality tapers off with age and older
criminals constitute a minority in prison.   There is little information about the later life of these men.   Law enforcers
feel that some criminals grow more experienced and adept
with time and are not so frequently caught, that they also
tend to limit themselves to less risky activities.   Social
agencies dealing with offenders know that some older ones
become skid row derelicts. Others become unskilled workers
– cleaners, night watchmen etc.   Still others find unconven-
tional but honest ways out, while a very few even manage to
merge well with the community.   Research into the natural
history of persistent criminality presents much difficulty.
Parole board executives try to maintain contact with offenders
who spent much of their youth and early manhood in prison.
Still it is not easy to keep tabs on those men who have kept out
of trouble, and have no wish to return to crime; they prefer to
live in honorable anonymity.
Our most rewarding research so far has been to follow up
men we have come to know in the past twenty years, first in
the penitentiary and later on the outside, and sometimes

again in the penitentiary. We have watched the changes in their personalities and in their criminal careers, and noted whether they failed or succeeded in leaving the criminal milieu. When we first saw some of these offenders, they were only fifteen while others were in their twenties, thirties, and even their forties.

Some signposts might be considered characteristic of phases in the criminal career. A significant one marks the passage from juvenile delinquency to adult criminality. The length of juvenile delinquency may be long or short, depending on when the pattern of persistent delinquency was first established. By the time some juvenile delinquents reach an adult prison, they already have behind them an apprenticeship of many years. (20)

The aggression discharged in persistent juvenile delinquency is diffuse and random, attacking whatever obstacles are in the way. It is repetitive and compulsive, because the release from tension is at best brief. Delinquent acting out becomes "addictive." Though profit may also be desired, it is not the delinquent's main goal. What dominates is the need to discharge aggressive impulses. This free-floating, almost motiveless, delinquency of the true juvenile delinquent is very different from the reactive, short-lived delinquency that can occur in the crisis of adolescence. Persistent juvenile delinquency is not part of the learning process, and is affected neither by punishment nor by reward.

Many changes take place in the character of the delinquent and in the form of his delinquency before he passes on to adult criminality. The purposeless striking out against the world and destruction for its own sake end. Delinquency is no longer mainly a way of releasing tension. Profit is now its chief aim.

The young criminal becomes selective. He may even specialize. His criminality narrows and localizes itself, and is reflected not only in his choice of offense, but also in his choice of criminal associates. He is no longer part of a loose gang, but forms partnerships. His aggression is channeled to achieve a defined goal such as theft or armed robbery. In some areas he becomes better socialized, and may be quite honest in personal and social exchanges. This narrowing of the field, the localization and specialization are three characteristics which indicate the change of aim, direction and selectivity in the passage from juvenile delinquency to adult criminality.

By the end of adolescence, the persistent juvenile delinquent will have acquired a set of antisocial values that will be with him for many years: he will think of criminals as "we" and of others as "they." Starting in his twenties, sometimes even before, he experiences a strengthening of bonds with the criminal world — a well-knit society with its own tradition and folklore, its own standards and code, and — despite its apparent non-conformity — its own conformity. In his late adolescence and early twenties he is usually confident, sure of himself and of his success. He thinks of himself as successful even though he gets caught. Important to his pride is the fact that he has successfully committed many offenses for which he was *not* caught. He is resigned to paying the price of a sentence. He will spend years in prison, sustained by memories of past successful offenses and fantasies of those he will commit in the future.

Criminality is bound to fail in the long run. Since the persistent offender spends most of his time in prison, he eventually loses his sense of achievement. He has failed at becoming a successful criminal and is disheartened by the sense that he has no future, that he has no true friends, no one to love and depend on who will reciprocate. In his late twenties or thirties, aggression — which previously was easily discharged in acting out — no longer gives gratification. Instead it leads to further frustration. Drives are increasingly converted into anxiety, depression and other autoplastic symptoms. (10, 50, 18) This awareness of failure and sense of malaise are important to identify, for they represent "saturation points." At this time the persistent offender, whose aggression until now had kept him from being really depressed about himself and the world, begins to suffer. These saturation crises mark the start of the process of abatement of criminality.

Depression is not the only mechanism in this process, but it seems to be the most easily identifiable and the most impressive. The inmate not only allows depression to invade his consciousness, often for the first time, but he also uses it to test reality. Depression permits a persistent offender to make a true, though painful, contact with the real world. He begins to look more objectively at criminal society and with decreasing hostility toward the non-criminal world even though he may feel he cannot cope with its values and demands. He may continue to express resentment against law-abiding society, which he feels rejected him and would not help him on his own terms but at the same time he shows a growing wish to come to terms and to belong. He sometimes even exaggerates the goodness of non-criminal society.

As he grows more aware of failure he returns to his past and remembers his family. Looking back from a distance of years, he judges not only his family but himself. He may remember that though they seemed to have failed him, some-where there was love and commitment, not only from his mother, but even from his father, whom he had thought to be overbearing and harsh. He faces the idea that no matter how much he may find to criticize in them, he was a bad son who brought them sorrow. Guilt often becomes exaggerated, and he sees early parental figures as all good while he is all bad — neither, of course, being true. (14)

At such saturation points, depression can reach psychotic proportions. For many of these men, however, a depression opens the way to maturity late in life. They work through their depression with all the mechanisms involved in mourning: sadness, anger, guilt and many others. They come out of it having gained, if only partially, a new capacity: to accept their loss and their lot. This permits them to advance and enables them to make meaningful relations, thereby protecting them-selves from further retaliatory impulses against the world. In time these relations may even permit them to join the law-abiding community. At the least, a saturation point depression accomplishes something of value, because it often puts them into an emotional crisis in which they must ask for help and accept it and, providing they have enough strength, insight, and resourcefulness, they may yet climb out of their pit.

What determines the length of criminal processes? In our view, the extent and depth of ego involvement is the main factor. It is clinically sound to assume that the more damaged the ego, the longer it will take for criminality to abate. The earlier persistent delinquency begins, the longer it lasts. While this statement is valid for adult persistent offenders it is not an absolute rule. Some adolescents, deeply and persistently delinquent, abate early. The effects of imprisonment must also be considered. In the latter part of their criminal career men who have spent many years deprived of liberty will commit offenses not so much because of criminal impulses, but because they are not equipped to live in freedom.   At this stage they are more habitual prisoners than habitual criminals. (12)

The systematic attempt to evaluate and treat offenders is relatively new.   Clinical criminology, a recent discipline, needs much development.   Its aim is to integrate all available knowledge for the purposes of diagnosis, prognosis and treatment.

Clinical criminology requires a frame of reference from which theories and practice can be developed.   One of the most difficult terms to define is crime itself which should not discourage us when we recall that in medicine the terms "health" and "disease" are also among the most controversial.   We require an uncontroversial, clinical, all-purpose definition.   One acceptable definition might be that crime is "an ego activity, punishable by law, as an act or an expressed intention against an established legal code."

The only addition to the generally accepted idea of crime is the psychological concept of the ego.   The ego is that conscious aspect of the personality which is in contact with the external world.   Therefore, the use of the term does not contravene any function of law (which judges the act), nor does it create problems for workers who study the man who acts.   While instinctual drives (the id) and a system of internalized values (superego) play their part, it remains that the ego, the conscious part of the personality, is the doer.   Thus, to add the term *ego* stresses that the act is committed by a person.

The term ego does not imply that the classification that we will propose for treatment and research in clinical criminology is a psychiatric one, merely that it is useful for evaluation, treatment and research.

The quality and frequency of delinquency are only partly a measure of ego involvement.   To these must be added duration, that is, the age at which the ego first became involved.

To formulate a true classification, we have begun with the age when the delinquency or criminality first manifests itself, as well as its extent and depth i.e. whether it was a response to stress, or persistent.   There are three major types of persistent delinquency: primary, secondary, and late.

Primary delinquency is a *fixated* pattern of delinquency

39

first established in latency, changing in pattern but continuing into adolescence. With manhood it transforms itself into persistent adult criminality. Offenders of this type are called *primary delinquents.*

Secondary delinquency is a *fixated* pattern of delinquent behavior which is first observed some time during adolescence. It, too, transforms itself into persistent adult criminality. Such offenders are called *secondary delinquents.*

Late delinquency is (a) a *fixated* pattern of criminal behavior which started after maturity, and (b) *incidental or episodic* criminal behavior occurring at any time in maturity, without any significant early history of delinquency. Those with persistent patterns are called *late* delinquents. Those with incidental patterns are *late offenders.* (17) Offenders who recidivate, but who have some significant crime-free periods are called *episodic offenders.* (13)

Such a classification permits us to locate the time when an adult offender first became delinquent, and is of great importance for prognosis and treatment. The type and severity of the offenses give us few clues about the offender. But knowing when he first became an offender and knowing the quality and duration of his criminality are of great value. Primary, secondary and late delinquents are all persistently criminal but the personality differences between primary, secondary and late delinquents are great, and important factors in their treatment. (The personality of an offender whose social behavior is more or less normal but who commits an isolated criminal act is quite different from that of one engaged in persistent criminality, no matter what the age of onset.)

The first fifty offenders who were admitted to the Diagnostic and Treatment Center were primary and secondary delinquents.

4. Therapeutic Community Inside a Prison

*No one can escape some degree of regression
in adapting to the loss of freedom.*

The concept of a total treatment plan in which patient or
inmate, professional staff, administration, and all others are involved, has attracted much attention.   Since Maxwell Jones's
initial therapeutic community after World War II, the principle
has become widely applied. (34, 35, 36)

What is a "therapeutic community"?   The term has
suffered from indiscriminate use. Improved living conditions,
some staff involvement or other desirable changes are now too
often called milieu therapy or a "therapeutic community."
Therapeutic community should refer to a very specific technique
in social treatment, a milieu where all relationships, whether
established during working hours or recreation, are deliberately
used as a social learning experience.   It is assumed that the
patient or inmate has potential which may foster growth, and
that the treated person, in using his own potential, can become
therapeutic to others as well as to himself.   What is new in this
concept is that the treated person works along with the
professionally trained.

The therapeutic community involves the training of total
staff: professional, administrative and correctional.   Though
these groups do not follow exactly the same programs, there
must be a basic training common to all, so that the philosophy
and aims of the therapeutic community are well understood
and integrated.   Contrary to conventional therapy, it goes
beyond a one-to-one relationship, and beyond group therapy,
where several relate to one therapist as well as among themselves.
Community living is systematically used to employ fully the

potential inherent in each individual for his own reeducation and for that of other participants in the community.

In a therapeutic community everyone is concerned with treating everyone else. This would not be acceptable in a democratic society, since such freedom would interfere with the individual rights of others, such as the right to privacy. Seen thus, the therapeutic community cannot be viewed as a democratic one, even though it gives its members the right of participation, disagreement, debate and other democratic privileges. In fact the fullest and most outspoken expression of thoughts which is encouraged in psychotherapy may not be compatible with the democratic way of life. The latter assumes some restraint and control, and some limits to expression. If all such exchanges were allowed in daily democratic practice as much as in a therapeutic setting, life would become highly unpleasant and sometimes intolerable. In a therapeutic relationship disasters do not occur because it is agreed that unlimited outspokenness will be confined to the therapeutic group and during its duration only.

Unchecked expression in society can be destructive, but without exceptional permissiveness a therapeutic community could not achieve its purposes. Psycho-therapeutic technique, based on the freest expression, does not aim at negating democratic thought. On the contrary, rights of expression go beyond democratic limits in order that persons may learn the controls that permit maximum freedom. (Freedom is here defined as the maximum fulfillment a person can achieve with a minimum of restriction to himself, and with the least possible interference in the fulfillment of others.)

The freedom of expression in a therapeutic community, which goes far beyond that found in an open society, can best be described as an experience in communality much like that found in primitive societies, such as among Eskimos before the advent of the white man. Interestingly, the Eskimos used a kind of playful verbal acting out as a means of solving problems. Such a communalistic society is at times very near to an ideal democracy.

A therapeutic community is also not unlike the shared life of a nuclear family, one of whose objects is to teach children how to live in the larger community.

The therapeutic community has a potentially wide range of applications. Not only must criminals recognize and accept their needs and those of others, but so should those mentally and emotionally disturbed individuals who are neither able to tolerate the stresses of society nor enjoy its satisfactions.

The therapeutic community technique has been used for different types of individuals, such as psychiatric patients, both certified and voluntary, and in various settings, in special schools, homes for the aged, and the like. It should be realized that when one establishes a therapeutic community it must be designed taking into consideration the milieu and the people for whom it is intended. (4, 5, 46, 38, 43)

A therapeutic community in a penal institution should begin with the premise that it is working under conditions of legally enforced deprivation of liberty as a form of punishment or as a means of protecting society. No matter what principle is involved, the prevailing atmosphere is one of punishment. Some mental patients are detained under similar conditions, but the great difference is that the procedure leading to certification is not punitive even though the patient may interpret it so. Involuntary placement should be determined solely for medical reasons and for the shortest period possible. The mental patient is deprived of liberty in a medical setting, the prisoner in an authoritarian one. This is an important difference provided that the mental hospital makes full use of medical knowledge and is mindful of the human and civil rights of its patients. Enforced living, however, in any setting where men are deprived of their freedom raises the basic relationship of men to the depriving environment. (29, 58, 7, 51, 45)

An atmosphere approaching a therapeutic community for persistent and/or dangerous offenders in a prison started as early as the 1930s when Georg K. Stürup introduced this concept at Herstedvester in Denmark. His experiences have been summed up in a recent book called *Treating the "Untreatable."* (55) After World War II Doctors P. Baan and A.M. Roosenburg established a true therapeutic community in a prison setting at the van der Hoeven Clinic in Utrecht, the fame of which has attracted visitors from all over the world.

Although intended as a means of reform as well as punishment, prison becomes a way of life, forcing a highly artificial milieu on an individual, a negation of the one into which he will be reintegrated. Since this is accompanied by a great loss of responsibility no one can escape some degree of regression in adapting to the loss of freedom. (42, 22, 11)

There are many reasons for this regression: dependency; the enforcement of either isolation or gregarious living; the suppression of heterosexual outlets resulting in repression, sublimation, or recourse to masturbation or homosexual practices. In these conditions sexual fantasies undergo changes in quality.

One source of regression is the need to detach one's self from life outside. We say "need" advisedly because if an inmate held fast to all his emotional links, life would become extremely painful, to the point of deep depression and even psychosis. Though all connections are not cut, the emotional energies, removed from the outside world, must now be cathected to the realities of prison life. An incidental offender, with strong family and social ties, must necessarily give up some links, but will, prior to release, painfully reach out for these links and recover his hold on the outside world. The persistent offender, on the other hand, usually has few links in society, though he may have had many in the criminal milieu. He finds his anger at the world reinforced by imprisonment. In associating with others like him in prison, not only does he regress but his fixation becomes more deeply entrenched. For incidental offenders paranoid feeling may be slight, or it may be acute but temporary. For the persistent offender, however, the regression that accompanies the detachment from life outside prison goes as deep as a return to a split in object relations into good and bad; the criminal world is good and society bad.

* *

In a therapeutic community "acting out" poses important problems, especially when dealing with persistent offenders. As therapists, we did not believe that the solution was to suppress acting out, as is the practice in a maximum security penitentiary. Rather, the alternative is to design a setting where much acting out will be tolerated and dealt with by other than authoritarian means. If the inmates are to understand the sources of their behavior they must be allowed to express it. Suppression only masks symptoms. This is the challenge in designing a therapeutic community for men with a long history of acting out against

44

person and property. Here the great permissiveness that is generally allowed must be restricted, with regard to physical harm, by mutually accepted rules. Such rules are no guarantee that physical harm will not occur. When it does occur violence must be dealt with as an emergency and not allowed to increase. Whenever violence occurs the success in dealing with it is measured by how much the men learn that other alternatives are possible.

The problem of physical acting out was believed to be so important that, while being trained, the correctional officers were confronted with prisoners who had a history of violence outside the prison, and of stabbing and taking hostages inside. For the prisoners these sessions were an exercise in finding out whether they could have avoided violence. For the correctional officers they were a way of trying to find out how they could have prevented it or might have dealt with it once it occurred.

While we know that some psychiatric patients could be violent, their acting out is generally different from that of the violent criminal. The psychiatric patient can be managed by isolation and/or medication; in this way the symptom and the disease can be dealt with at the same time. In contrast, the violence of the persistent offender with a chronic behavior disorder is an ongoing character trait. Medication and isolation may be used as temporary aids, but these do not go to the root of the problem. Of course, even though violence is forbidden, a therapeutic community for persistent offenders must be ready to cope with it. To suppress members or withdraw them from the community is to refuse to deal with the symptom and to negate the principle of the therapeutic community.

In setting up such a community, one must always remember the prevalent paranoid thinking in penal society, which creates two camps, the guards and the prisoners. The inmates are very much aware of how they feel about correctional officers and the society they represent but the officers are not so much aware of their own suspicion, distrust and fear. Moreover, they are not fully conscious that they represent the authority of society not only in the form of physical custody, but also that of a rejecting world. For a therapeutic community to succeed, correctional officers must know their own feelings before they can change their role.

The therapeutic milieu is a taxing and challenging one for both inmates and officers. It is difficult for persistent offenders to change when they have been in and out of prison for many years; their prison wisdom becomes a handicap on the outside. It is also difficult for the officers to change. Many of them may have spent more years in the prison setting than the inmates themselves. Thus they have become accustomed to depriving others of liberty.

The function of correctional officers in the past was to ensure that inmates did not escape and that discipline be maintained. A new objective must be to develop staff who, though remaining authority figures, also learn to help the prisoners. Parole and probation services are or should be well aware of how hard it is to combine authority and counseling, and correctional officers now face this challenge. It must be recognized that at the outset inmates will not likely trust even the best-trained and most well-meaning officers enough to participate in a therapeutic relationship with them.

Of all prisoners, persistent offenders are the ones who have developed the most extreme distrust. They dislike authority in any shape or form, particularly as embodied in correctional officers. This hostility is reinforced by the fact that the larger part of their adult life is spent in prison with similar inmates.

A training program for correctional officers should be many sided. It should include a knowledge of human behavior, emphasizing its application to living situations, rather than intellectual awareness. Though there is a place for straightforward teaching, other educational techniques must also be used: seminars, audio-visual equipment, sociodrama, etc. These, however, cannot replace actual contact between officers and inmates, and the training of officers must be accompanied by direct involvement with the prisoners. Methods used for training doctors, social workers, and other clinical personnel who during their internship or field work come in contact with patients or clients should be utilized. This involves group interviews between officers and persistent offenders in an atmosphere of freedom. To the outsider this may seem obvious. But until now it has seldom, if ever, been applied in the prison system. One wonders why this technique has been so long delayed. It can be explained only by traditional prejudice where the spirit of custody and punishment overshadows all else. Needless to say, even the most intensive training program is only a beginning. Continual renewal in the light of experience and new developments is a must.

In discussing therapeutic communities in a prison setting, Maxwell Jones suggested that the first members should be first offenders with short sentences, relatively mature and likely to respond well to treatment. Such a choice, he believed, would also improve the training of staff and volunteers, so they would be better equipped eventually to deal with the more difficult offenders. In this pilot project we chose instead persistent offenders.

After studying many such offenders in a conventional penitentiary setting, sometimes over a period of more than fifteen years, we have come to feel that despite what looked like an ongoing, irreversible pattern, there were in fact crucial saturation points at which intervention might have helped. Until now it has proven very difficult to reach confident young persistent offenders because they are fortified by mechanisms which suppress much of their depression and anxiety. By the time they reach their late twenties they have years of an unsuccessful criminal career behind them which they cannot deny. Though they have succeeded in committing many offenses they have not managed to remain out of prison. The first penitentiary sentence may be easily endured, but succeeding ones grow harder and longer. In their late twenties, they consciously become aware of disappointment and failure, not only as criminals but in their inability either to marry or to sustain a marriage, or to make and keep friends. They feel lonely and alienated even in their own criminal world. This often results in a depression which they experience quite sharply. They then begin to think of other solutions. This crisis is a *saturation point*. (9)

Many persistent offenders succeed in getting out on their own — witness the fact that there are markedly fewer men in their thirties in the penitentiary, and fewer still in their forties and fifties. Many return to prison, not because they are anti-social, but because they cannot find a way out. Often, for example, they cannot adapt to work and they drift back to the criminal milieu where they are accepted without question. Hence some of these men become habitual prisoners. Their handicaps in getting a foothold in the community lay in their defective social background, their difficulties in making personal ties and in adapting to consistent work. It would be challenging and valuable to attempt a therapeutic community for a group of older persistent offenders (in prison one is old at thirty), who, if they could not make it on their own, would likely become persistent failures.

PART II:
THE FIRST SIX MONTHS

1. Breaking the Silences

What is to be feared is silence between the watcher and the watched.

Nothing is to be feared more than a "silent" prison. Though the expression may seem strange it is not a difficult one to define. It is a special silence that one can literally hear and feel, even during the shouting back and forth, from one cell to another, that goes on between prisoners. It can be observed in the shops where inmates engaged in animated conversation suddenly become silent when a guard approaches. A silent prison is one where inmates do not communicate in their own language with guards, with the usual profanities and scatalogical expressions that prisoners use. The officers, too, have a vocabulary and in a silent prison, that also is set aside. It does not matter whether prisoners and guards speak to one another in anger, kindness or understanding so long as they speak. What is to be feared is silence between the watcher and the watched.

Some of us in the McGill group had firsthand acquaintance with what prison tension and riots mean. In 1961 there had been a general hunger strike at the St.Vincent de Paul Penitentiary located just off the island of Montreal. The strike was ended by harsh repression, including corporal punishment. A year later this same prison was nearly destroyed during a riot in which all the shops were burnt to the ground. The main cell block, a Pennsylvania type of citadel, barely escaped the same fate; one of its wings was already in flames when firemen intervened. In the period between the hunger strike of 1961 and the major riot of 1962, St. Vincent de Paul was a "silent" prison. We were not surprised therefore to see the Official Report on the Attica riot allude many times to the kind of silence just described. For instance in describing classes taught by inmates, it says, "Class was led by an inmate . . . when an officer or civilian entered, the class usually became silent." (2) Another illustration: "In the exercise yard, inmates began to get together in groups to talk about their problems . . . The officers watched the growing discussion circle in the yard nervously, but were reluctant to force the issue by trying to break them up." It would seem obvious that the time was well past when officers and prisoners could discuss together. This tragic silence is even more ominous in the following description also taken from the Attica Report:

> Although not overtly threatened, officials who
> singled out an inmate for discipline began to
> find themselves acutely and uncomfortably
> aware of the hostile glares of many inmates.
> Instead of retreating from a confrontation,
> inmates realized they could intimidate many
> officers simply by standing fast. They soon
> learned that they could communicate their
> hostility and their resentment and their
> unacceptance merely by their silent, ominous
> presence together. The politics of confrontation
> had come to prison.

This was precisely the kind of silence we had experienced at St. Vincent de Paul in 1961-62 during the months between the hunger strike and the major riot that erupted like a roar in the silent prison. Many inmates at the Center knew the power of silence and this we were to discover.

The Center was not to be run without rules and discipline, but we deliberately started off without written regulations because we felt that all rules and their application to the daily routine should (and would) emerge on their own. The usual disciplinary rules and regulations that prevail in the maximum security penal institutions would not apply here. The kind of problems that rules and regulations may evoke is seen in the following (again from the Official Report of the New York State Special Commission on Attica):

> . . . Rules at Attica were poorly communicated,
> often petty, senseless, or repressive and they were
> selectively enforced . . .

Even when rules were clearly defined, the strictness of their enforcement varied from officer to officer, depending on each one's experience, perspective, and personality. For example, some officers insisted that inmates stand at the front of their cells for roll call; others allowed inmates to remain in bed or seated, as long as they were visible. Some allowed quiet talking in line; others did not. Some were rigid and insensitive, others understanding and patient.

Another example shows how favoritism, discrimination and harassment were displayed (this example is by no means peculiar to Attica):

The possession of heating droppers (i.e. any kind of handmade electrical appliance that can be used to heat water or warm food) was generally permitted, but some men considered troublemakers or who were otherwise disliked were punished when the devices were found in their cells on shakedowns. Inmates widely reported that special searches were made of disfavored inmates' cells, in order to find the same contraband which was ignored when in the possession of others.

Arbitrariness, pettiness, and harassment by themselves did not, of course, produce the Attica tragedy. Indeed, this type of routine is a way of life in most of the overcrowded penitentiaries of North America, and inmates, as well as correctional officers, learn to live with it, in a sort of mutual conning where the inmates "neutralize" the pettiness of the authority by an "underground" system of their own. Extensive disciplinary rules and regulations not only permit arbitrariness in their application; they give guards plenty of room to find cause to make official complaints about inmates. Whether these complaints may or may not be justified, statistics show that inmates have little chance of winning an appeal once such a complaint is entered. On this the Attica Report noted: "Of the 3,219 complaints considered in 1971, only six were dropped at the hearing. The others resulted in punishment or, when considered more serious, referred to a Superintendent's hearing."

As far back as 1939, a Royal Commission to Investigate Penal Systems in Canada (47) pointed out that at St. Vincent de Paul Penitentiary in 1934-35 and in 1935-36 there were respectively 1,967 and 1,537 offenses charged without a single acquittal in either year. A similar state of affairs prevailed in the six other maximum security penitentiaries then existing in Canada. St. Vincent de Paul, under such a regime, passed some thirty consecutive years without a riot. We mention this only to show that rules, even unfairly applied ones, do not by themselves provoke a riot. They can, however, foster resentment and a sense of outrage that, when added to other factors, cause riots. And they certainly impede the rehabilitation of prisoners who already feel life has been unjust to them.

In 1966 we were not so well acquainted with disciplinary practices of New York State prisons as we were with those in Canada. However, we knew enough about maximum security penitentiaries to decide that we wanted none of the types of rules and regulations that were common in the prisons from which the men came. At the Center a great amount of time was left for leisure, and we were determined not to make an offense out of behavior, acts or words, that might be classifiable as impolite or improper, but were not actually delinquent. We also avoided rules about personal deportment, including dress, hairstyles. An offender is not serving time in prison because he wears his hair long or short, with or without sideburns.

We did not even make attendance at work a rule but simply a moral obligation. Not to be obliged to work in a system where "forced labor" is a basic tradition was probably the most revolutionary aspect of the absence of rules at the Center. We were well aware that many penologists consider work attendance a fundamental rule and that the absence of this particular rule would present a challenge to both inmates and officers. We were aware not only of the problems, but also of the many solutions that would have to be found from the first day when fifty persistent offenders and forty correctional officers would come together and attempt to co-exist under such a minimal regime.

2.   The Therapeutic Community at Clinton

*In prison language, the perimeter was maximum
security, but the life within was minimum security.*

When it started in October 1966, the Clinton Center
housed fifty inmates: this number was increased to 100 the
following year.   Inmates were to remain there, prior to
release and parole, a minimum of six months and a maximum
of eighteen, the average stay being about a year.
The aims of a therapeutic community vary with the
participants and the setting.   Reeducation and resocialization
were stressed at Clinton because we see them as being
inseparable.   In reeducation the emphasis is on the individual
vis-à-vis his milieu; while in resocialization, the milieu itself
contributes to shaping the individual.   Both are important
when working with persistent offenders, for one soon
discovers that their individual psychopathology and the harsh
reality in which they grew up were hardly likely to lead to
good social and individual adaptation.
We agreed from the start that the Center would not
specialize in the treatment of persistent offenders guilty of only
one type of offense such as sexual offenders, chronic alcoholics
or drug addicts.   However, in the second year of operation
some sexual offenders serving indeterminate sentences were
admitted.   At no time, however, were there so many such
offenders that the Center veered from its original intent — the
treatment of persistent offenders regardless of their offenses.
Those responsible for selecting the inmates for admission
to the Center were familiar with the McGill classification of
criminal processes, their evolution and abatement.   A set of
clinical criteria was drawn up to serve as a guide or as a

practical tool to help in selecting persistent offenders eligible
for either admission to the Center or to serve as a control
group.   The men were selected according to general criteria
with only two absolute conditions.   They had to be :

(1) persistent offenders; and

(2) eligible for parole within eighteen months.

The other criteria were broader and more flexible:
There was no strict age limit, though the suggested range
was between twenty-five and thirty-five, with a preference for
inmates in their mid-twenties.

Inmates had to be motivated for treatment, i.e., to ask
for it, or actively take advantage of it when it was offered.

Good behavior in prison was not in itself a reason for
accepting or rejecting a candidate, nor did chronic disciplinary
problems in a character disorder disqualify an inmate if he was
willing to take part in a special intensive program and was
eligible for parole.

A history of psychiatric breakdown, provided it was not
a chronic state nor present at the time of selection, was not a
barrier to admission.

Although well-motivated offenders were preferred,
persistent offenders who were known to be passive individuals
were not eliminated.   In these cases the goal was to arouse
motivation and induce awakening through active participation
in the life of the community.

A pattern of violence was not in itself an obstacle to
admission.   Such prisoners could be admitted to the Center
in the hope that their behavior could be controlled with an
intensive program and the energy used in "acting out" could
be channeled toward reeducation.

Good motivation along with disappointment with
criminal life and a consciously expressed desire to change
were useful criteria.

The first four to six weeks was a probationary period and
if a man showed that he was not really suited for the program
he was returned to the regular prison.   Such a return was not
considered as a punishment by either the Center or the prison,
nor did it preclude later readmission to the Center.

Inmates were made aware that the Center would not be a

place for relaxation and that work would be very much part of their daily life. They would be expected to work no less than if they were in a regular prison — and possibly more. The difference would be in the regime of life: inmates would be given as many responsibilities as they could handle. The entire staff, professional as well as custodial, would be directly involved with them in these responsibilities.

Though acceptance for the treatment program might result in parole, it was no guarantee. Only the Parole Board could decide if and when parole would be granted. Inmates were expected to accept treatment for its own sake, whatever the possibility of a parole. Most of them tended to feel however, that parole was owed to them because they had fulfilled the conditions of treatment. The staff had to bear this in mind when inmates at the Center were not granted parole.

Since persistent offenders tend to reach a peak in their criminal career in their late twenties, this was the age used as a guideline for selection. However, men with a severe record of persistent delinquency starting in early childhood have deep-seated character disorders that might not peak until their thirties; therefore they were accepted at that age. Clinical judgment was the deciding factor.

Discontent with themselves was a characteristic that made older criminals eligible. They were anxious and depressed, and they felt their life had been wasted. They might not be hopeful about their future, but at least they were looking for some solution. Revolt against society was present, but there was also the realization that society alone was not to blame. We viewed this state as indicating a certain amount of self-criticism and an ability to appreciate the criticism of others.

Seeing the past with bitterness was another characteristic. Most of these men had been beaten by life for one reason or another, but by now this had resulted in their realizing that if they were to have any life at all, they would have to reevaluate their lives at some stage. Wardens or other members of the staff who knew certain persistent offenders over the years recommended promising candidates. They were often aware that an inmate was ready for help and had a good chance of making the grade if given timely assistance. Such estimates were carefully considered.

* *

The setting was a maximum security one. Within this outer frame, however, a living milieu was devised to give the greatest possible freedom. In prison language, the perimeter was maximum security, but the life within was minimum security. Patterns of daily routine were established to resemble as closely as possible those in the community outside. While the greatest possible freedom of movement and choice in the personal order of their lives was given, certain obligations had to be accepted. These were presence at community meetings, attendance at group and individual therapy sessions, participation in committees and — most vital — turning up for work on one's own without being paraded or regimented. The inmates spent the shortest possible amount of time locked in their cells, from 11 p.m. to 6 a.m. seven days a week. This was in direct contrast to conventional maximum security penitentiaries where inmates usually spend sixteen hours per day — more on weekends — locked in their cells.

Dannemora State Hospital has no surrounding walls, only those of the building itself. If the administrative wing of the hospital once had barred windows this is no longer true. The windows are now of steel frame. On the other hand the cell blocks, shops and recreation rooms all have large barred windows.

Unit I, set up in the old part of the building, consisted of two sets of living quarters, one per floor. In each set there was enough room for twenty-five men, nineteen of whom had individual cells, plus a dormitory, broken up into cubicles, accommodating six men. Ample space allowed each man to arrange his cubicle to give at least a minimum of privacy. The twenty-five men had their own dining room and common rooms, and long high-ceilinged corridors underlined the impression of lots of space.

Unit I had a great advantage, one seldom found in modern penal institutions — a feeling of space in which to move around. This, besides the freedom of movement allowed inmates (sixteen hours a day outside their cells), was an important factor in helping them live together. When groups of men live together and there is room to move away, they will do so rather than fight with one another. If, on the other hand, they are crowded together, there is increased risk of fighting. In this program, freedom of movement promoted security rather than danger. This important factor is often ignored in modern prisons: men deprived of freedom should have enough space to either meet together or avoid one another.

Next to Unit I a once-large dormitory equipped with modern plumbing had been transformed into a huge shop. As in the housing units, the shop's windows were larger than normal. No modern architecture would have provided as much airy space as this serviceable old building.

Unit II was not as pleasant to live in as Unit I, though its inmates could also move about freely. The shop was essentially the same, but the housing quarters were not immediately adjacent. Since the cells had been built on the outside wall of what were once two big dormitories, each had its own large window. In this unit the showers and toilets were communal.

In both units, some of the space was used for art studios. The inmates also used a well-equipped and recently built gymnasium. It was somewhat paradoxical to find that we could transform an old building to suit a modern program.

The daily program was more or less as follows: 6 to 8 a.m. was devoted to waking, washing, showering, breakfast, making beds and tidying cells, all of which was the responsibility of the inmates themselves. At 8 a.m. they were expected to report for work.

Work was considered of prime importance, but the main concern was not the acquiring of skills. The emphasis was rather on good work habits, responsibility for work, self-discipline and toleration of the inevitable daily frustrations. In our culture, work is seen as part and parcel of life, a social relationship, a way of being in the world. Most of the men in the prison therapeutic community had acquired at least two, and often more, well-developed vocational skills in the course of their prison sentences, but had been unable to exploit them on the outside. Instead of specific work skills we stressed establishing work patterns: punctuality, acceptance of supervision, and mutual tolerance. As we expected, this proved an unending source of conflict at every level, but it also became an important therapeutic agent, taking up a great deal of the time at the community meetings.

It was not surprising that during working hours there was a good deal of acting out on the part of the prisoners. We were acquainted with maximum penitentiary regime and we did not feel there was merit in enforced punctuality where anyone refusing to go to work was reported to a disciplinary court. Allowed to go to work on their own a great number of inmates were habitually late. When asked why, they gave such answers as "I don't like work," "I didn't feel like going," "Why should I work?" "I'm bored," and so on. Tardiness was one specific area where acting out was allowed so that we could deal with the symptom rather than suppress it. Other examples of acting out in work, such as insolence and leaving the shops, were also dealt with as symptoms.

A daily community meeting of inmates and staff, professional and correctional, took place five days a week, usually at the end of the morning work session. The therapeutic community was not a decision-making body but a therapeutic tool, though suggestions might be made on which the administration could choose to act. As everyone was involved in the community, any decision — popular or otherwise — could be fully explained and discussed. After each community meeting, the staff met and had a post-mortem. This enabled the staff to deal with immediate problems as part of a continuing in-training program. In this, as in other techniques, Jones's formula was closely followed.

This meeting was followed by the midday meal during which the inmates were responsible for eating on their own within a prescribed time limit before returning to the afternoon work session.

Individual therapy was the only therapeutic activity carried out during shop hours, but all such interviews were by appointment, and no inmate was expected to leave the shop for longer than the interview itself. For individual therapy, each inmate was assigned to a therapist but it should be stressed that the object of individual therapy was to foster group therapy, and the object of group therapy was to foster community therapy. Important as individual therapy may be in the solution of personal problems, the opposite approach, that of stressing individual rather than group and community therapy, would negate the principle of the therapeutic community. In some therapeutic community programs, all the therapeutic resources are centered around the community meeting. In the Clinton Project, because the staff dealt with inmates with chronic acting out disorders, we felt that personal as well as social therapy should be combined in the order of priority described. Group therapy meetings took place once a week with groups of eight to ten inmates, plus a therapist and correctional officers.

Committees, composed of inmates and of professional and correctional staff, are an essential part of the therapeutic community. There were house, shop, arts, handicrafts, sports, and other committees. (It should be emphasized that the committee is not in itself a decision-making body, but a group of community members who discuss specific problems and offer suggestions and recommendations which are placed before the community meeting and, if accepted, are carried out by the administration.) All problems and personal frustrations encountered in community activities were dealt with on the spot, so that it became a therapeutic experience in resocialization. This is one of the reasons why staff form such an integral part of the committee.

We chose this formula for Clinton even though we know that in other therapeutic milieus committees are composed only of inmates who bring their recommendations to the administration. The staff felt that this particular group, composed of two interlocking, sometimes clashing components — inmate and staff — offered valuable occasions for encounters that should be exploited.

An important feature of the Clinton Project was that the inmates had considerable free time during the day, in the evenings and on weekends. Much of the therapeutic activity necessarily took place then; and the greatest impact of the program lay in how this time was used.   It is here that the correctional staff played a major role. They were with the inmates during evening shifts and on weekends when much activity went on: adult education, participation in arts and crafts, organized sports, etc. On Saturday mornings there was a period of sociodrama and other role-playing events. In all this "free time," inmates and correctional officers were encouraged to discuss their problems as they arose, and to have interviews with one another as in any other therapeutic community processes.

3. A Special Breed of Officers

Whatever they were, they were not just forty
pasteurized, homogenized bottles of milk. They
were forty men with characters of their own.

At the invitation of Dr. Ludwig S. Fink, then Assistant to
the Director of the Dannemora State Hospital, Dr. Cormier was
a frequent visitor to the hospital in 1965-66. The New York
Correctional Services were awaiting the outcome of the Baxstrom
appeal. (Baxstrom v. Herold, 383 US 107 1966) Final
decision was rendered in February 1966. They knew that if
the appeal was successful, the decision could result in considerably reducing the hospital's population. With this in
mind, the New York State authorities, though their decision
was independent of the case's outcome, invited the McGill
Clinic in Forensic Psychiatry to cooperate in improving the
Dannemora State Hospital which was used for convicts who
had become mentally ill while serving sentences.

On our first visit we had the usual guided tour with the
hospital officials who apologized and offered explanations for
most of what we were seeing. We exchanged ideas on how things
might be changed.

The guards were already receiving courses in psychiatry,
especially in group counseling. Actually none of this knowledge
could be put into practice, even though many of them were
sincerely motivated to be more than keepers of mentally ill
inmates. There was in fact some awkwardness whenever Dr.
Cormier used the word "guards." Once during the first or
second visit, he was politely reminded that this was not the
appropriate term. They could accept that penitentiary inmates
referred to them as "screws," "hacks," "dogs " and "blueshirts,"
but that a McGill University professor should refer to them as

61

guards when the correct term was "correctional officers" they considered to be a breach of protocol, if not downright rudeness.

This incident, one among the many during our early visits to Dannemora, took place in our initial encounters with the correctional officers. Some are worth recalling as it is through them that we came to know the forty officers who would eventually become our colleagues and friends.

On another official visit, we witnessed something none of us had ever seen anywhere before. We were approaching the doors to one of the vast common rooms. Just after the classic sound of a key in a prison lock, the door opened onto a large, extremely long room characteristic of old asylums or hospital wards. The attending officer suddenly gave a tremendous shout as if he meant to be heard a mile away. It could neither be described nor imitated and we came to refer to it as "the indescribable yell." As soon as we entered the room, two or three officers, somewhat like a guard of honor, joined the official party. We could see the patients scurrying hastily away from the center of the room toward the walls on either side. The officials could then proceed serenely down the center of the room. We walked slowly, wanting to observe as much as we could. The slow march was interrupted only by the exchange of ideas. For some of the psychiatrists the walk posed items of clinical interest. Scattered here and there, the occasional patient could be seen lying on the floor while a few others postured near the numerous supporting columns. One of the accompanying psychiatrists pointed them out and gravely observed, "Catatonic schizophrenics, evidently," with an air that seemed to say, "What else could they be?" In due course we reached the opposite door of the room. Again there ensued the classic sound of the lock clanging. The door opened, the officials filed out, and the visit was terminated. But not quite. As the door was closing, the "indescribable yell" rang out again. We could almost visualize the scene in reverse, this time the shout undoubtedly signaling the return of the patients to the center of the room where they could mingle with their guardians, undisturbed — until the next official visit.

These were our first encounters, albeit silent ones, with the correctional officers. So well were they trained to guard officials that we had no occasion to talk to them meaningfully. Our visits became more frequent during the spring and summer of 1966, when the Center was being actively planned with an opening set for that October. The McGill staff soon became members of the family and the day arrived when we were able to enter the common rooms without an accompanying "indescribable yell."

The main purpose of our visits was to get to know the officers. We also had some interest in the mentally ill inmates with whom they were working even though the Center we were planning would be treating persistent offenders only. It was during one of the pleasant informal visits that it occurred to us to ask about the singular "indescribable yell." It turned out that it was to protect the officials. No one could remember how or when the ritual got its start.

During these unofficial visits we noted that there were markedly fewer catatonic patients lying about on the floor or assuming stances near the columns. We remarked on this to the officers. One of them explained: "You know, when officials arrive, some of the patients just find it a lot simpler to fall down on the spot and go into an 'acute catatonic state' rather than have to go racing over to the wall . . ." We could not suppress a smile as we thought back to the "catatonic schizophrenics evidently" diagnosis. Behind this diagnosis, so reassuring to the officials, there could in fact have been a truly dangerous paranoid patient. But, since the correctional officers knew the distinction between the catatonic patients and the occasional dangerous mentally disturbed inmate, the officials were indeed well guarded. During these later visits we jokingly referred to the correctional officers as the "official guardians," a title to which they did not object.

A correctional officer was always present during psychiatric interviews at Dannemora State Hospital (this applied to other professionals as well), and some psychiatrists resented this practice; at least one fought it openly. Unfortunately, most of them accepted it unquestioningly, and we may assume that they felt it was a necessary protective measure. This was a saddening thought. For many years some of us had been interviewing offenders and mentally ill inmates with no guards present and we had never felt that such protection was necessary.

By the time that several hundred so-called dangerous patients had to be released from Dannemora State Hospital we understood a lot more about the Baxstrom decision. The professional staff of the institution were released from many of their fears. In retrospect, some years later, we know that these fears were unfounded since the 960 Baxstrom patients returned to society in orderly and uneventful fashion. (31, 53, 54, 52) Many of the correctional officers, who guarded the psychiatrists as well as their patients, were well aware that this would be the case.

We were well into the summer of 1966 and signs of autumn were becoming evident in the Adirondacks on the road from Montreal to Dannemora, but we of the McGill staff had other matters on our minds. Commissioner Paul D. McGinnis and Peter Preiser, Executive Director of the Governor's Special Committee on Criminal Offenders, were by now well acquainted with the proposed program for the Center, and they were determined that it be implemented with the briefest possible delay. Dr. Cormier remembered the final discussion in August when, though very enthusiastic about starting a program based on research done at the McGill Clinic in Forensic Psychiatry, he found himself ruefully remarking, "I already work fourteen hours a day" only to be greeted with the rejoinder, "Well, you still have another ten! " The contract was signed with opening day designated as early in October.

It is not unusual to hear professionals who are venturing into a new correctional program which differs widely from the traditional pattern say, "I wish we could start with brand new staff who have never worked in prison . . . The old guards are always in the way." We never subscribed to this view. We know that many correctional officers become more institutionalized than the inmates, but we also know that administrative and professional staff too (presumably with more knowledge and experience — too often, armchair experience) can become more *imprisonized* than the guard at the gates.

Forty correctional officers were to be selected and trained, a task that proved to be far less complicated than we had anticipated. No criteria had been set for their selection. Therefore, we began by meeting in large groups with the guards already employed in the institution. We would outline the program in a formal way and each meeting terminated with a question period and discussion, especially on points which were entirely new to those who had been trained under maximum security conditions: no punitive quarters or cells; sixteen hours a day, seven days a week, out of the cells; a mixed professional staff (a first for New York State); no writing of misconduct reports; no frisking of inmates or searching of cells without the

complete cooperation of the inmates and without having stated
the reason; complete freedom to circulate within the living units,
common rooms, studios, gymnasium; toleration of all forms of
aggression, except for physical. Was this all a dream or utopia?
The more these aspects of the program were explained, the more
questions were asked. In the end, the forty correctional officers
believed they were not so much volunteering for a program as
meeting a challenge.

A good remark to open our description of the forty officers
at the Center might be to say they were not New Yorkers, i.e.
from New York City, nor did they wish to be. For a New Yorker,
to come from the upper part of the state is to be "rural." This
idea was not unfamiliar to us in Montreal since we tend to regard
as provincial anybody in Quebec who does not come from
Montreal. For a metropolitan New Yorker, what else can you be
when you come from a small town or village? It feels good to
be a New Yorker, something special in the Empire State. Some
of the prisoners, as well as some migrant New Yorkers now living
in the upper part of the state, often held the rural origins of the
officers against them.

How can correctional officers with a rural background
understand inmates coming from New York City, which sees
itself as the most complex metropolis in the world and even
takes pride in being referred to as ungovernable? New York,
where great universities are within walking distance of the
largest ghettos, where life is dense, hyper-animal and hyper-
human, super-rich and super-poor, holy and evil.

"Rural" was never a term that came to mind when we
described our forty correctional officers. They might be
citizens of a small town in an upper state area, but in Clinton
County they were considered the region's middle class. With
the prevailing salaries and security provided by being civil
servants, they were able to do a lot more with their money than
if they had been living in New York City.

Culturally, many of them were frequent visitors to
Montreal. Some even had French names, such as Champagne,
Rabideau, Racette, etc. For the latter, perhaps coming to
Montreal was more or less consciously felt as a return to their
origins. Despite their names, however, none of them spoke
French. In fact, with one exception, none could recall ever
having spoken French at home. This was in contrast to the
Canucks living in the small textile and manufacturing towns

of New England, where French is a language still heard in the streets, even though the distance from Montreal is much greater. Our men were more likely descended from French-Canadian families living near the border who had crossed the 49th parallel and become Americans sometime during the last century, when American doors were wide open to immigrants.

Statistics on the age of those who elected to work on the project are meaningless. Some were in their thirties, most in their forties, some in their fifties or older, but none were near retirement age. As a group they were mainly middle-aged men with a special past — years of life spent working with criminal mentally ill prisoners.

That they were not young was an advantage. For many years they had had little to say but had heard a lot in countless interviews during which they guarded the psychiatrists. Each of them had special memories from the long years spent with criminals. Yes, they had used force to restrain agitated, violent patients or those believed to be dangerous; they had removed patients bodily to the isolation ward. (Paradoxically, they often had to do the same when they brought them out again later.) The older ones among them had witnessed the advance of psychotropic drugs and were very pleased that force was now seldom necessary.

In speaking about the use of straitjackets, and what has come to be known as the "chemical straitjacket" i.e. tranquil-izing injections, they indicated that they felt their use did not leave much challenge for real work — the patient was either quiet and had only to be watched, or he was violently agitated and assumed to be dangerous. If the latter, their function was to restrain him. We had heard guards boast about doing this in the past but we never heard any of the Dannemora guards brag about having to subdue X, Y or Z — patients known either for agitation, violent outbursts or dangerous behavior and we assume they did not like having to do it.

In temperament, they varied as any group of individuals might. Some were impulsive, always ready for the give and take of argument. Others were quiet. Some were even passive. Nonetheless, their inner clocks worked well and the right question or solid objection would emerge at strategic moments. The ones who stand out most in the minds of the McGill group were those who, right from the beginning, were referred to amicably as "shit disturbers." Though they were not prepared to give or

66

take any crap, they were ready to clean up the mess (including their own) when there was one. These were the ones who were active in the program, keen, observant, at times even belligerent. It did not take them long to get to know the characters they would meet among the persistent offenders. Whatever they were, they were not just forty pasteurized, homogenized bottles of milk. They were forty men with characters of their own.

In joining a program where establishing relationships with persistent offenders would be their basic tool they did not pretend to be anything special, though they must have felt somewhat different from the rest of their fellow officers.

This impression is reinforced when we read what has been said about the correctional officers in the Official Report of the New York State Special Commission on Attica: "Most officers perceived themselves as custodians who were there to enforce the rules and to keep the inmates in line, not to help solve their problems. They were not trained to counsel inmates and they generally lacked the motivation to try." The consultant psychiatrist for the Commission interviewed thirty officers, and stated that these were men who did not purport to be social workers. Like most civil servants, they had been attracted to their posts by job security and the promise of a pension. He testified: "These are really quite decent people, these officers I have met, and I mean no derogation of them when I say they have no particular skill for the kind of work that they're doing, if indeed rehabilitation is to be the goal and not just custody and safekeeping." (2)

It is possible, indeed highly probable, that if we had selected forty officers at random from among the many hundred working at the prison, we might have come to a similar conclusion. But our officers chose to come. We simply explained our program to groups of officers, and in the end we had the forty officers needed for the project. We never felt that they considered themselves to be out of the ordinary. They were simply a group who wanted to meet a challenge and change their way of living with the inmates. They were well aware that they would be stripped of all custodial "gimmicks" to keep a prison "cool." They knew they would have to work with men who knew all the prison "gimmicks" to keep a prison "hot" and that they would have to rely on human relationships only.

We often wondered how these forty officers so rapidly learned the techniques that resident psychiatrists take years to

learn. Many stated that working with the mentally ill inmates
had given them a different outlook on men. This appeared to
be true. The experience certainly contributed to making them a
a special breed of correctional officers. It must at the same time
be recognized that working with the mentally ill, who are also
prisoners, does not always mobilize feelings of compassion and
empathy. Often, quite the contrary. These officers who
began the two-week intensive teaching program of group
and therapeutic techniques started in the autumn of 1966.
Though they were fast learners, we knew there was one thing we
could not teach them. In the difficult process of helping men
who wish to change, we are often confronted with a more
difficult task, that of changing ourselves, a reality which must be
discovered and accepted individually.

This group of officers, mainly middle-aged men, was
preparing to work with a group of adult persistent offenders.
Both these groups were men who had reached a stage in life
when, as W.C. Fields so aptly and humorously described it,
"there comes a time in the Affairs of Man when he must take
the bull by the tail and look the situation squarely in the face."

4.   Introducing the Officers

Persistent offenders, newly come from citadels of security, found it strange to be greeted with a handshake from the officers and given a personal explanation of the attitudes and minimal rules in effect at the Center.

The captains and guards were the first to have to learn new styles.   The first captain to work with us in training the officers, Captain Anderson, was promoted and transferred a few months after the Center opened.   Until a permanent posting was made, Charles Davis, a captain of the officers at Dannemora State Hospital, served also as acting captain at the Center.

Then, in August 1967, Frank Wald, a captain from Attica, was named to the Center.   He was 61 years old, with 35 years experience in the department, 25 of them at Attica.   At a staff meeting shortly after his arrival, our minutes show that he remarked: "A lot of the inmates say that we need a set of rules." Dr. Fink lost no time in emphatically replying, "This is one thing we don't see eye to eye on.   Rules should be simple and kept to a minimum."   Later Capt. Wald stated that the Center should be like some other institutions where "You get one chance and if you blow it you are done."   Dr. Fink took this up immediately and remarked that "We are not running a reformatory here.   This is a therapeutic community."   Dr. Fink's statement was followed by Art Rabideau's comment that "we had a great community meeting yesterday after two inmates were separated from a fist fight."   Capt. Wald thus became acquainted with our new way of doing things.   A fist fight between inmates is usually what is most feared in ordinary penal institutions.   At the Center we felt safe in resolving the matter by discussion rather than punishment.

Capt. Wald took all this in stride. He learned to let his men go their own way with a minimum of interference and

most of the inmates called him "Pappy" Wald.   He was transferred back to Attica not long before the tragedy occurred
there, and during the riot distinguished himself with his courage,
compassion and cool-headedness.   The New York State Special
Commission on Attica had this to say about him in their official
report: (2)

At the time of the riot:

Capt. Frank ("Pappy") Wald, the senior uniformed
officer at Attica . . . and two other officers retreated
into the C block office.   They could not lock the
door, but jammed it shut with a piece of heavy wire.
Inmates . . . tried to force open the door . . . tried to
burn them out . . . as well as trying to flood them
out with fire hoses . . . but the door was jammed
shut and they couldn't get out . . .   In Captain
Wald's words: ". . . if the door had opened I felt
quite sure we would immediately be massacred . . .
I looked out . . . and saw a black inmate that I
knew . . .   He said, 'Place yourself in my hands,
you won't get harmed.' . . . one officer . . . didn't
want to give up because he thought sure we would
be killed . . .   I said, . . . 'I am going to give up.   I
am going to accept this man's word'."

After being taken to the yard as a hostage, inmates came up to
Captain Wald and told him they needed medical help and "you
are the only one who can get it."   He was taken to A block
gate and shouted to the correction officers in the administration
building, describing the hostages' injuries and asking for medication and a doctor, a call that did not go unheeded.

There were other officers who played major roles in the
early development of the Center.

Art Rabideau had fourteen years of service at Dannemora
State Hospital when he joined the group of officers working at
the Center.   Art was ambitious, perceptive and outspoken.   At
staff meetings he was certainly the griper *par excellence*, and
we were the subject of his complaints.   Many officers questioned
and criticized the professional staff, and rightly so, but with Art
it seemed a specialty.   He disliked the formal lectures, pre-
ferring the seminars and audiovisual methods used in the
officer-training period before the opening of the Center.   Like
many of the other officers he enjoyed the initial experience, in

spite of the fact that he was upset because he did not feel the officers were given enough status.

Although he was not easily depressed, he had a sort of let-down feeling, perhaps impatience, that in the first months of the Center's operation the officers could not become involved in therapeutic relationships with the inmates as rapidly as he felt they should. At first the inmates had a sort of blind trust in the professional staff and an equally blind distrust of the correctional officers. Art said later: "I began to enjoy the program again after the professional people started to throw problems back to the officers."

Art was soon joined in his griping by Paul Williams, the first bearded professional at the Center. A later addition was Josh Zambrowsky, the first"mod"therapist at the Center.

Ray Casey had nineteen years experience at Dannemora State Hospital when he joined the program. He was put in charge of the shop, perhaps the most difficult assignment at the Center. Ray was a jovial, impulsive person, who welcomed the challenge to put himself in the "hot seat." He apologized when he felt he had gone too far but remained firm and uncompromising when he felt he was right. This was true of his attitude to both inmates and staff. Behind his impulsiveness and outspokenness he was very sensitive; he was as prone to anger as to depression. At parties he was joyful and exuberant. Ray was the officer to whom many of us felt closest.

No matter what the situation Ray expressed his feelings. He was not embarrassed to say that at the beginning he felt strange when faced with handshaking and saying good morning and good evening to the prisoners. On the other hand he found himself quite naturally going out of his way to do little things for the inmates. He was not ashamed to admit that when first in contact with the complex state of relationships between officers and inmates he often found himself waking up at night in a cold sweat or with nightmares. But he survived well. Perhaps he is best described by his own statement: "In my heart there was never a conflict between maintaining security and being helpful."

Working with Ray Casey as a co-supervisor in the shop was Lindon Payne. He had been employed at Dannemora State Hospital for twelve years before joining the Center. These two men could not have been more dissimilar in character. Lindon was a quiet, soft-spoken man of even

disposition.   While Ray's fluctuations of moods matched
those of the inmates, Lindon could be relied on to remain
calm.   This in no way implies that Lindon could not express
strong feelings or change his mind.   For instance, describing
the Center when it opened, he said that it was "next to
Paradise."   Later, when griping had become a daily routine,
he found it "hard to live with" the inmates.   Lindon and
Ray, with their opposite characters, were both highly
regarded by the inmates: Lindon because of his consistency,
and Ray because he was outspoken but able to apologize
when he went too far.   The inmates always knew where they
stood with both.   They also knew how to approach either,
depending on the circumstances or moods and tempers
prevailing.

It is interesting that although at first Dennis felt inadequate, poorly equipped, not ready to deal with inmates
who were acting out, he was, in fact, one of the officers who
dealt most efficiently with such situations.   He seemed to
analyze himself more than the others and believed that an
officer working in such a program was necessarily involved in
changing himself.   He once said that at first he saw security
as an important feature but later it no longer seemed so
important: "It is human relationships you are forming here;
security is not really needed."   He was also the officer who
wrote the most extensive notes on his interviews with inmates.
At times they were practically verbatim reports.

Charlie Hayden had worked for four years as a prison
officer and fifteen years at the Dannemora State Hospital
before joining the staff at the Center.   Over six feet tall, he
was certainly the most impressive-looking of the officers,
especially in winter when he wore his blue greatcoat with the

gold stripes indicating his rank on its sleeves and his officer's hat trimmed with gold braid. Like most of our officers he was a devoted family man with a keen interest in his daughter's musical education.

Charlie was the one who described the early days of the Center in the most glowing terms, but in the same breath he admitted how short its duration was: "The first ten days were ecstasy! " He was the first to sense the griping that was to come. Though he had found the first ten days exciting, he became very annoyed at the "outrageous demands" of the inmates, their beefing, their lack of courtesy and their bad manners in general. Charlie was concerned with all these problems, but he needed to consolidate things. Unlike Art and Ray, Charlie enjoyed a good lecture rather than seminars. He probably regretted that reeducation of persistent offenders could not be achieved by a formal method of teaching them how to live on the outside. For this reason he sometimes felt sad that progress was slow and that so many of the inmates were unable to be neat and tidy. But he also had the ability to wonder if his expectations were perhaps too high. At times, however, he had a tendency to let things go.

In many ways he was the officer who felt most acutely the difficulties of being both a correctional officer and a therapist. With great honesty he once acknowledged that he felt quite ambivalent about reporting the delinquency of an inmate who stole five pairs of pants as this was somewhat like "squealing." In this Charlie understood very well indeed how correctional officers can easily, and even without being aware of it, live according to the code of the inmates they guard.

To believe that fifty persistent offenders would be able to communicate and discuss with almost as many correctional officers within a framework of minimum rules, and that everything would run smoothly right from the start, would have been unrealistic. Fortunately we had no such expectations. To live with a minimum of rules is, at best, difficult to achieve in any social group; to have assumed that it would be easy in prison would have been utopian. But it was a challenge, and so we went ahead and replaced the hundreds of heavy-handed rules applied from morning to night in maximum penitentiaries by a few general guidelines. We also knew, of course, that at some stage some rules would be necessary, not necessarily disciplinary ones, but rules regarding the living units, the shops, the recreational area, and above all the increased amount of free time the inmates would have on their hands. But we wanted such rules to arise from the practical experience of staff and inmates having lived together. Cocky as we were, we realized that we should always be aware of what we were doing and what was happening.

Before the Center opened we suggested to the officers that we make it a rule to bid the inmates good morning and good evening the same way we greeted each other. We also mentioned that when an inmate arrived or departed from the Center, it would be appropriate to shake hands with him. Some officers saw this as a gimmick, but we saw it as the normal type of relationship that exists in factories, workshops, and offices, among friends and neighbors. It was a way to reestablish the manners that disappear in a prison setting. Of course, some guards greet inmates they happen to like, but in general inmates and guards are people who pass each other in silence.

At first the greetings were self-conscious and gimmicky, but as time went by casual, more natural forms of greeting developed, with each person using his own style. Persistent offenders newly come from citadels of security, found it strange to be greeted with a handshake from the officers and given a personal explanation of the attitudes and minimal rules in effect at the Center. Some wondered uneasily if they had not really been transferred to the "nut house" wing of the Dannemora State Hospital complex.

During those first weeks the atmosphere could be described as one of camaraderie. The inmates arrived in groups of three or four and it took about a month to fill the two housing quarters of Unit I. The staff had time to give each a great deal of individual attention and those first inmates remarked on their being treated as "human beings." They felt comfortable, if somewhat strange, in their new surroundings.

Obviously these good feelings were not going to last forever. Gingerly at first, but with growing intensity, the mood in the community meetings became one of griping, bickering and bitching. Anything and everything seemed to be the subject of complaint. Food was almost always, and not without some justification, on the list along with haircuts, salaries, mail, library books, lights in the rooms, telephone books and medical care. Some of the demands were irrational

and impossible, but others were quite realistic. Unfortunately
the men wanted everything to be done at once. They could
not come to grips with the fact that the staff had to contend
with the administration as well as the prisoners. The result
was a new wave of griping about delays.

Griping also went on among staff members. It is not
easy for people who have always thought in terms of "we"
and "they" to develop a sense of belonging to a community.
At first there was a proliferation of "we's" and "they's." At
times there were three "they's" in a community meeting:
they, the inmates; they, the staff; and they, the administration.
Not surprisingly, there were as many "we's": we, the professional staff; we, the officers; and we, the inmates. How long
did it take to weld them all into one group? It can be said
that about six months after the opening a community existed —
and it continued to exist for nearly six years.

By the end of the first six months, a few inmates had
left and new ones had arrived to take their place. Like those
before them, the newcomers started to gripe. However, by
this time the community meetings were strong enough so that
"we " the inmates and staff were old-timers and knew that this
was a phase new arrivals had to go through, and we welcomed
them to the community. They soon integrated. The
incessant bickering and griping of the first three months
gradually leveled off. True, people continued to bitch to
some extent, but this is part of life in any community. How
some of the correctional officers survived the events of the
first six months will illustrate just how well staff and inmates
integrated into a *real community*.

5. Training the Staff

*Where there was a tendency to overindulgence,
there was also a tendency to take old-style punitive
measures in a crisis.*

Essential to any therapeutic community is the training of
personnel. The program set up for the training of the officers
made simultaneous use of lectures, seminars, audio-visual media,
and clinical demonstrations — including interviews with
prisoners. Once the community was established we felt that
training would be an on-going process. As the officers
participated in community meetings and case conferences, they
would be expected to keep clinical notes on the inmates and to
consult with professional staff.

In his training the correctional officer is unavoidably confronted with contradictory situations. His first and most
important function is the security of the institution. Inmates
must be detained and they *must* observe the rules. Rules vary
in strictness from maximum to minimum, but the principle
remains that the institution is maintained as an authoritarian
regime. Though correctional training has greatly improved with
the years, its programs still rest on security and discipline.
Needless to say, a therapeutic contact between officer and
inmate does not just develop under these conditions. It has to
be taught.

The aim of our program was to train officers to create a
truly helping relationship, while at the same time keeping control
of the situation. Parole and probation services are well aware of
how difficult it is to combine surveillance and counseling.
Correctional officers were the ones now facing this challenge.

It must be accepted that persistent offenders, with whom
the well-trained officers will interact, will not be inclined to

trust guards and participate willingly in a therapeutic relationship. They dislike authority in any shape or form, but most particularly the oppressive authority of the prison.

Of all prisoners, persistent offenders are the ones who have developed the most extreme collective distrust of guards. Thus the two groups confront each other, each having been deeply influenced by its prison experience.

Since the objective was to involve the correctional officers as an integral part of the treatment program, they required training similar to that given to the professional staff. The group at Clinton had already heard lectures on the principles of human behavior and on group counseling.

None of the forty men had fewer than ten years service, the average being fourteen. They all had experience either in correctional institutions or in prison psychiatric hospitals. They volunteered because of their particular interest in the program; they wished to take part, and they met the requirements.

After four months of operation, we felt that a good deal had been accomplished. Though hostility between the two groups, inmates and officers, was still present, it was producing no major crises. Because of our contact in individual and group therapy, we were aware of the inmates' feelings. They acknowledged that the officers were different, but they were still not prepared to accept them completely.

After four months, however, we did not know as much about the reactions of the officers as we did of the inmates, though it was evident that a great deal was going on. The most intensive interaction took place during recreational periods in the evening and at weekends, when the professional staff was seldom present.

A way to find out what the correctional officers thought about their training and performance was to interview them individually. One surprising fact that came to light was that for a number of the officers the training program had, to a large extent, been forgotten. Poor recollection was usually related to areas where the officer had trouble in functioning or to a personal problem. An extreme example was the officer who said that it was not he but the professional staff who was helping the prisoner, thus contradicting what had been empha - sized again and again. Other officers were so imbued with their responsibility that they bent over backward to be indulgent to the inmates. In the first example, the basic concept had not penetrated; in the second it had gone beyond its scope. Most of the officers had got the message, but with varying degrees of understanding.

The overall feeling about the training program, especially in relation to abstract concepts such as theories of behavior and psychodynamics, was that it had not been well assimilated. Officers must be taught, and understand, complex psychological theories, which are the basis of all reeducation programs. We introduced seminars followed by free discussions, especially on concrete problems dealing with practical issues within prison life, as well as audio-visual media and films designed for training followed by discussion and these were well received. Also highly rated was sociodrama which involved role playing as a method of training.

We tried a new technique as well, which can be compared to medical training where the intern participates with the doctor and both work together at the patient's bedside. Officers-in-training, along with two members of the professional staff, interviewed persistent offenders who had been selected because of their different types of personality and criminality. The professionals conducted the interview at the start, but left it to the correctional officers to intervene and carry on.

The inmates were encouraged to raise questions with the correctional officers just as they would with professional staff. Problems were collectively discussed. This kind of training proved to be very valuable. Though they had worked many years within a state psychiatric hospital for psychotic inmates, or in penal institutions, it was for them a new experience. We feel that this method should be worked into any program which aims at involving officers in a therapeutic, reeducative process.

The officers' reaction to the Center can be divided into two stages. The first period lasted two or three weeks after the actual opening of the Center. The officers were enthusiastic, fresh from training, eager to try out new concepts and had high expectations of success. This somewhat artificial enthusiasm at the beginning was reinforced by the prisoners themselves who reacted similarly to the new setting. Their pleasure should have been anticipated and the correctional officers alerted to the effect of placing prisoners in the freest prison setting they had ever known.

Looking back on this period of harmony, we realize that we failed to warn the officers that the inmates' satisfaction was

78

not related to a response to the officers' special training but to freedom of movement, individual choice, the variety of the program, and the attraction of better housing.

When the novelty wore off, the inmates returned to their old habits and began to act much as they had in other prisons. When occasionally they displayed overt hostility, the officers found themselves in the dilemma of either using their new techniques or reverting to their previous practices of handing out disciplinary reports. This conflict between the accustomed expedients and the new training created anxiety for the officers as they entered the second period. The real test was now approaching. How would the two groups interact when the novelty had worn off?

During the second period, the work of running a therapeutic community with all its problems commenced in earnest. We observed five types of reactions to disciplinary problems and to the fact that the officers were for the first time in their working life close to the inmates.

1) These were officers who, though at times tense and worried about the program, kept faith throughout and tried their best to use the knowledge acquired in the training program. They recognized in their tension and anxiety a warning that they would have to cope with an emerging problem. No matter how troubled they might be, these officers retained optimism.

2) Some officers tended to be indulgent and permissive when there was a problem requiring action. They excused conduct which should not have been overlooked, believing that this was in the spirit of the therapeutic community. They went overboard on the question of permissiveness.

3) As therapeutic community techniques could not sufficiently control difficult behavior or rapidly produce results, some officers wanted to return to old methods, and depending on where they placed the blame, they were in turn aggrieved at the inmates, the staff or themselves. None of them really wished to restore the previous regime, but the temptation was always present in an emergency. Where there was a tendency to over-indulgence, there was also a tendency to take old-style punitive measures in a crisis. They were not aware that their overindulgence had contributed to the crisis.

4) This reaction was a temporary state of discouragement: the program would not succeed, it was not worth carrying on, it should be "debunked" and dropped. Though such emotions

were frequent, they were usually resolved following a good community meeting, an informal discussion with professional staff, or an unexpected return to good behavior on the part of the inmates.

5) A certain number of officers tended to remain passive and somewhat detached throughout. They were onlookers rather than participants. They were not entirely passive, as they invariably followed the lead of a stronger colleague. Their passivity was apparent when they were in charge. Such persons work best under stimulating leadership. This type of attitude does not rule out ability to work in such a setting since their passivity did not hide hostility, aggression and negativism.

A number of correctional officers denied or did not acknowledge that they were an integral part of the treatment program. They continued to feel that it was carried out by the professional staff, in spite of continued assurance that they were the central force since they spent so much time with the men. The idea of participation remained foreign to them even when their role was obviously therapeutic. It was hard for them to understand this and to acknowledge that their work was as valuable as the professionals'.

Despite these reactions the majority of officers turned out to be constructive and active participants. It should be noted that the program was also new to the professional staff and as the professionals became more secure in their own work, tension and anxiety in the officers were lessened.

6.   The First Arrivals

By suggesting rules and punishments harsher than the
ones they claim to be the victims of, the inmates were
not only identifying with the aggressor by showing
they could become better aggressors than their keepers,
they themselves became super aggressors.

Prior to the official opening of the Center, it was decided
that minutes of all staff meetings, community meetings and
committee meetings would be systematically recorded.
Because this would be time-consuming, the work was divided
among the professional staff, correctional officers and inmates.
From the more than 500 typewritten pages covering the first
six months of the Center's existence, events, problems, and
happenings, some joyful, some sad, were selected which give a
broad insight into the feelings of all those involved.

The first inmates reached the Center on October 6, 1966,
arriving in groups of four or five.   These first arrivals found it
rather strange to have such a large staff to look after them.   By
October 10, the first community meeting at which minutes
were recorded took place.   There had already been enough
good mornings, good evenings and handshakings to confuse
everybody.   The inmates were still somewhat bewildered by
it all.   The meeting was rather slow going.   A few asked for
information about the gymnasium, correspondence privileges,
visiting and so on, but most of them remained silent or replied
only to direct questions with answers that were brief and to
the point.   Paul Williams notes that at the meeting, as often
happens, one particular inmate, *Chuck D.*, appointed himself
spokesman for the group.   Words came easily to him.   His
questions were straightforward, direct and aggressive.   He
enumerated five points, clearly and precisely, asking whether
the group would have an immediate reply.   These five points

became the theme of the griping to be heard in the sessions to come.

In these first community meetings the staff had a tendency to take the lead. Consequently, at the staff meeting that followed it was suggested that the inmates be encouraged to speak up. At the meeting of October 12, we started asking the inmates how they felt about being at the Center. Five or six of the twenty had a few good words to say about it. They felt comfortable, they felt that they could talk reasonably freely and that they were being treated as human beings.

A revealing discussion occurred at this meeting on the subject of frisking. Not all the officers were "true believers" and some had failed to grasp the guidelines that had been laid down during the training period. For instance, it had been made clear that frisking was to be used only if there was serious reason to feel it was needed and only with the co-operation of the inmate. A staff member, not identified in the minutes, said the inmates expected to be frisked when leaving the shop to go to an interview. Some correctional officers felt that special safety measures should be taken when a woman was doing the interviewing. Since they had "guarded" male psychiatrists during interviews at Dannemora State Hospital just a few weeks earlier, they found it hard to get used to the idea of a therapist, especially a woman, being alone with an inmate during an interview. Needless to say, the professional staff voiced strong opposition to any such suggestion. No frisking took place. The correctional officers themselves had the right to interview inmates and had the practice of frisking before interviews been initiated, they would have been in the curious position of having to frisk the inmate they were about to interview.

The uneasy relationship which had existed between the officers and the female staff since the training period was gradually improving, but the paternalistic attitude toward the women was still there. Initially, some officers felt uncomfortable when they saw inmates eating with knives and forks rather than with a spoon as had been the case at Dannemora State Hospital. So it was understandable that they should also feel disturbed by the idea of a woman being alone in an office with an inmate.

At the meeting of October 13 the inmates began to request commodities that they could not enjoy in other penitentiaries but which were certainly allowable at the Center. At one meeting they pointed out, not without reason, that if we expected them to do their own laundry they would need ironing boards. It had been hoped that automatic washing machines would be available at the Center, but no one had thought of ironing boards. To help "iron" out various problems of this nature, Lydia Keitner, a social worker, was appointed co-chairman of the inmates' housekeeping committee along with one of the inmates. From her they learned what it was like to deal with a popular, well-liked but very determined woman, one who would stand for no nonsense.

Another reasonable suggestion at this meeting was that individual lamps be provided in all the rooms. There was no difficulty in giving this a clear affirmative answer since it had been agreed before the opening of the Center that inmates could continue to read or to work on their hobbies as long as they did not interfere with the rights of other inmates to sleep. Because the Center had started in the middle of the fiscal year, there was no budgetary provision for the purchase of the requested lamps. The staff gave repeated explanations for the delay in providing them, but this was always a good subject for complaint. Though unreasonable and quite annoying, the nagging produced some results. A clever administrator succeeded in amending the budget, and the lamps were obtained in January.

By October 14, a number of committees were operating, especially the basic ones such as housekeeping, sports, recreation and art. However, it did not take long for the inmates to feel at a loss with so much free time on their hands and so few rules to guide them. Some of them could not grasp the idea that personal responsibility for one's behavior is the best set of rules that man can have. It is interesting that they and not the guards made a strong plea for a "list of written rules and a set of penalties for violation of the rules." Furthermore, they talked of "the necessity of a special officer to enforce these regulations." We were not ready to give way to anything that would mean even a semblance of a return to the way of life found in the penitentiaries they had come from. Some officers too were beginning to feel that possibly, if not all the previous rules, at least some of the "good ones" should be reinstated.

Fortunately the more militant officers sided with the professional staff in this matter.

At the meeting of October 17 a real griping session started over matters that could and should have been resolved in short order by the shop committee. There was no doubt in anybody's mind that smoking could not be permitted in the sewing shop because of the fire hazard. Adjoining this shop was a large room that was formerly a communal lavatory from which the plumbing had been removed. This room had tiled floors and walls, with large windows looking out on one of the inner courtyards. It was a really ideal spot for a smoking room. Nonetheless, some of the inmates persisted in smoking in the shop area. Some of them gave the clear impression that they enjoyed doing so for the sheer pleasure of griping about restrictions. They also seemed to want to see how far they could go before the axe would fall. This led Bill Dupras to remark that the inmates at the Center certainly were different from the patients of Dannemora State Hospital — they were more like a bunch of children.

The subject of smoking, both in the community as well as in the shop itself, gave rise to much discussion. In the end the inmates worked out a system of rules and punishments for infractions. Alfie B., one of the more troublesome inmates, took it upon himself to speak for the group regarding the smoking regulations. They unanimously agreed for a first violation an inmate should be obliged to wash all the factory windows, about a day's work for a fast worker; for a second violation, he would have to scrub the floors of the shop, which amounted to more than a good day's work. However for a third violation the severity of the punishment would diminish. The penalty then would merely be the loss of either a morning or an afternoon break, this being the twenty-minute work-period stoppage which inmates were allowed during the day's work schedule. The recommendation was no sooner made than it ran into trouble from a source its backers never expected — the staff, who informed the inmates that if they wanted this kind of regulation they would have to return to the penitentiary since this was not, nor would be, the *modus operandi* of the Center.

In truth such a suggestion from an inmate who came from a strict maximum penal institution did not surprise us. Most of us were acquainted with the experience of the van der

84

Hoeven Clinic in Holland where at the beginning it was found that, when inmates were asked to suggest punishments, these were more severe than what they were actually receiving and protesting against.

This is a good example of how people identify with those they consider their aggressors. By suggesting rules and punishments harsher than the ones they claim to be the victims of, the inmates were not only identifying with the aggressor by showing they could become better aggressors than their keepers, they themselves became super aggressors. All that had been asked of the inmates was that smoking be done in the smoking area yet *Alfie B.* took it upon himself to draw up a whole set of rules and punishments. What surprised the staff was that everyone went along with his suggestion. In all honesty, we must admit that we on the staff derived a certain pleasure in turning down his resolution in spite of the support of his fellow inmates.

The rules about smoking remained simply: there was a time and a place to smoke; this applied equally to guards and prisoners; and the officers and the shop supervisor would remind anyone of this when necessary. The inmates in turn missed no opportunity to point out whenever an officer broke the smoking rules. To their credit, the officers took account of these rebukes. On one occasion *Morris T.*, one of the most rebellious prisoners in the Center and one who was usually negative about the guards, came to their support by stating they should have the right to smoke wherever and whenever they wanted. During the discussion, it became obvious to all concerned that this sudden generosity towards the officers was just a means of inducing them to break the rules.

Eventually griping about smoking faded away and something else took its place. The inmates' need to complain in the first three months at the Center was such that one subject was dropped only when another surefire one appeared to replace it.

7.   Some of the Silences

*Silence could be a symptom, an expression of feelings
and moods, a form of language, even a right, and . . .
nothing was gained by putting an end to a meeting
just because nobody had anything to say.   If the
inmates did not wish to talk, it was up to the staff to
learn to understand their silence.*

By November we were used to the community meetings
starting with a long silence or, conversely, starting well only
to bog down in a period of silence.   Both prisoners and
officers discovered that silence has many meanings.   Silence
between two individuals can be aggressive, like the angry
silence with looks that speak volumes; sad, like the silence
which looks deep within oneself; and loving, like the silence
between two people where words are not necessary.   These
are but a few of the many well-known meanings of silence.
The silence of a group has as many meanings as the silence
of individuals.   We were in the process of discovering ways
in which inmates used silence, but we did not know as yet
how to cope with it.
   On November 11, one of the inmates opened the meeting
by stating that since this community meeting was not planned
he would rather not have one.   Two more inmates seconded
his view.   Dr. Theodore Eftihiades, who was chairman of the
meeting, said that he would close the meeting after he had
made a few announcements if there were no discussion within
five minutes.   Later, he and the professional staff agreed that
his offer was a mistake, but one from which we learned something.   In actual fact the meeting was not closed, and the
request was seen as a stimulus to voice demands and complaints.
The minutes state that in general the meeting was very active,
and a great deal of anxiety and discontent were expressed by
the inmates, mainly about the visiting room and their own rooms.
   The following week, the inmates were ten minutes late

in arriving for the meeting. It began with a prolonged silence. Neither staff nor inmates seemed to have much to bring to the floor. When the discussion petered out, the meeting was closed fifteen minutes before its usual expiration time. At the staff meeting afterward, all recognized that it had been a big mistake to close the meeting early. It was agreed that if the inmates had nothing further to say, the staff members should have been able to come up with something. It was stressed by a not-too-silent Dr. Cormier, as well as by others, that silence could be a symptom, an expression of feelings and moods, a form of language, even a right, and that nothing was gained by putting an end to a meeting just because nobody had anything to say. If the inmates did not wish to talk, it was up to the staff to learn to understand their silence. As to the staff's silence we had to do our own soul searching. Never again did staff members take the initiative of putting an end to a meeting because of silence.

We knew that the inmates had recognized our mistake and that it would be only a matter of time before we would be told about it in no uncertain terms. After all, if a member of the professional staff had the right to dissolve a meeting, why not the officers or the inmates? We realized that we had set a precedent and could anticipate the day when an inmate would take this initiative — even if no staff member again tried to put an end to a meeting.

The anticipated day arrived quite soon — on December 8. The meeting started slowly. Nobody seemed to want to discuss any of the subjects that were suggested by the staff. *Alfred E.*, one of the inmates, became impatient and proposed a motion of adjournment on the grounds that there was really nothing to talk about, thus repeating the reason given by the staff member for closing the other meeting fifteen minutes early. This time however, the moderator, Burl Bailey, rightly said that the daily community meetings could not be adjourned although this had erroneously been done in the past. A heated debate ensued to the effect that there were two sets of rules, one for "them" and one for "us," that when the staff wanted to stick to a schedule they did so, but that when the inmates wanted to do something they didn't have the same rights. The staff had to admit that it had been a mistake on their part to have allowed the meeting to close early but that this would not occur again.

The staff, by accepting this criticism, opened up the meeting to a great deal of discussion. There was much to discuss for the rest of the meeting and we received a good number of well-deserved and sometimes well-administered blows. The fact that some of the officers had been reducing the inmates' gymnasium time by fifteen minutes was cited as an example of how the staff arbitrarily changed the schedule when it suited them. Other complaints were voiced, but the staff was not ready to sit back and be hanged for its shortcomings. In the end, the inmates were gently reminded by a senior member, Miriam Kennedy, that all these complaints had to be seen in the context of a community of which all were members. For the inmates, too, had been trying to shorten the work schedule and had requested that the number of community meetings be cut down. At no other meeting did the staff receive so many punches and try so hard to hit back. A bitter exchange between both sides led to the best contribution of the session. Officer Dennis Champagne voiced his objection that everyone was using the words "we" and "they" too frequently, leading to generalizations. He thought we should be more specific and use the word "I." When an inmate talked about an officer, or an officer talked about an inmate, individual names should be used rather than "they." Use of the pronouns "we" and "they" make it difficult to break down the barriers between people since nobody knows who is talking about whom. This intervention contributed a great deal to the start of a new era where the members of the community were not pronouns but nouns.

In the staff meeting that followed, the staff was very downcast because it had been subjected to so much hostility. Pessimism reached the point where some of them even expressed the thought that trouble could be expected. Fortunately this did not materialize. The staff, who had been sailing along serenely, had to realize that they had collected what they deserved, a good dressing down. Joseph Doe, an officer on the night shift, intervened to say that one thing he remembered vividly from his training period was a remark by one of the psychiatrists that the only way to learn from mistakes was to recognize them as such. Officer Doe had worked at the Dannemora State Hospital for about three years. Before that he had been employed as a

guard at Clinton Prison for sixteen years.   Having had so
much prison-guard experience he had found the training
program given prior to the opening of the Center offered him
little new in the way of practical knowledge, but he had
learned that he would have to master the art of "self-control."
He said he began to appreciate the training he received only
after the Center had opened.

In retrospect that meeting taught us all how to agree or
disagree as persons, on a one to one basis, rather than as groups.
After it, anyone using the collective "we" or "they" would
immediately be checked so that individuality could be retained.

* *

Dormitories were certainly not our choice, in fact were
nobody's choice.   However, since the Center had only thirty-
eight cells, we had to have recourse to two dorms, each
accommodating six inmates.   Each housing unit of Unit I
had a dorm.   It was settled from the beginning that the last
twelve arrivals at the Center would have to live in a dorm.
When inmates were liberated and cells became available the
senior dorm member would move to the empty cell and a
newcomer would take his place.   The dorms had dividing
partitions about four feet high and one foot deep, equipped
with built-in shelves and drawers so that each man could at
least have a territory he could call his own and could
decorate it according to his taste.   He also had a personal
locker and a small table with a reading lamp similar to those
in the cells.

A dormitory committee was set up to deal with problems
bound to arise among the twelve inmates who would be living
in the dorms.   It eased the gap between the staff and the
inmates when incidents arose.   The Committee consisted of
one professional staff member, Lydia Keitner, two correctional
officers and four inmates.   It was within this Committee that
we saw the beginning of the erosion of what is usually referred
to as the "inmates' prison code," and two particular dorm
incidents illustrate how it contributed to consolidate life in the
community.

One incident related to a housekeeping problem.   One of

the dormitories had difficulties with two of its members who were not keeping their area clean. Things had reached the stage where the resultant smell was a nuisance to the other inhabitants. Two of the inmates on the committee were very ill at ease about naming the men responsible: they considered it squealing, spying or even worse. Mrs. Keitner asked how we could deal with this problem and help these two individuals if we didn't know their names. The other two inmate members agreed that there was no point in hiding the names but it was quite a hassle to convince the two dissidents that no punishment or squealing was involved, that it was simply a matter of helping two people who were not doing their share thereby causing annoyance to others. Common sense finally prevailed and *Mark L.* and *George S.* were named.

Mrs. Keitner finally asked why the hell they had made such a fuss about naming people whose names everybody knew anyway since they had been the subject of open discussion at the community meeting the day before. The two inmate members who had fought so hard for the principle of non-squealing had quite a laugh when they suddenly realized that they had been so worried about the prison code they hadn't remembered that the men had already been identified. They then agreed that prison code or not, these two individuals would have to learn to keep their corner clean, if not for themselves at least out of consideration for the other residents.

The second dorm episode is a trivial one in itself, but it involved the whole community when the members of one dormitory took it upon themselves to appropriate a table from the dining room. (It was a small table from the dining room, not a "dining room table.") There were more than enough tables in the dining-room, and the whole incident could easily have been overlooked if one of the officers had not realized that beyond the appropriation was a real community issue.

At the community meeting of November 17, Officer Charlie Hayden brought up the matter by emphatically stating that the table should be returned to the dining room as it was the property of the community as a whole. Many used this as an opportunity to attack Charlie and accused him of being against them no matter what they did. Words such as nasty, hostile, aggressive, among others, were generously used, but there was also an outright accusation that he was trying to ruin the program by not letting the inmates think for themselves.

The whole thing degenerated into an outpouring of accusations and insults between Charlie and the more verbal inmates. The flaws in their argument appeared when they insisted that the table was needed to write letters in privacy when, in fact, the table had been used the previous night in order to play cards.

This meeting took place just after Capt. Davis was appointed acting captain at the Center. He was acquainted with our program mainly by hearsay and he frowned at the mention of the card game, especially when it was established that the game included participants from outside the dorm. Nobody mentioned gambling, which was of course prohibited, and in fact there was none. But to the more security-minded officers the possibility of gambling is always present. There were, however, two very relevant issues: first, the appropriation of the table, and second, the violation of the rule agreed upon that each cell was, so to speak, the private home of its occupant and the dorms restricted to the inmates living there; these private quarters were not to be used for meetings, receiving guests, or other group activities. Four large common rooms provided ample space for the fifty inmates to congregate, to play cards, ping pong, read or study. These two issues were therefore referred to the Dormitory Committee which dealt with them at a meeting that same day. It was agreed that, if the dorms needed a table or two, a request should be forwarded through the appropriate channels. Tables were provided in the dorms soon afterward.

Once the issue was settled, emphatic demands for apologies were insisted upon by both sides, especially by Charlie Hayden who had raised the issue in the first place. Whether or not apologies were made is not important. What does matter is that the incident proved that forthright discussion, even with harsh words, does not hurt anybody, especially if in the end a responsible group such as the Dormitory Committee is able to deal with the problem and solve it.

This whole incident would not have been worth reporting in itself if *Alfred E.*, the shrewd and intelligent spokesman of a group of inmates, had not put his finger on a real issue when he asked Charlie where he had obtained the information

91

about the table in the first place. We have already mentioned Charlie's ambivalence about "squealing" over the theft of five pairs of pants; he had not yet resolved it. He replied that the complaint was confidential, that it had not come from an inmate, but from a night officer. This answer set off a reaction like a stick of dynamite. One inmate shouted, "You have your own code, but you want to break ours," and a chorus of protest broke out. The only way out of this impasse was — if one may be forgiven a pun — to put all the cards on the table. The inmates were right in insisting that this was not part of the game we had agreed to play. The "Table vs. Charlie Hayden" became, in a manner of speaking, part of our jurisprudence.

Capt. Davis's first encounters with the community meetings did not seem to perturb him unduly and, during the period that he was with us, he seemed to adjust to behavior which at Dannemora State Hospital or any other penitentiary would certainly have been the subject of disciplinary action: appropriation of state property, verbal aggression, lack of respect for officers and an attack on the whole correctional system. Here he saw it handled without punishment during a one-hour community meeting and another committee meeting later in the afternoon.

The aftermath of these incidents was even more important than the incidents themselves. Our program and methods were largely inspired by and, in some details, certainly followed a medical model. We did not want the correctional officers to write disciplinary reports on inmates. Instead they wrote clinical reports and it was unfortunate that the word "report" was used at all in this context, for these were really progress notes similar to the notes a nurse writes on medical charts. For that reason, the clinical reports were considered as confidential and mainly for the use of the professional staff when dealing with the inmates in interviews, group therapy, or in handling incidents in the day to day life of the Center.

In a staff meeting about two or three weeks after this matter was first raised, the officers openly questioned the writing of confidential reports. The most outspoken were Art Rabideau, Ray Casey, and Charlie Hayden, who made a strong point saying that by establishing a system of confidential clinical reports we were creating a group of strangers among ourselves, thus reducing our effectiveness. If reports or progress notes on the inmates were to be written the inmates should be made aware of the contents of these reports and should be free to discuss them with the officers. Harsh words were exchanged between the professional staff and the correctional officers. The professionals didn't quite agree with Ray Casey's statement that we used whatever material suited us and left the correctional officers vulnerable to criticism.

It had always been recognized that the officers had the hardest task in the community, namely, that of being there every day. It now became abundantly clear that it was not fair for an officer to be singled out if only part of his observations were used by one professional or another and the report not dealt with as a whole. If the material was to be useful in the reeducation of the inmate, it had to be used *in toto*, not in bits and pieces taken out of context. The argument involved a basic principle which was brought to the fore by the officers. This meeting proved to be a veritable turning point in the relationships between correctional officers and the professional staff.

If in law a decision has to be confirmed many times before it becomes jurisprudence, ours was now clearly established. Progress notes on the inmates were no longer to be restricted to the use of the professional staff. Thereafter all such material was to be freely used by inmates, officers, and professionals alike. It was indeed part of the officers' duty to write the progress notes, but it was also part of their responsibility to discuss these observations with the inmates. The professional staff felt justifiably proud of the correctional officers who had questioned the validity of this aspect of the medical working model.

8.   The First Christmas

Nobody has ever studied how much inmates owe one another in terms of help in remaining free in society.   Emphasis is always placed on prison as a school of crime.

The first Christmas party, which was held on the afternoon of December 20, 1966, was a very informal and pleasant gathering of staff, officers, inmates and a few invited guests. The secretaries attached to the project at McGill, and those who worked at the Center, were present, as well as the wives of some of the medical staff.

The festive group partook of food and soft drinks, and enjoyed two or three hours of music and song, including both folk singing and rock since the Center had by then obtained various musical instruments.   There was even some dancing when two of the participants gave way to the beat of the music and decided to liven the proceedings with a little go-go dancing.   Staff, inmates and visitors were amused and delighted.   But we had no inkling of the burlesque situation to which this first party would give rise.

It was only the next day that the staff became aware of the rumors circulating and felt that perhaps they had been the cause.   This was the first time there had been fifteen women in the Center at the same time.   Within a prison such a peaceful and agreeable gathering could possibly be referred to, tongue in cheek, as a "wild" party.   In any event, talk was rife and the incident was magnified out of all proportion. Regardless of how or why it happened the conscience of some citizens of Dannemora must have been sorely troubled that night.

As a consequence, a telephone call was made to Albany and the rumors reached the Commissioner.   There was immediately great concern about "a busload of go-go girls" from Montreal having invaded the Center for a Christmas party. Dr. Cormier received a telephone call from Albany demanding to know what had been going on. And indeed, from the rumors heard in Dannemora, Albany would have had real reason for concern. In the telling, the short skirts of the secretaries had become very short indeed, the few dance steps became a floorshow, and the more people talked about it, the more it took on the air of a real "scandal." The Folies Bergères of Montreal had invaded one of the prisons at Dannemora. Dr. Cormier and Commissioner McGinnis had a good laugh over the telephone when the whole thing was placed in its proper perspective, and Dr. Cormier's wife was indeed surprised and amused to find she had achieved the accolade of being promoted to a spot in the chorus line.

Such was the first Christmas party at the Center: the first and the last great scandal to hit Dannemora. Christmas came to the town pleasantly, as it does to towns set in the mountains, with perhaps just a touch of sadness and disappointment. People no longer really believed that the Folies Bergères had come to town, but one suspects that on one of the Twelve Nights of Christmas some of the inhabitants nourished a wish that it might have been so.

The rumors spread in the town had reached the inmates and it was they who were most hurt by them. In the community meeting of December 22, one of the men asked if there had been anything amiss in their behavior. Abe Ferstman emphatically replied that there was no need for any inmate to fish for a compliment as he felt their behavior had been beyond reproach. For the staff the whole thing became "The Go-Go Episode."

Christmas and Easter became regular occasions for celebration with a party. The spontaneity of the first one gave way to more careful organization, especially after a drama group was formed at the Center by the Art Department of Plattsburgh College, and putting on a play at Christmas and Easter became a tradition.

The Christmas season is short in prison. There is no hangover to recall the day that was before yesterday. On December 27, the daily community meetings resumed as usual, and during that session Dr. Cormier suggested that the inmates be actively involved in a research project he had in mind which was very much at the core of their adult life, namely, their work history, record and habits. Basically, the proposal was that a group of nine inmates, subdivided into groups of three, interview one another on every aspect of the subject. Within the smaller group, two inmates would interview the third until the investigation was complete. The interviewee would then become an interviewer, and so on. By the time the investigation was ended, each inmate would have been an interviewer and an interviewee, i.e. a research worker and a research subject. This was to be entirely voluntary and Paul Williams and Susan Waters would be advisers as to methodology.

There were many volunteers for the investigation, but it was agreed that for a start we would use one group of nine inmates only. When they had completed their investigation, they would report to the community and we would then decide on whether to continue. (We did, in fact, continue and the project was completed.) Any doubts that inmates might not be able to interview one another soon disappeared. It was very rewarding to see groups of three inmates interviewing each other in offices assigned to the research. As far as we know, this was the first time that inmates conducted social research on themselves. Most of them were proud of their work despite the fact that they were often astounded by their findings. No, they were not the good workers they usually claimed to be, as will be seen in the chapter on the work habits of the persistent offender based on the data they collected on themselves.

The New Year break was as short as the Christmas one. On January 3, 1967, community meetings resumed. There had been a kind of truce during the holiday season, but at the community meeting of January 5, discussions resumed in the style that had previously prevailed. This meeting was a rather important one in the light of what was to happen a few days later.

Charlie Hayden was upset and disturbed by the fact that the inmates were extremely resentful when he asked them a question, and they refused to answer him. Ray Casey expressed the same sentiment. He had noticed lately that, in the shop, inmates plainly refused to talk to him, some putting it in very clear terms: "I don't want to talk to any officer." *Aaron D.,* a very intelligent and articulate inmate, expressed discontent with the officers who, he said, claimed to have changed their attitudes toward inmates though in fact they had not really changed at all. And so went the discussion about inmate-correctional officer relationships. Three inmates were quite verbal about their grievances, but two others, who came to their defense, stated that they had had many experiences with the correctional officers of the Center who, in general, were considerate and asked them to do things instead of ordering them. Lindon Payne, with his usual calm, agreed that most likely there were some officers who found it difficult to relate, but that this was a two-way process since some of the inmates had similar difficulties. The minutes of the meeting quote, but do not identify, somebody who philosophically stated, "Nobody expects that everyone will love everyone else. We are simply expected to live with each other the best way we can. This is one of the basic principles of this community and the community outside." This silence between officers and inmates was quite different from the one existing at Attica prior to the riot there. This was a silence that could be discussed. Nobody, however, could foresee that in five days another kind of silence would reign over the community.

On January 10, the inmates maintained complete silence throughout the community meeting. It is difficult to describe this meeting: it was not a completely silent one, since the staff spoke and asked questions. But there were no replies from the inmates. Dr. Fink called it a cold silence, a description which was appropriate to the winter season.

Therapists know how long an hour of silence can be with an individual patient. However, silent patients always communicate in some way or other. A facial expression can be understood; sadness or anger can be observed, as well as tears or the effort to suppress them, some movement of the body, a twitching of the lips, shuffling of feet, a movement of fingers. In teaching this is referred to as non-verbal language, but we were faced with the non-verbal language of fifty persons, simply not talking, smoking as if they were alone, looking this way or that as if they did not know each other like fifty strangers waiting at a bus stop. Even the more experienced staff members had never really dealt with such a situation before.

Whether we dealt properly with this silent community we do not know. We just did what we could at the time, but we do not feel now that we handled it in a way that can be used as an example in teaching.

Dr. Cormier was chairing the meeting that day (the inmates later said they had selected that particular day because they wanted him to be present when the silence came) and he broke the silence with a general question: "How are your interviews about work history getting along ...? " None of the inmates answered. Dr. Eftihiades remarked that the men were trying to say something by their silence and he wondered if it would not be easier and more effective if they were to use words. According to the minutes other staff members felt that the inmates were"protesting" possibly against the food or the numerous requests that had remained unanswered lately. No matter what any staff member said, nothing succeeded in breaking the silence. The fifty men continued to look very much like fifty strangers at a bus stop. The silence became contagious and spread so that most of the staff fell silent as well. Dr. Cormier said that, as a member of the community, he for one did not want to be involved in a community silence about which he had neither been consulted nor informed. Had he been told what it was about, he might well have been a participant. Paul Williams mentioned that, as far as he knew, this was not a concerted, premeditated plan of silence. It struck him as regression. Another staff member went so far as to mention sabotaging the program, but fortunately nobody took him up on his comment.

The minutes report that "for the most part the staff appeared sad, unhappy and disappointed." The writer might also have added the word "worried." What if the silence were to go on and on and on, like a hunger strike?

When the hour was up and the meeting was adjourned there was a general feeling of relief. Everybody started talking at once, staff and inmates alike, the inmates especially commenting on the remarks they had heard. It was difficult that day for the staff not to bypass the rule (established among themselves) that they leave the community meetings promptly in order not to be late for their own meeting which usually followed immediately. Everyone was late for the staff meeting that day and no one made a remark about it.

Seen in retrospect it can now be said that we faced a mature silence on the part of the inmates. Afterwards, some of them told us quite frankly that they had not wanted it;

others said that they had followed suit.   But there was a lot of truth in saying that it was not an organized demonstration, that it had just happened. Nobody felt that there was any need for an inquiry as to who had instigated it.   On the part of the staff it was simply accepted and understood that silence is, after all, a right.

Why this particular silence?   Behind it were probably all the reasons suggested, except that of conscious sabotage. Looking back on it, we see it as a necessary pause.   Staff and inmates had been speaking more and more personally to each other.   Traditional officer-inmate codes had been eroding rapidly .   The inmates may have felt they were being "led" or "forced" into a new relationship decided on by others.   They may have needed this way of asserting their independence before taking a further step in community living.   From then on, there was a marked move toward more direct interaction and interpersonal relationships, including clashes, that brought life to the community.

On January 16 *Clem B.* told Paul Williams that he wanted his name removed from the volunteer list of the assessment program.   He could see no value in it for himself nor for any other inmate who would be involved with him. He felt that if the staff wanted information, they could get it from him directly.   He was followed by inmate *Curt L.* who said that he, too, was not prepared to discuss his personal life with other inmates and that he saw no value in discussing his work performance with them. Paul Williams simply replied that the project was absolutely voluntary and anyone could withdraw if he wished.   However, the nine inmates who had made up the first group working on this project had reservations about this.   They pointed out that since *Clem* and *Curt* were not yet actively involved in the program, they were scarcely in a position to evaluate it.   Comments were added by four other men who had been working on the self-assessment program.

All agreed that it was both interesting and beneficial. *Gianni F.* said that inmates could withhold information and *Frank G.* stated that everyone was free to do so, but that he had found members of his team were divulging almost everything, sometimes going far beyond the area of work.

The time had now passed when one was afraid to use names.   Therefore, when the question of housekeeping

99

came up on January 19, it was natural for inmates to complain that the shower stalls and toilets were not being kept clean and to question those responsible. An angry *Clem B.* maintained that he did his job properly, but that he was not going to clean up after inmates who decided to have a shower or shave during the day leaving the place in a mess. On that point he received the support of the whole community.

Another discussion centered around certain inmates who were behaving like minor pashas. The fact that they received more food and money from their families made them the so-called "wealthy members" of the community. Thus they were in a position to have the poorer or more subservient prisoners do their work, wait on them and serve them breakfast in bed. Both the pashas and their subordinates were taken to task.

In many ways it was fortunate that, during his first days at the Center, Capt. Davis was exposed to behavior that would not only have been frowned upon, even at Dannemora State Hospital, but dealt with by severe disciplinary measures. We have already described the "table incident." It was soon followed by the first really serious fist fight at the Center. Both incidents happened at night, and the night staff had not had the counseling and the benefit of community and staff meetings, as the day staff had.

At that time the correctional officers were rather edgy and nervous. There had already been one fist fight, but it had erupted during a ball game shortly after the Center opened and could be ascribed to the heat of competition. It was immediately obvious that it was the sort of scuffle that might break out during any game anywhere. When there is a fight of any kind in a prison, the belligerents usually have to answer to a penal tribunal. At the Center, however, everybody was able to accept that, if a fight was simply an incident related to a game, the referee's decision should be the final and decisive one.

But the fight now in question occurred inside the Center. Since it was the first real fight the inmates would be observing how we dealt with the matter. The professional staff and the correctional officers, even those who were keen on the new techniques, felt that if disciplinary measures with adequate punishment were not taken, fist fights would become a daily occurrence at the Center. Art Rabideau emphasized the point that there was no use in trying to see the two opponents as equally responsible. One of them, *Alfred E.*, was quite aggressive verbally, but he was not the type to get into a physical fight. He was a difficult but likeable character and, though he was withdrawn from the Center at one stage, he was later reintegrated. *Jeff K.*, on the other hand, was an annoying type, demanding and given to provocation, mainly because he was weak and always in need of help, pity and support. It was not surprising that he provoked such impatience as to precipitate a fight. The actual fight was, from the reports of the night staff, a minor affair of short duration. The officers did not have to intervene, the inmates taking it upon themselves to separate the combatants and talk them into settling their problems by more peaceful means. What complicated the problem was the rumor which spread, and persisted until it was regarded as fact, that *Steve M.*, never known to be a conformist, had said that he was just waiting for the outcome, and if it was to be dealt with by therapeutic techniques he had "some problems to solve." We ended up dealing with the fight in the same way as we dealt with other incidents that we considered serious. Each fighter first had an individual interview with the Deputy Director and also with a psychologist, Bill Derby. Then both were asked to have a joint interview with him on the understanding that the whole matter would be brought to the community floor. Anyone acquainted with prison life will recognize that a prisoner would much prefer to be dealt with by a captain, even if the punishment is two or three days "in the hole," than to undergo open discussion.

The most comforting result of the incident was the fact that the correctional officers became convinced that the inmates did not want such incidents at the Center. After all, it was the inmates who had stepped in to separate the belligerents and talk to them.

All later fight incidents were handled in the same way. A few acts of real aggression causing bodily harm occurred and where these were deliberate, both the professionals and correctional officers agreed these were not to be tolerated. But to the best of our recollection, only two inmates were ever withdrawn from the Center for causing bodily harm.

By the end of January the problem of stealing — either in the form of appropriation of state property or of theft from another inmate — was being more and more discussed. One incident concerned pairs of pants missing from the shop. The inmates denied involvement of any kind. However, Lindon Payne insisted he had caught two inmates carrying pants out of the shop. One inmate made the humorous comment that whoever took the pants was perhaps just trying to cover his nakedness. (At this stage the men were wearing ill-fitting and worn clothing.) For the first time an inmate stood up and confessed. *Syl A.* said that he was the one who had taken the pants from the shop; he was embarrassed and awkward while talking about it. Feeling that he had done the wrong thing he had accordingly returned the pants. A discussion followed about how stealing in this case reflected a real social problem, namely, that the question of the inmates' clothing had not yet been solved. Much of the clothing had come from Dannemora State Hospital where it seemed that the mentally ill were less concerned about the appearance and cut of their clothes. Part of the stealing was related to this problem, but there was also a "racket" aspect to it: the better-qualified tailors in the community could alter the stolen trousers and dispose of them on the black market. Another aspect of the "racket" consisted in ripping up the worst looking pants in order to speed up the process of getting new clothes. While all this was being discussed, not a single person accused another of being a "stool pigeon." We had a problem and we dealt with it.

By now there was more man-to-man discussion at the community meetings and some of the officers asked that, when they were working in their offices, the inmates respect their right to privacy in the same way that the officers respected the privacy of the inmates' rooms. A little earlier in the life of the community this kind of request would have given rise to angry discussion. Now it was dealt with as a reasonable request.

That the staff were a group of individuals and did not react as a "we" group was made obvious when, on administrative decision, two inmates were removed from the Center. It was known that most of the therapists did not agree with the move, since it was not felt that the misbehavior of the two individuals warranted such an extreme measure. This difference between the staff and administration usefully demonstrated how there could be open disagreement by some members of the staff with decisions taken by other members without a breakdown of the working structure. To witness this disagreement was quite reassuring to some inmates who had been worrying about whether from now on they would have to be careful to use

102

polite language in community meetings, to watch themselves
so as not to get angry and yet be angry enough not to look stupid.
In other words, the removal of the two inmates had been seen
as a threat to the community's freedom and had become a
serious problem. It was fortunate for the health of the community
that most of the officers agreed with the professional staff that
these two inmates need not have been removed and that there
was no united front against the inmates.

One of the problems that came more and more to the fore
was how to define delinquency in the therapeutic community.
This question was brought up as much by the inmates themselves as by the staff. It was resolved by referring to our
original stand — a delinquent act in the therapeutic community
is an act that is considered delinquent in free society.

The Center was now four months old and discussion was
getting easier and more open. At the meeting of February 8,
Aaron D. asked Ray Casey why his attitude toward the
prisoners had changed. He had been a man with much understanding, but he had recently become a "man of the book."
Several inmates joined forces with *Aaron.* In response, Ray
Casey said that he would prefer to answer this question the next
day. Meanwhile he asked the inmates to think things over and
to try and see for themselves what had really made him change
his attitude.

A good part of the community meeting the next day was
devoted to Ray Casey's explanation. His reply was addressed
to the audience in general. He declared that he was discouraged because no matter how much he put into the program,
he felt that the inmates were not living up to expectations in
spite of being given a fair chance and being treated as men. He
claimed that he was discouraged the most by the fact that the
inmates tried all kinds of manipulation to get out of work. He
felt that he had done his share, studying to be able to change
his attitude and to understand the philosophy of the program.
He had reached the conclusion that what he really needed was
a book on child psychology. His relaxed attitude and fair
statement elicited an encouraging reply from inmates. *Jeff K.*
and *Aaron D.* said they recognized that he could be discouraged
at times and they urged him to carry on his work. *Gianni F.*
maintained that Ray had no reason to change if he believed in
what he was doing, but that he should realize that it would take
a long time "to change someone like me."

Meanwhile stealing had become more widespread. Around this time complaints began about inmates stealing from other inmates such things as tins of fruit juice, candy bars, soap, etc. When *Earl Y.* reported that he had been robbed, several others echoed his complaint. *Clem B.* suggested that perhaps they should keep their rooms locked, but another inmate said he did not like this idea. All agreed that it was more than just a question of locking doors. It was actually a question of who among them were the thieves. One inmate remarked that, assuming only one person was guilty of the many thefts, "a person of his calibre will not do anything about rectifying his misdeeds."

This kind of theft in prison was the most difficult type of delinquency we had to deal with. Though the inmates had reached the point where they could report the theft of public property, it was quite another thing to deal with personal theft. This type of theft arouses much anger, and in regular prisons it often leads to serious fights, knifings, and so on. Many aspects were discussed: why did they react so angrily to this kind of stealing when, in fact, many of them were in prison for having inflicted just such thefts on others.

In a very useful discussion, the inmates raised several points that, from a clinical and criminological point of view, were quite correct. They pointed out that, among other things, most of them do not know the person from whom they stole on the outside; they were merely looking for an object to sell. What made theft here at the Center a personal injury was that the thief had to be a member of the household, a friend. They pointed out that this kind of stealing is frowned upon in boarding schools, army barracks, lumber camps, and so on. We agreed that the distinction was valid but we suggested that they give a lot of thought to ways of dealing with the problem. Later on a thief was identified and the situation was handled by individual discussion. Curiously enough, the way the inmates dealt with the issue was by a principle that society finds difficult to understand: that of restitution and reparation to the victim.

An incident occurred in March which illustrated how great was the improvement in the relationship between inmates and correctional officers. Inmates were still at times suspicious of their guards and, as the officer in charge of the shop, Ray Casey had the most difficult job of all. The minutes of our March 1st

104

meeting report what happened as follows : *"Mel W.* asked Mr. Casey to explain a certain behavior that he noticed happening this morning in the shop. Three officers had surrounded one of the inmates in the shop in a way that reminded him of guard behavior in a regular prison. He was upset and wanted an explanation. *Dirk E.* seconded *Mel W.* and also appeared to be very concerned with what had happened. Casey answered bluntly that, being in charge, he could move around in the shop as he wished. His answer served to increase the anxiety of the inmates at the meeting because nobody knew what was going on." Dr. Eftihiades asked for clarification as to what had happened in order to avoid misunderstanding. Casey stood up and declared that he acted in a suspicious way toward a certain inmate because he had reason for doing so, that this particular individual had been found to have nine pairs of pants in his possession in the dormitory, that at another time he had been found carrying a package out of the shop which, as it turned out, contained something that he had not reported. Asked to identify the person, Casey said that he was referring to *George S.* His explanation appeared to have made a deep impression on everybody. *Alfred E.* said that he understood how Casey became suspicious, because he knew that *George* acted in a suspicious way so that he could ridicule Casey afterward. *Dirk E.* and others commented that it was very wrong of *George* to play tricks on Casey. When it was clear that *George* had tried to put Casey on the spot, many inmates rallied to Casey's support. They criticized *George* for playing such a dirty trick on a man who always acted in a straightforward manner. Only one inmate did not understand the real issue. *Gianni F.* declared that as Casey had not produced the nine pairs of pants as evidence, he had no right to treat *George* as a guilty man. At this point another inmate explained to *Gianni* that there was considerable difference between the legal procedure that he was used to and the way we dealt with problems in this community.

As spring drew near, an atmosphere of tenseness developed, and with it came another fist fight. This one is mentioned not because of the fight itself, but because of the reasons behind it. We were now used to dealing with minor outbursts similar to those that occur in factories or restaurants, and this one was again stopped by the inmates themselves.

The fight arose from a difference of opinion regarding scoring in a bowling tournament. As in an earlier incident, the two men involved were interviewed, and no further punishments were imposed. The problem of scoring was one of long standing. An arbitration committee of the most knowledgeable bowlers of the Center was appointed to draw up a set of rules and their recommendations were to be considered final. It was clearly stated that tournaments which were now being organized with outside teams would be impossible if there were constant disputes over the rules.

The officer in charge of security and discipline on the night shift told the staff meeting that the Warden thought the men involved should be locked in their cells immediately after such an episode. The Director of the Center replied that it must be left to the discretion of the officer in charge to judge the situation. It was up to him to have the participants withdraw to their cells if he felt there was any danger of the fight starting up again. There was no question of locking the men up as we had no punitive cells. This incident illustrated again how much Capt. Davis and the officer, who were in charge of discipline and security, respected the spirit of the community.

The entire meeting of March 14 was devoted to one issue — how much more difficult life could be at the Center than in a regular penitentiary. The writer of the minutes noted that there was much participation, and that the discussion was orderly, rational and, in his opinion, very mature. Abraham Fertsman, a therapist, mentioned that *Del A.*, one of the inmates on his caseload, wished to leave the Center and that while this was a personal decision, it was also one that concerned the community as a whole. Many men expressed positive feelings about *Del A.* They were sorry that he was leaving, but felt it was his decision to make be it for better or worse.

Del himself was especially annoyed at *Enrico T.*, one of his close friends, who had reported this matter after a personal conversation they had had. *Del* saw this as a breach of confidence. *Enrico* said his only concern was for his friend, that he wanted to help him make up his mind and to allow the community to express its views. *Del* had confided that he wished to return to a penitentiary to have a "part-time job." What he really meant was that he found it hard to do time at the Center where he was constantly being confronted both by his own thoughts and by the community. The natural reaction of the other inmates was that *Del* was simply running away.

The whole question of leaving the Center was discussed in

106

depth, not only in relation to *Del*. Several inmates said that they felt that if they were to leave the Center, this would affect them negatively when they appeared before the parole board. Most of the discussion took place among the inmates themselves. *Ralph C.* placed the issue in its proper perspective when he said that "It is possible that withdrawing from this program could affect parole. But premature withdrawal is even more likely to affect the chances of succeeding on the street, and this is where the real question lies."

In support of *Del*, several inmates affirmed that time goes by more quickly in a regular prison. "But what then? Doing time sixteen hours a day in a cell, don't you find that devastating?" asked Paul Williams. They agreed that it might be devastating, but at least they were left alone. *Ralph* again stated that it was more difficult to do time at the Center than in a regular prison, that we have more time on our hands, more time to speak to each other and to face each other, not only every evening but during the long weekends. There was also the risk of being put on the floor in the community meetings or of having to discuss one's problems in group and individual therapy. In the end, *Del* remained at the Center, and was eventually paroled, but we were very much aware by this time that many inmates found it harder to do time at the Center than in ordinary prisons.

About this time inmates were given a questionnaire that they were asked to answer without signing their names, and 85 percent mentioned that at one stage or another they had thought of leaving the Center. This problem came up from time to time in community meetings, but it seemed to be discussed more among themselves. Much has been said about subgroups or cliques in prison, but inmate groupings based on friendship or shared interest are not necessarily a clique, although this is how they are too often interpreted in penitentiaries. In a setting like ours men can discuss their problems. We do not believe that 85 percent of them seriously contemplated leaving the Center, but we do know that the question of finding it hard to do time at the Center was a favorite subject of conversation in their free time. Most solved this problem through these informal discussions. In a community like ours where as much freedom as possible is given, a lot more goes on than what we observe.

Nobody has ever studied how much inmates owe to one another in terms of help in remaining free in society. Emphasis is always placed on prison as a school of crime and some partnerships and planning for new crimes do start in the prison. If the inmates in our community wanted to use their free time for that purpose, they had more of it than in any other prison. Yet there is no indication that they did so. In fact, the indications are to the contrary. So many of them helped each other that we would not claim that the help we sometimes forced on them was more successful than the spontaneous help they gave one another.

One thing that helped us in our work was the good sense of humor of many of the inmates. We would never claim that a prison is a happy life, but we can certainly say that we had some good moments at the Center, sometimes even joyful. In prison, like in school, any Saint's day or birthday of a great man is a good excuse to ask for a holiday and some of the inmates decided to ask for St. Patrick's Day and who could possibly argue the case to the director better than a man with an Irish name, Ray Casey. The answer, of course, was no. This wasn't too surprising as everybody works on St. Patrick's Day. But what surprised and delighted everyone was when *Alfred E.*, a tall black man, said in a very serious tone: "I am Irish — how disappointed I am not to watch the parade this afternoon." It was near closing time for the shop, and as the laughter died down we all joined to sing "When Irish Eyes are Smiling," with a sense of comradeship more usual among old school chums or friends than prisoners.

The inmates were in rather a good mood around that time. A few days later, one of them stood up toward the end of the meeting, and with a pad and pencil in hand, announced that he had taken the minutes of the meeting, and asked "What should I do with these minutes? Maybe after the community meeting inmates should have an inmate staff meeting."

We selected March 30 as the date to end the six-month period we have been describing in the early life of the community. A period of six months was chosen as we knew that by then we were a community that had survived its growth crisis and was entering adult age in a state of good mental and physical health. The community meeting that day was like many others, constructive but in no way spectacular. (There were, in fact, very few meetings that were devoid of interest.) In order to acknowledge that the plastic arts program was in full swing, it was announced that three of the inmates *Nick G.*, *Sean D.* and *Dirk E.* had been awarded special prizes and a public exhibition of their work.

Easter came early that year and the drama group, which was young and active, presented a very successful evening of theater. The inmates were planning ahead. Mention was already being made of plans for July 4, a holiday for inmates in all New York State prisons. There was even some joking about the many holidays for inmates and Dr. Fink asked when there was going to be a special staff day.

One important discussion took place at the meeting. The tone was casual, almost as if we were afraid to discuss the subject. One of the inmates asked Dr. Fink if there was any truth in the rumor that Ray Casey was leaving the community. Dr. Fink shook his head, to indicate a negative reply, but the question was then put to Ray himself, who explained that he had once decided to leave the Center but had reconsidered. He explained that his initial decision was not because of anything to do with the inmates but because of an administrative problem which had since been resolved. There was a very positive response from the inmates, with cheers and applause, a great homage to Ray. More important, however, was the fact that *Alfred E.*, with his usual shrewdness, remarked that if Ray Casey had thought of leaving for personal reasons, that was certainly his own affair, but if it was because of difficulties between himself and the administration, then it was a matter to be discussed in the community.

In the staff meeting that followed, Dr. Fink was in the somewhat embarrassing position of having denied by a gesture a rumor that was confirmed by the subject himself. Everybody sympathized with Dr. Fink's position, but by the end of the discussion, all, including Dr. Fink, agreed that Ray had done the right thing in stating what he did on the floor.

This meeting, arbitrarily selected as the end of our narration about the first six months in the Center, could not have been better if we had picked it deliberately, but it just happened that way. Both in the community meeting and in the staff meeting afterward, staff and inmates showed all the maturity of being citizens of a community.

So ended the first six months. What happened in the

Center was as different and at the same time as similar as the transformation that the two seasons, fall and winter, brought to the impressive Adirondack landscape outside. Having seen these changes in the Center, we could now look forward to a first anniversary.

PART III:
AREAS OF INTERACTION

1. A University Goes to Prison

*Since the programs were demanding psychologically,
an individual remaining with the activity usually did
so for reasons of individual benefit and social
integration.*

From the time the Diagnostic and Treatment Center
started, faculty from the State University of New York College
of Arts and Science at Plattsburgh took an active part in supervising activities and instructing inmates.

They were involved because we wanted to improve the
inmates' knowledge of themselves, their understanding of
others as individuals and of society in general, their adoption
of mature and socially acceptable values, and, through these,
their behavior. A special objective was to supply them with
a satisfying leisure time activity for future years in society,
one which they could do reasonably well.

The faculty-supervised program consisted of evening
classes in drama, art and photography, physical education and
sports, and in something conveniently known as the "Wednesday
Evening Series," a set of meetings bringing people from the
College and surrounding area to the Center for discussions on
various topics. This series was the first structured evening
activity attended by most of the newly arrived inmates. It was
instrumental in leading them into other evening activities.

Although the faculty members had the approval of the
College their activities were independent of their jobs. The
group comprised three full professors, three holders of doctoral
degrees and three of master's: their selection blended consideration of personal interest, indications of which activities
would be both desirable and feasible, and a judgment as to
which persons were best suited in temperament as well as in
professional competence.

112

Though the instructors spent as little as two hours per week at the Center, they came to feel, and to be regarded, as members of it. They occasionally took part in its other activities and volunteered time beyond what their duties demanded. It seemed that the more time they spent, the more the inmates accepted them into the community. This being the case, utmost care had to be exercised in selecting stable persons for this faculty role.

Evening activities were all voluntary. The inmate was free to choose instead television, card games or his private room. The inmate who chose to attend was doing something which others considered to be for his own good and which was socially approved. The choice often symbolized the desire to rejoin society on its kind of terms rather than to remain in open conflict with it. No doubt some inmates allied themselves with an activity for spurious reasons, such as to look better to the parole board. Even if this was the case, the program had a chance to appeal to them. Since the programs were demanding psychologically, an individual remaining with the activity usually did so for reasons of individual benefit and social integration.

The supervisor of each activity submitted a report for each regular session. These reports detailed the behavior of each inmate, as well as plans and remarks on general participation. The individual reports, ranging from a sentence to a page, were placed in the inmate's clinical file. His therapist thus had the advantage of another source of therapeutic information. The inmates were aware of these reports. At first there was some delicacy in establishing the role of the faculty member as a person whose interests truly lay with the inmate and not as a spy for the institution. The only possible policy for assuring the inmates' acceptance of the instructor's report was complete honesty. The report had to be candid, accurate and free of emotional bias. Therapists avoided mentioning the reports to the inmates who gradually recognized that they were not hurt by them.

Instruction moved forward unimpeded and faculty members enjoyed the confidence of the inmates as well as that of both the professional and the correctional staff. The degree of participation and, perhaps more important, its quality were significant signs to the therapist of what changes were taking place in the inmate. The acquisition of a skill or activity by the inmate was in itself an argument favoring his having had the opportunity to take part.

The most formal evaluation of the program was a survey covering a ten-week period beginning with the first week of February 1970. At that time the inmate population was about ninety. Physical education involved thirty-one men regularly and another ten men occasionally. Art and photography drew twenty-three regulars and three others on occasion. Drama involved nineteen regularly, six occasionally. At that time there was a music activity, since discontinued, which engaged two regularly and six occasionally. A year later the Wednesday Evening Series drew about twenty-five regularly and another twenty-five to forty occasionally. Some men regularly took part in more than one activity. The survey showed that twenty-two of the men then present took part in no activity; thirty-six took part in only one activity; thirty-two took part in two activities; one took part in three activities. Thus the faculty-supervised program reached about four-fifths of the inmate population in at least occasional involvement and nearly half of it in regular involvement.

Physical education was the most popular activity with most of the faculty personnel and inmates. A professor supervised a program involving a dozen individual and team sports, both indoors and outdoors, with some emphasis on carry-over value to later life. Two assistants and a number of correctional officers helped the supervising instructor with this program. One evening a week was devoted to unstructured sports and physical activity, another to intramural team competition, with still additional time for bowling as either a personal activity or a team sport. Frequently, on Sunday afternoons, basketball or softball teams from the nearby community played against inmate teams representing the Center. Inmates enjoyed this contact with people from the outside.

The general aim of the sports and recreation program was to provide laboratory experience in citizenship through participation in various forms of physical activity. Specific aims were to provide opportunities for inmates to maintain and improve their physical and mental health; learn the important values developed through team spirit, cooperation and the sense of belonging to a group; and to learn new skills and establish a habit of regular participation in physical activity.

114

Surprisingly, we found that the inmates were not physically representative of the overall population. They seemed, with noticeable exceptions, to be less coordinated and to have less than average physical prowess. The instructors suggested that their physical inefficiency might have caused some of the maladjustment which ultimately led them to crime. The instructors further observed that frustrations of all kinds became evident on the gymnasium floor, certainly more often than in a high school, college or YMCA. They readily noticed individual progress in their acceptance of referees' decisions, and in their ability to regard these as being objective rather than as the implementation of personal ill will or as the hostility of "the system." It was also observed that they became less combative in adverse game situations.

A strong contributing factor to the success of the program was the sports committee. It brought together the inmates, the supervising faculty member and one or more correctional officers. The committee assisted in solving the problems that arose in a changing population of inmates. It designed tournaments and other features of the sports program, saw to its internal operation and selected timekeepers and other aides. Strangely enough, the inmates generally preferred college staff to referee their competitions rather than other inmates they could select from among themselves. Perhaps this tendency showed confidence in those who had authority. On the other hand, perhaps it indicated that inmates were suspicious of their companions' objectivity. In spite of these reservations, one inmate with prior officiating experience was well accepted as a game official. He served in that capacity for more than a year before his release. Recognition of officiating skill was probably the stronger factor in his selection.

The physical education staff offered some other observations. The program created a climate for general counseling which the formal clinical situation did not provide. Team sports provided a setting in which meaningful participation depended on group cooperation. In the highly competitive sports activities, the men had the chance to see each other at their worst. Weaknesses and strengths in the character of individuals became readily apparent. In fact, the fear of "looking bad" in front of others tended to prevent inmates from trying new recreational activities. However, when they did get involved, they enjoyed themselves. In addition they appreciated instruction since it helped them to improve their competence in the sport.

Defeat, inadequate performance and adverse referee decisions led some "problem" inmates to show ill feeling. They openly blamed the officials, the college instructors or their teammates for their poor showing. Athletic awards, a feature of most athletic programs, provided a strong incentive for improvement. Trophies and certificates handed out at appropriate times before an outside as well as an inmate audience pointed up the accomplishments of successful competitors. These were so treasured that, on release, some men were seen getting on the bus with a bundle of belongings in one hand and a sports trophy in the other. Consequently, certificates were used to recognize other achievements, such as the successful completion of short courses in photography, computer technology and dramatics.

Weekly art instruction was provided by a faculty member assisted by two undergraduate art majors. Each of the two residence units had its own painting and photography studios as well as darkroom facilities. The inmates set up these spaces themselves. They issued the supplies and looked after other mechanical aspects of the activity. Photography was generally taught in small groups. A class of beginners took lessons for two to three months in the use of the camera and the darkroom. Occasionally, advanced classes were taught for graduates of the beginner class.

Drawing and painting were taught on an individual basis since talent, previous experience and dedication varied greatly. Most of the men did their painting on their own time rather than on class evenings. Some of them painted only in the privacy of their own rooms, occasionally producing a finished product for criticism by fellow inmates, the instructor or his assistants. Some of the instruction was visual with the instructor or one of his assistants painting in the studio along with the inmates. The art-student inmates participated as critics in the instructor's appraisal sessions. They occasionally taught new recruits the fundamentals in paint mixing or canvas stretching. The use of student assistants enabled a modest expansion of the program into ceramics, sculpture and glass painting. These activities filled the gap between art and a hobby.

Although the use of student assistants was an economy, they were not employed in preference to extra faculty members entirely for that reason. They were open-minded and receptive, they were "good listeners," and they were alert. They were generally sincere and honest in their interactions with the inmates and related well to them. Though accomplished in their media, they were not so far ahead of the talented inmates as to be unapproachable. Thus in their work they showed work goals that were attainable by the inmates.

The work of the men in the art and photography classes yielded data of therapeutic significance. The fact that one man painted nothing but realistic rather than abstract works, or copied only photographs or other illustrations rather than composed something of his own, gave useful data to the therapist. Progress in changing his approach to painting and to seeing, relayed by the instructor in his reports, reflected attitude changes of broader significance.

The art program made much impact on the inmates in the Center. The walls of their rooms and residence corridors were covered with their work and created an effect of stimulation and excitement that went a long way to shift emphasis from the underlying institutional nature of those walls. This display made it evident to new inmates that many of their new colleagues found satisfaction in participation in the arts.

How much the inmates participated was revealed at the annual Department of Correctional Services art show for 1972 in Albany. Of nearly 100 inmates present in the Center, fourteen submitted works to the show. Seven sent photos, five submitted paintings, and two entered both photos and paintings. One inmate submitted six paintings. Although an inmate now graduated from the Center took a first prize in the Albany show and others received awards, art continued to be offered primarily to appeal to the inmate who would "just enjoy painting." It was neither an attempt to enhance the spirit of competition among those with talent nor to provide a vocation for the most successful.

The drama program was particularly important because, besides inmate participation, it provided needed spectator recreation for the entire community. Though instruction was provided on a one-night-a-week basis, during the final week of developing a production, the instructor might be on hand five or six evenings to guide the play through technical rehearsal, dress rehearsal, and two or more performances. Inmates necessarily devoted much extra time to their productions since they had to memorize their parts and rehearse with other actors in order to keep to the production schedule.

Many more inmates were drawn into the productions besides the actors, since there were stage and house crews.

Because there was no auditorium, existing space had to be adapted to stage productions. Curtains and lighting had to be provided and flats had to be built. The inmates made most of the costumes, and improvised a good portion of the stage setting and properties for each production, although some borrowing from "outside" was permitted.

The instructor brought in actresses to play the female roles, recruited from among college students interested in the theater. The girls were carefully watched at first. Problems in the inmates' adjustment were predicted and to some extent they did arise. However, strict adherence to the theatrical purposes of the sessions overcame the difficulties. Since the price of any inappropriate behavior on the part of the inmates might be to lose the privilege of having women present, the transition from all male to mixed productions was made with the utmost propriety, and the presence of females became a well-established feature of the program.

The drama activity progressed at an almost unbelievable rate at the Center. At first, holding a book and reading a two- or three-minute skit was about all that could be expected of an even relatively uninhibited inmate. The first shows produced were mixtures of privately developed musical numbers and comedy routines but gradually the instructor focused attention more and more on serious dramatic literature. He moved the inmates from round table play reading to acting out of scenes, to one act plays, to full length dramas, and finally to having an inmate director. Similarly, an inmate technical director became responsible for lighting, sound and other effects and supervised other inmates as crew. The inmates always selected their own plays from scripts brought in by the college instructor. Through their own growth they saw the need for further improvement from steady rehearsal throughout the week to taking direction from a fellow inmate for the sake of the production's success.

The effects of the dramatic activity were obviously of great social value. Another respect in which this activity was greatly beneficial, although the results were less readily seen, was the dramatic content of the works produced. Critics as early as Aristotle stressed the importance of the character's moral purpose. In order to play a character, an actor must understand it through analysis that is partly intellectual, partly intuitive. The analysis is made in some moral framework, most naturally that of the actor himself. His basis of comparison for

118

comprehending the character, in other words, is his knowledge of himself. Dramatic study therefore focuses some attention on the actor's own inner makeup helping him to know himself better. An actor has to have a sympathy for the character in order to play it believably to himself if to no one else. Regardless of whether he approved of the character, the inmate had to discover a way of understanding it in order to make its behavior plausible. Inmates had to play roles such as that of policeman. Doing this successfully meant a growing insight into human nature. There was also the necessity to control body and voice in order to "be" the character of the play. The following quotation, written by a fellow inmate, was taken from *The Insight News*, the Center's community newspaper: ". . . W. has gained a great deal from the drama class. He has learned how to relate to people through acting. He is a much stronger person now and is not afraid of people anymore. He has successfully overcome the challenge of talking on stage to an audience."

The Wednesday Evening Series had two different formats during the Center's first five years. At first it was a compulsory activity, the only evening activity so designated. In its original format a faculty member secured a visitor to be the evening's speaker. He told the inmates about himself, the kind of work he did, his interests, and he offered his views and displayed values relevant to his life. We wanted to show inmates a cross section of society that was realistic but whose members did not resort to conduct that would lead to imprisonment. These were not people without problems, but rather people who had found socially approved ways of defeating or living with problems. This program was very successful for a time, but gradually fell victim to several factors. When it was no longer compulsory, attendance became erratic, though the change was in the spirit of a therapeutic community and no doubt a sound one. Eventually too the supply of articulate guest speakers was exhausted because of the area's small population and the faculty member who ran the project had great difficulty in finding enough "spare" time to maintain community contacts and keep a flow of new speakers.

In its second format, instead of one evening speaker there were several guests, each having a part in the program. Most of such evenings were devoted to an informal panel discussion. When there was only one guest, there was only one chance for each inmate to react to him personally. If the inmate was not

119

attracted by the speaker he closed off his responses, and afterwards attended less often. On the other hand, if a group were coming in, the chances to relate were greatly increased. Groups also increased the opportunities for contact with women. Such experiences were needed to help fill the gap before inmates rejoined society.

To reinforce the concept of the Wednesday Series as directly serving inmates' needs and desires, an inmate committee was formed. Its role was to suggest topics and issues for discussion and what kinds of visitors were desired; to publicize forthcoming sessions and to give out advance information; to provide a chairman for the session and to act as hosts representing the Center community. The evening became a chance to make social contact with various persons from outside. Thus the program helped "build bridges back to society."

The change of format showed good results. Townspeople , college students and faculty were brought in as panelists to discuss subjects in which they had special competence or interest. The inmates were at once enthusiastic about the new opportunities to meet face-to-face a variety of new people. It gave them occasion to practice "social graces," one of the subjects which they wished discussed. Other favorite topics were crime, justice and imprisonment; home, family and sexuality; race relations in its many aspects and guises; and social issues.

In the question periods following panel discussions or short talks by visitors, inmates were able to air their own views and challenge the opinions of others to an audience representing society at large rather than the prison. They could approach visitors during coffee time and get better acquainted, argue issues or ask for impressions. The atmosphere during the outsiders' Wednesday visits was always warm and cordial and the inmates were zealous in making the visitors feel welcome and wanted. The visitors tended to go through a short period of sizing up the situation and dropping their preconceptions of what "cons" were like. On discovering the inmates to be fully human and often very likeable, they entered into warm exchanges.

Some experimenting went on as to what size and composition of speaking panels and extra audience would be best. Visitors of varying ages, sex, races, personalities and interests were needed to provide a social spectrum, and to give the

120

inmates opportunities to see people interact socially. This was
one more way in which inmates achieved greater insight into
themselves and greater motivation toward socially acceptable
ways of living.

Originally, a program in music was a part of the evening
program. Though music is thought to be a universal language
and therefore likely to succeed, that very fact is partly why
instruction in it could not succeed. Three instructors tried
several different approaches and all failed. The reason seemed
to be that music permeates the culture of the prison population,
and every man in some way had as much music as he wanted.
Thus the instructor had no role. The instruction in music was
therefore left to one or two professional or otherwise highly
competent musicians, some of whom always seem to be among
the inmates.

* *

It should be stressed that the role of the State University
of New York faculty in the evening instructional program was
not intended to be clinical, nor did they regard it as such.
Drama, for example, was not taught as psychodrama or sociodrama but simply as theater. Theater itself, with its constant
use of the actor-character relationship, is inherently a tool of
therapy and obtaining insight. The function of the drama
instructor is not to analyze the inmates psychologically but to
analyze their acting performances. In this way the instructor
can try to add to the inmate's understanding of a fine art,
without transgressing upon the vocation of the clinical professional. In this, he undoubtedly helps the inmate to understand himself further. These same principles applied to each of
the faculty-supervised programs.

Although instructors in the evening activities were not
clinicians, they were not ignorant of clinical objectives and
setting. As they gained experience they learned to instruct
objectively and impartially, while simultaneously observing
and evaluating the students themselves.

The faculty-supervised program, particularly the Wednesday
Evening Series, served also as an avenue of contact with the State

University College and the surrounding area. The program helped to inform the public of the values of the therapeutic community in the prison; to promote interest in correctional vocations; to supply well-prepared workers to correctional fields; to enhance the value of the Center program by recruiting the interest of faculty and citizens; and to promote awareness of opportunities for university research on the rehabilitation of criminals .

There were at least two additional values in the use of students as guests and assistants. In fact, many students who visited the Center were influenced toward careers in crime prevention or correction. Furthermore, the students dispersed to their homes throughout the state and were a source of "good press" for the Center's program. They represented a new generation of voters and taxpayers, from whose base the development of correctional progress would have to be made.

Females from outside the prison were first introduced when wives of correctional officers and professional staff were invited as guests to parties: the Christmas and Fourth of July parties and the anniversaries of the Center's founding. Next, the drama instructor sought and obtained permission for his wife to serve as an actress in an inmate production, so that plays need not be confined to an all-male cast. Gradually, two, then three or more actresses were permitted inside. Then in the Wednesday Evening Series, women came as guests according to the nature of the evening's discussion topic. This progress has shown clearly that there was little to fear — the Center was probably one of the safest places a woman could be at night outside her own home. Further it led to actual contact of inmates with that half of humanity to which an imprisoned man normally has no opportunity to relate, yet with whom he must have peculiarly delicate relations in order to succeed as a member of society. The Center had here introduced a new and fruitful, if at times difficult, factor in the therapeutic program.

The problem arising when visitors, particularly female visitors, are introduced lies in the tendency of inmates and visitors to set up one-to-one relationships, in contrast to the necessity that visitors be guests of the entire community. The former is not in the interest of rehabilitation in a therapeutic community while the latter is. Hence, before arrival, visitors were asked to be available for conversation with all inmates equally. The problem increases when the same outsider makes repeated visits. Such visits could have been prohibited, but some visitors understood that they should avoid one-to-one relationships and took such a wholesome and fruitful interest in the community that it was unwise to exclude them. The difficulty is in selecting who among equal citizens should have the privilege — for so they regarded it — of repeated visits. It must be emphasized that the problem was not one of security or of administrative inconvenience, but rather of therapy. A new and serious one-to-one relationship injected into an inmate's life, a new emotional attachment, can interfere with his therapy, and may affect that of others. The success of the community as a therapeutic agent may be endangered by the presence within it of new, private relationships. These are problems that are inherent in the further liberalization of prisons in general, and of the therapeutic community in particular.

Unlike their colleagues in the behavioral sciences, the faculty taking part in the evening instructional program were able to do little research into their experience at Dannemora, though their weekly reports might yield valuable findings. Since many were already actively engaged in artistic production or other contributions as well as teaching, they would have required finances and time to work up research results. This is particularly hard to arrange in years of austerity budgets. Grant support from those interested in developing this research would be helpful in meeting this difficulty.

If the therapeutic community at Dannemora is regarded as a pilot project, the question naturally arises: should such liberal-arts supportive activity be a part of the therapeutic program if the principle of the therapeutic community is extended to a full-scale prison?   Ideally the answer is an unequivocal yes. The effect upon the paroled can at best be measured only subjectively, and appraisals of these activities by professional staff, correctional officers, inmates, and participating faculty all concurred in valuing the program highly. The activities did not reach every inmate, nor even reach the others uniformly well. Yet clearly they contributed a cultural stratum to the fabric of the community that could not be supplied by magazines and TV. They permitted the inmates to participate in activities which western civilization attests to be valuable, activities that contribute to making a man a whole human being, rather than just a worker (or a fugitive from work) in the economy. If arts activities are lacking in a prison therapeutic community we feel

something should be found to serve this cultural function.   It
is hard to imagine what that could be, other than what was
provided at Dannemora.

But how might such a program of cultural activities be
worked out in a full-scale prison?   Clearly, it should have the
same relationship to the work program that it had in the
Dannemora situation.   Such a program is effective partly because
it is *separate from* economic work; the problem it addresses is
the problem of using time outside working hours.   The inmate
has decisions to make that are partly conditioned by the fact
that it is his *spare* time, his *free* time that he is committing.
This would seem to point to evening arts programs staffed by
persons from outside the prison rather than daytime programs
operated by full-time employees.   The difficulty is in finding
enough competent persons to staff a college-based program in
the appropriate evening hours.   Obviously a prison has a better
chance of succeeding with such a program if it is located near a
big population center with large universities or many colleges.
The most practical direction for a large prison would probably
be toward broadening the variety of activities, rather than simply
multiplying the Dannemora activities fiftyfold.   The prison
population of a larger institution would undoubtedly supply
more inmates with common interests in a greater number of
activities and with better performance in them.   One may easily
imagine, for instance, that sculpture, ceramics, special aspects of
music, writing, public speaking, more specialized forms of
physical education and even dance could be successfully begun.
But if any prison were seeking one particular activity with which
to start a limited program, we would strongly recommend drama.
However, everything really depends upon finding competent
people to supervise each activity and the judgment of those in
charge of the overall program must be depended on to evaluate
the strengths and weaknesses of potential instructors and their
suitability to working within a prison therapeutic community.

124

2.   A Man's World

What was to be feared was not the awareness of living in a homosexual world, but the denial of this reality.

Most authors who write about prison life mention that sexual offenders are in the lowest rank of prison society and are usually ostracized.   Why this stigma?   Is it anything more than a psychological construction, a kind of unstated agreement between both the watcher and the watched to single out one type of offender whom they use for their own interests and purposes?   We believe from our observation that the watchers keep this segregation alive to serve their custodial and psychological concerns.

We do not deny that there is prejudice against homosexuality in our society.   True, it has decreased substantially during the past decade, and there is even the beginning of acceptance.   Even before the present trend toward a less prejudiced view of homosexuality, we felt it was wrong that the biases of society should be transplanted into the prison world.   Homosexuality and sexual deviations in prison are different in quality and origin from similar practices in free society, despite the fact that they have much in common.

When later we deal with the problem of delinquent acting out at the Center, we deliberately will not discuss the question of homosexuality.   This is not out of prudery nor the naive belief that homosexuality did not exist in the community.   We always assumed that such behavior or practices were inevitable.   Indeed, in a world where there are not heterosexual outlets for sexual gratification, only three avenues remain open: total abstinence, masturbation and homosexuality.

We never had any written rules nor did we discuss standards

as to what was permissible in the Center; we simply acknowledged generally that sexual life is something that is private. On
the other hand, it was quite clear that sexual behavior that
would be considered criminal in free society, rape or assault
for instance, would be considered as such at the Center.

We hoped that staff and inmates would from the beginning
accept this attitude, which we saw as fair and just. We also
hoped this attitude would help everyone understand the legends,
prejudices, sexual acting out, ostracism and discrimination
against sexual offenders or deviants in prison.

In a world where, despite wishes and drives, heterosexuality
is impossible, no jailer has ever, to the best of our knowledge,
written a definite rule that would reflect this reality in such
clear terms as "heterosexuality is forbidden." Whether heterosexuality is forbidden or simply not possible, its absence changes
the thinking, the affect, the drives and the unconscious
instinctual forces that partly shape man's behavior. Jailers and
prisoners are both aware of this, but they are bewildered when
it comes to dealing with the consequences, such as the deep
disturbances and changes in individual and collective affect,
thinking and behavior. (27, 30, 32, 59, 48, 6)

We all realized that homosexual conflicts and fears
were often at the root of restlessness, angry moods and unpredictable behavior. Some men were closer to one another
as friends or possibly as couples, and this closeness drew unavoidable comment and speculation from both staff and inmates, comment determined as much by their own fantasies
as by what they actually knew. Within the community we
knew that, given the great amount of space available and the
freedom of movement, expression of feelings, including homosexual practices in private between consenting adults, was
eminently possible.

Our real concern was that in a prison world homosexual
tensions, fears and anxieties are the lot of both the keepers and
the kept. The guarded show their feelings through fear that
they may not escape the retaliation of their guardians: whether
the guardians punish or tolerate what they see, or go out of
their way not to see, they are, whether they wish it or not,
emotionally involved. The owners of harems were well aware
of this when they selected eunuchs to be guardians, but even
they were naive as the literary evidence suggests eunuchs were
not as sexless as their employers thought.

126

We wanted our staff to be alert to this homosexual reality in which they were living; we wanted it to be a subject of open discussion among ourselves. What was to be feared was not the awareness of living in a homosexual world, but the denial of this reality. Tolerance, permissiveness, acceptance of homosexuality may be desirable on the part of the guardian, but these same feelings can be as unhealthy as their opposite when they are dictated by dormant or half-awakened homosexual wishes and fantasies. When one is conscious of one's feelings, behavior can be checked by one's own controls or helped by outside ones. We like to believe that this was the prevailing climate in our community on sexual and other matters involving passion, but we must recognize that to live with a mind fully illuminated by insight is not always easy. We were aware that both the watcher and the watched could dim the light when life was simpler and more comfortable in shadow.

The fact that there was no expressed taboo against homosexuality and that it could be freely discussed created a climate where we did not in fact have to deal with any serious sexual misbehavior, such as rape or assault, during our six years at the Center. For that matter, we can recall no instance where sexual practices were the object of repressive measures. This is not to say that homosexuality and the tensions, fears and anxieties or defenses against homosexual wishes and fantasies did not affect the behavior of the inmates or the attitudes of the staff. Homosexual problems were discussed more often at staff meetings than in the community meetings. These discussions increased insight and this led to an easing of fears by the staff and to a healthy attitude toward unavoidable sexual deviance. We believed that homosexual practices should be viewed with the same tolerance that now generally prevails, or should prevail, in free society: intervention is not called for as long as homosexuality does not interfere with social life or the rights of other individuals. This is no different from attitudes toward heterosexuality, where no one intervenes unless individual rights or social norms are infringed upon.

We do not want to leave a false impression that we knew nothing of the sexuality in the community. But we weren't on the watch for it, and so it simply appeared on the landscape as it should. As individuals, of course, the staff knew a great deal about the inmates, who easily confided in them on such matters.

Here the sharing was not equal; the inmates were very much left to their fantasies about the private lives of staff members, though in some cases their fantasies or intuitions were not far from the truth.

Inmates could discuss marital problems, divorce, separation, affairs, in or out of prison, without actually referring to their sexual practices at the Center. Most of them preferred to discuss this aspect of their life with individual therapists and, in cases of homosexual relationships, some preferred to discuss it with a woman therapist.

Such discreet attitudes, however, were not the rule when a man had a history of sexual offenses, either the last one for which he was sentenced or earlier ones in his record. This was the legal criminality, the known delinquent problems for which he had been sentenced to prison, and the staff felt free to bring this up in group discussions or at community meetings, not for the sake of divulging it but to help an inmate discuss an important matter that he was consciously avoiding.

It is not only misleading but an error to state that most persistent offenders were initiated into homosexual practices when they entered an adult prison. Many case histories indicate the contrary. The persistent delinquency of youth, the forerunner of an adult criminal career, is not determined by a psychopathology that involves only the transgressing of social rules or laws. Persistent delinquency involves the total personality of these youths (adult persistent offenders in the making) at periods of development where psychosocial as well as psychosexual development is burgeoning. It is difficult to imagine that youths so deeply involved in social deviance would not also be involved in sexual deviance. A study we made of fifty young severe delinquents revealed that during their adolescence, apart from the offenses that brought them to juvenile courts and institutions, 62 per cent of them were deeply involved in sexual deviance, such as homosexual prostitution, homosexual practices, early pimping and so on. (20) The sexuality of these young offenders went far beyond the norms of sexual practices among "normal" adolescents who, in their search for sexual identity, not unexpectedly indulged in sexual deviations. The sexuality found in the persistent delinquent youths could definitely be described as of a pathological polymorphous type. While acknowledging that the early institutionalization of some did not help them to find a secure sexual identity, one would be

128

clinically unsound not to recognize that for the severe delinquent youth psychosocial and psychosexual pathology often feed each other.

This does not justify their being detained with older sexual or deviant offenders at this early stage in the development of their criminal career. It is important that young offenders entering prison be placed with others of the same age, not as a means of preventing homosexuality but so that the sexual deviancy of their youth at least be confined for a time to their peer group.

We must also bear in mind that involvement of staff in active homosexual practices in youth institutions or the passive participation of others who obtain pleasure from witnessing such practices is a problem. Youth institutions that select fully mature adults as guardians and counsellors can help some youths to develop sexual identity despite their total immersion in a man's world. That such institutions for delinquent youth should be a man's world is certainly a deplorable tradition which is only now beginning to be corrected. Staff composed of males and females and the setting up of some coed establishments are new and welcome improvements in such institutions.

In working with adult persistent offenders whose careers started in childhood or adolescence, we also found that sexual deviance was a dominant feature of the juvenile phases of their careers, and included male prostitution, pimping, and even the hatred and ostracism of homosexuals in spite, or because, of their own latent or overt homosexual concerns.

Many persistent offenders, therefore, enter prison already initiated into deviant sexual practices and their role as prey or predator becomes clearly evident in a prison milieu. But others live as peacefully as they can the only love relationship that is possible in present day prisons, a homosexual one, temporary for some, permanent for others.

We did not want the Center to become known as a treatment center for sexual offenders: first, because that was not its aim, and, secondly, because we did not believe that closed specialized centers for the treatment of sexual offenders are clinically justifiable. In the long criminal records of our first fifty inmates, there were, as expected, case histories of previous sexual offenses and involvement in sexual deviancy. There

129

was only one of the fifty whose last conviction was for a sexual offense. *Mark L.* was a recidivist rapist with no other type of offense on his record, and he was serving a sentence of one day to life (a type of sentence which has now been repealed in New York State). This type of sentence singled him out at once as a sexual offender.

At first the staff was quite sure that he would be ostracized by the other inmates because of this. Those among us with more experience in penal societies were convinced that if this happened the responsibility should fall on us rather than on the inmates. But the inmates did not pin the label of "rapist" on *Mark L.* They treated him with contempt for another reason. Unlike most of his fellow prisoners, *Mark* came from a middle-class background. In the community he was a "rich" prisoner, receiving from his family the maximum number of food parcels, gifts and money allowed under prison regulations. He paid poorer inmates to do his dirty work when it was his turn to mop the floor, handle the garbage or do household chores in the community. However, it took only a few community sessions to put an end to his exploiting practices and we may add that those who had agreed to sell their services were not exempt from blame. From then on, *Mark* joined the ranks and any ostracism to which he had been subjected gradually disappeared. But each time that his exploitative traits of character showed up, he was reminded of them. However, the community did not attempt to find in the fact that he was a recidivist-rapist an excuse for a new ostracism.

In *Mark's* group therapy session there was a mild attempt to help him with his sexual problem but each time it reached a certain point, the subject of discussion got shifted to other matters. The therapist knew that two other inmates in the group had been previously convicted for rape, but neither of them volunteered the information. The situation remained on this level up to the time the therapist directly opened the subject. When the group was once more shying away from it, he asked: "How many rapists are there in the room?" It took many maneuvers before anyone came up with an answer. The subject went around rape, wishes or fantasies, ". . . after all everyone can think of having a jolly good time . . . ", ". . . I fuck many girls when I walk on the street . . . ", ". . . What's your feeling about the women therapists and the attractive mini-skirted students who visit the Center? . . ." At the end, everybody accepted that at least mentally one could be more or less a rapist, or even better, an irresistible ladies' man (as many of them liked to present themselves when talking about their sexual prowess). It was in this atmosphere that it became known that there were not three but four rapists in the group. (The therapist had not been acquainted with the record of a newcomer.) Only *Mark L.* had been found guilty of more than one forcible rape. As for the others, the rapes happened with some degree of victim participation. Although *Mark's* problem was different and the group seemed to fail to understand him completely, they conveyed to him that if he were to repeat his crime, perhaps rape with a degree of victim participation could be considered an improvement compared to forcible rape. Even if the group could go no further at this stage *Mark* was certainly no longer alone within the group, or in the community. It is our observation that both the watchers and the watched psychologically build up segregation and ostracism against the sexual offender. This in turn is fostered by many correctional systems which push the prejudice to its logical end by constructing special closed institutions for treating the dangerous sexual offender. At the end these places are filled, with only a few exceptions, with ordinary, non-dangerous sexual offenders, who after all, compose the majority of such offenders.

Right from the start the discussion of *Mark's* case contributed a lot to tackling this prison-made psychological segregation that serves the needs of the watchers and the watched rather than being based on real dangers. After the first fifty subjects, admission of sexual offenders to the Center was unrestricted. We were not looking for sexual offenders, neither were we avoiding them: we simply accepted them.

Eventually, there was real change among the watchers, well illustrated by the attitude of Dennis Champagne, a senior officer who was at the Center right from its start: "I used to think that if a guy committed a crime against a child or something, that he ought to be hung up by the balls but when you get to know (him) as a person, you start to realize the type of problems that he's got . . . This makes your attitude become different . . . My feeling is they should still be in jail but should be treated humanly. . ."

As the attitude of the watcher changed, the attitude of the watched also changed, as shown by the statements of two inmates who were admitted to the Center four years after the

131

opening.   When questioned as to how the type of crime committed affected the way officers related to them, *William D.* said: ". . . sex crimes are the only real ones . . .   In prison, there's this hierarchy by the type of crime you commit . . . all the way down to sex offenders . . . here the officers don't seem to have that kind of viewpoint — they don't see sex offenders as being low-down degenerates.   They see them as a sick mind." *Ross P.* added: " . . . that goes for inmates too . . .   I used to look at somebody who was in for a sex offense as being a piece of scum.   Here I don't.   I've learnt to look at them as somebody with a problem. . . the sad thing is that despite all this insight . . . if we were to go back to prison today we'd resort back to the old attitude toward sex offenders.   If we were to associate with a sex offender, we'd be outcasts . . . the same kind of outcast he is in prison, which is a lousy thing to be in prison . . . in prison you've got to go along with the tide of public opinion . . . if I go back to prison I'm not going to associate with a sex offender because I know that you, you, you and you would ostracize me because of it."

* *

For those who have visited many of the old prison citadels, the visiting rooms are the saddest part of the establishment.   The architecture of these old fortresses is generally so similar that when you have been in one you can anticipate what the next one will look like.   The visiting rooms are generally located on the periphery of the prison proper, so that the visitors do not actually enter the security area.   Some visiting rooms have been built as an annex attached to the wall of the prison, but no matter where they are located, the fundamental principle is that the prisoner is in the security area while the visitor is on the other side of it.   To achieve this, prisoners and visitors must be separated by a "curtain" as secure as the wall that surrounds the prison itself.   Needless to say there are no doors or windows in that curtain.   In fact — and here there is no play on words — it is an iron curtain, constructed of bars similar to the ones on prison doors and windows.

A table stretches away from this curtain wall on either side, the width of which is calculated so as to preclude the meeting of hands even when arms are extended.   Fully extended legs cannot meet either, there being a solid metal, or metal-plated wall beneath the table. In some prisons there are divisions along the table forming small cubicles. There are, of course, vigilant watchers on both sides of the curtain.

The visiting rooms themselves say a lot more than can be written about heterosexuality in prison. If one wonders if sex is forbidden or just not possible, the architectural design provides the answer: it is not possible, and it is forbidden.

No one questions that visiting rooms in a maximum security prison should be secure and no one would expect them to be doorways to freedom, but when it comes to calculating the length of two extended arms in order to ensure that two hands cannot meet, measurement is carried to an extreme. Such architectural calculation simply means that not only can two bodies not meet, but two hands cannot even clasp one another to communicate unspoken feelings. Besides all this, in many maximum security institutions prisoners and visitors are searched as well.

Nor does this description fit only the visiting rooms of the prison fortresses built in the last century. In any number of recently built prisons, opened only within the last decade, the above description still applies. To be sure, the materials are different. Instead of iron and steel, reinforced concrete or cement blocks with built-in bars are used, and the surface can be left as is or painted, even in bright colors. In some the "iron curtain" is now security glass, with 6- or 8-inch diameter speaking holes cut in the unbreakable glass so that conversations can be carried on. The principles are exactly the same; only the appearance has changed. As for monitoring conversations, the acoustics are far better in modern prisons; if need be there are electronic gadgets that can be pressed into service and some correctional systems admit to using them. Bright artificial lighting assures perfect visibility. One watcher can watch and watch and watch, where many were needed before.

This long description of visiting rooms may seem to have little bearing in a chapter dealing with sexuality in the prison therapeutic community, but one should remember that the persistent offenders at Dannemora had served their previous sentences in the old-style fortresses and were well acquainted with the type of visiting rooms described. The visiting room at the Center was certainly quite different from the ones they had known before. In fact, it was a novelty, not only for them but for the watchers as well.

The size of a large living room in an upper-middle-class mansion, the area had no partitions, and hands could meet and bodies touch. Had regulations permitted, it could easily have been transformed into a conjugal visiting room. In fact, this was never considered, much as we may personally favor some formulas permitting such encounters. We believe there are better places to make love than in prison. The best alternative to conjugal visits in prison would be to find an alternative to prison itself, but this will be part of our conclusions.

The Center's visiting room was also a multi-purpose room and served as a conference room, a music room, and a common room at night. It was an agreeable place with large windows looking out on the Adirondacks, and we could even see Lake Champlain from one of the windows. There were folding tables so that when conferences weren't scheduled more floor space was available. The best of all our common rooms, it was furnished with curtains and pictures on the walls, and it prompted many fantasies and ideas in the minds of visitors, and of the watchers and the watched. It was a meeting ground where, if you could not do the things you might wish, at least you could talk about them.

Before we comment further on events that happened in our visiting room at the Center, we would describe , for contrast, the visiting room at the Dannemora State Hospital. It was not only quite different from ours, but also very different from those in the old fortress prisons. A description of it will give the reader a good idea of the new kinds of responsibilities our correctional officers, who had at one time supervised the hospital visiting room, encountered at the Center.

The Dannemora State Hospital visiting room is a museum piece, almost a caricature. The hospital is now closed, so it is no longer used, but we hope that it will be preserved as it was when we first visited the hospital, for it merits being kept as a showplace. It was located in the security area, but not within the hospital's territory. On entering the hospital after passing the security gate, you were in an area where only staff were admitted, and visitors who had passed the usual security check. Even the inmates went through such formalities before being admitted to see their visitors.

It was a large, rectangular room with barred windows. The main piece of furniture was a long table, not unlike a refectory table in a monastery but somewhat larger and wide enough so that hands could not meet except with great effort. It would have served admirably in an executive board room with lots of room for papers, files and briefcases. On either side of the table were large high-backed, antique wooden chairs, eight or ten to a side. It goes without saying that visitors and inmates were on opposite sides of the table.

At each end of the room was what almost amounted to a throne: a base about three feet high topped by a large chair similar to those alongside the table but which, because of its position, assumed a regal or religious aspect. With the high ceiling looking like a sober gothic canopy over the "throne," one could imagine an abbot in the refectory of a monastery reading abstracts from mystic writers while the monks ate their meal in silence. One might also imagine a throne room except for the embarrassing detail that there were two thrones: the "thrones" were for two watchers who presided over the visits in solemn boredom. We never asked the correctional officers how they had felt sitting in such exalted positions and looking down on the prisoners and visitors, but we do know how they felt sitting on an ordinary folding chair in the waiting room at the Center, or just outside of it, when inmates had a visit and this was the subject of many discussions.

How did our visiting room bring together the inmates, visitors and correctional officers? It was so close to the entrance that although the visitors actually came into the Center, they did not get to see anything of the prisoners' quarters.

Basically, the visiting rules were the same as at Dannemora State Hospital, although the program at the Center was quite different. This sometimes created a number of funny situations and at other times gave rise to angry arguments. For a time the visiting room really became a symbol of all that was worth fighting for and the type of visits that inmates and their families could have. At the beginning, we did not talk much about rules. We knew we had a visiting room. It was a nice place, poorly furnished at first, but as time went on, with new furniture, draperies and pictures on the walls, it also served as the music room and became quite attractive. As this happened, both offenders and their visitors began to share with each other thoughts they had to leave unexpressed before.

As there were no written rules, the correctional officers just followed the same ones in effect at the hospital — the officer remained in the room and watched throughout the visit. We had hoped that the door might simply be left open, but the old rules prevailed at the beginning and it was some time before we could bring about changes. When the first visitors came, the correctional officers sat in the room, but since the observation was more discreet than what the prisoners had known previously, they did not complain at first. However, as time went on and the correctional officers got to know the prisoners well, it became embarrassing for them. They didn't like being there in the same room while an offender with whom they were on friendly terms was visiting with his wife and family. Some began to express the view (that became quite prevalent later) that they felt more like voyeurs than correctional officers.

Nobody had told the correctional officers how close the visitors might get to one another or whether a man might embrace his wife or children. Nor whether, if a couple happened to have a good relationship, they could pass much of the visiting time holding hands. As the correctional officers came to feel more and more like voyeurs, the prisoners began to ask for more freedom, a more intimate atmosphere. Thus it came about that the watcher's chair which had been just inside the door of the visiting room was moved just outside the door. This was an improvement, but for the one who had to sit there and pretend he was not looking into the room when in fact that's what he was there for, it presented a greater conflict than actually being in the room.

In spite of this uncomfortable situation, no one wanted to return to the old type of visiting room. As time went on, the correctional officers felt freer to walk around rather than remain glued to their chair by the door. Depending on the officer assigned, there was more or less freedom, although that freedom never went so far as to permit physical love-making.

A stir was created when one of the officers reported to the community meeting his concern when, rightly or wrongly, it was reported that one of the inmates had been seen with his hand under his wife's skirt. Some of the staff were quite scandalized by this comparatively minor incident, but most of them took it for what it was, a relatively untoward display of marital affection. In a regular prison it would undoubtedly have been punished by curtailment of visits, but the protest here resulted in a healthy and open discussion at the community meeting. While there was no question of conjugal visits in the community, this sort of discussion provided a healthy climate where reasonable guidelines, without any set rules of what was permissible and what was not, were established.

We mention elsewhere that most of our persistent offenders had unhappy marriages. Only three among the first fifty had marriages that had lasted for some time; the others were separated, divorced, or had lived in a number of common-law relationships. Sometimes the visits they received were in order to discuss a legal separation or divorce; other times the meetings were full of reproach about the lack of visits, worry about infidelity, and so on. On the whole we must assume that the men enjoyed receiving visitors, since they could have refused them if they had wished to.

In many ways we would have wished that the visiting room could have been even freer. Instead of having the correctional officers outside the door or walking nearby, we suggested that there might be a foot-square window in the door. (After all, nobody ever worried about the women therapists interviewing in rooms. People passed by continuously — inmates, staff, professionals — and it was easy to glance in and make sure that everything was in order.) By having merely a window in a door, there could have been the same sort of control without any system of official surveillance.

Our visiting room evoked other important emotions in the community. The most touching were the reactions of inmates when their friends received visits from wives or someone who had a particular meaning for them. Frequently the men prepared a treat for the couple. They would join together, use their commissary, and prepare special foods. It meant a lot to all the participants; far more than the simple but generous gesture in itself. The "banquet" was for some fantasized as the meal a man might share with a girlfriend before making love. For others, it was the ritual that goes with a wedding, an anniversary, a birth, or any other occasion for rejoicing. This need for festivities is probably as old as man, but here at the Center where the holidays of free men did not have much meaning it was a simple but touching celebration. We felt that everyone was trying to participate in the reunification of two people and perhaps find hope for themselves. This was probably the most meaningful fantasy for those men who had in the past experienced such difficulty living with a wife or a girlfriend.

As the community matured, some of the men wanted

their wives to see it. This was quite understandable. Unit I had been renovated: its cells in general being larger than ordinary ones, they were more like roomettes, and the occupants had exercised considerable ingenuity in trying to make their small space look like a living room. Many decorated their cells with their own paintings, pictures and slogans. Some were flamboyant, others reflected political ideas or showed awareness of being black. As men left and were replaced by others, the rooms acquired new styles and individuality.

It was a pleasure to visit this unit and pass from one cell to another, discussing the paintings and decoration and seeing how each man had arranged his small territory. The men were proud of what they had done, but we think their request meant more than just showing off a place. It was a wish that those close to them, their family, could come right to the heart of the place where they were sentenced to live.

We would have favored this request had the two units been fairly equal in amenities but Unit I was more privileged in terms of space and facilities. We don't believe such visits would have been damaging to the wives or children but rather that they would have served a useful purpose not only for the men requesting the privilege but for their fellow prisoners who would have made it a point to see that the Center was in tip-top shape.

This was the first time in all the years we had worked in prisons that we had seen prisoners ask that the people they loved be allowed to come right into the heart of the prison. We think it came about within the spirit of our therapeutic community, that it arose from all the arguing, fighting, confrontation, the putting of one another on the floor, and not from a "do-gooder" atmosphere. Our community was not freedom by any means, but perhaps our visiting room was the nearest thing to it.

3. Women in a Man's World

In prison what both the watchers and the watched
fear most is their own fantasies about each other.

We were a close-knit group at the McGill Clinic in Forensic
Psychiatry. It would be inaccurate to say that we were like a
family, but we did have a kind of common lineage. Most of the
staff had done part of their training at the Clinic either as
residents in psychiatry or as students in social work at the
master's level, so that over the years we represented several
"generations." There were three such generations on the staff
that could be clearly identified, and this was especially marked
among the women, all of whom were social workers. Miriam
Kennedy, the senior social worker, was a scholarly woman in
her teaching, training and treating, a woman for all seasons, so
to speak. She trained Lydia Keitner, who in turn trained
Ingrid Cooper and Betty Malamud. Ingrid trained Julia
Northrup. Perhaps a few years hence we may have Julia's
students on our staff.

Seven women on our staff were actively involved with the
Clinton project; many other women also participated. These
included social work students doing their field work at the
Clinic and students in criminology from the University of
Montreal who visited Dannemora during the course of the
academic year, some regularly. (The students were usually
equally divided by sex.) We also had visitors, staff and students,
from other universities that had made a visit to Clinton part of
their program during the years 1966 to 1972. Such visitors
spent a full day at the Center where they participated in all the
activities and meetings going on.

Many women from the State University in Plattsburgh took

part in the Wednesday Evening Series and the drama program. All of these contributed much to making the Center "hetero-sexual." "Heterosexualization" is perhaps a strong word if we think of what we wanted ultimately to achieve, namely, the involvement of women in prison work in every capacity. Nevertheless, we believe that at Clinton there were more women actively involved in the treatment program proportionately for one hundred inmates than in any other prison. This active, central participation of women was, to the best of our knowledge, unique in North America where male or female professionals most of the time remain in the administrative section, the periphery of the prison.

* *

At Dannemora, one of the most important contributions made by the women was in helping us all to handle the fears and fantasies which the watchers and the watched felt about each other. Here is how three of them — Lydia Keitner, Ingrid Cooper and Betty Malamud — described some of their experiences onto a tape recorder.

Mrs. L.K. - the Therapist-Teacher

Working in an all-male institution was not an entirely new experience for me. In Europe, and especially in the so-called socialist countries like Hungary, women have been involved in all aspects of professional and non-professional fields of work at different levels. Even as a child I had the experience of attending an "all-boys" private school with my brother, and later I was teaching in all-male army classes and other state organizations. Although I did not work in a penal institution, some of my experiences were very similar to it. Thus, the idea of working as a member of the professional staff at Clinton Prison was not a particularly threatening situation for me, although I was certainly aware that on this continent, and specifically in the correctional field, the presence of women is unusual. I also wish to emphasize that as a professional I have never made a point or distinction of being a woman so when I was asked to participate in the program my role was clear in my mind: I was to help inmates, correctional officers, the parole board and the entire program in our attempt to determine if a

140

psychiatrically oriented therapeutic community can work in a maximum security prison setting. The clarity of the goals of the program and the supportive help that I expected and received from Dr. Cormier and my colleagues gave me the assurance that I could handle the situation.

During the time that I was at Clinton very contradictory feelings were expressed toward me by the inmates in the program. To put it bluntly, a few took the extreme position of either loving me or hating me. I can report that the majority were able to handle feelings that a female therapist aroused. Some thought of me as the ideal woman, or as the wife who could have saved them from all this criminal life, and could even now assure them success in changing their lifestyles in the future if I were around to help them. This was an unrealistic picture of me, since I am not at all a person as easy to get along with as they seemed to think. But it did no harm if they saw me in a kinder light. It is quite normal for a woman in a man's world to be transformed into an ideal person. Women are so seldom seen in a men's prison that persistent offenders especially tend to see anyone who is there as THE woman of their life.

The difficulty came in helping them realize they were using me as a sort of crutch, or as some use religion — to "save" them. It was necessary to make the inmates understand that they would only change their lifestyle if they wanted to do it for themselves. I found this approach most effective for it also allowed me to remain realistic and objective in my work.

I often thought about this tendency to idealize women. Many men do the same thing in freedom, so it is by no means an emotional state found only among prisoners. Among persistent offenders, however, most of them treated wives, girlfriends, mistresses, prostitutes with whom they lived — in fact, nearly all women in their lives — as objects to be exploited for their own emotional satisfaction and often also for their financial needs and did not consider them "ideals." At the same time they usually thought of one woman somewhere as an "ideal" — often their mother and it would not matter if the "ideal" and the real mother had little in common.

A woman who works in a men's prison, whether she likes it or not, will be looked at by many pairs of eyes. Each man uses his pair of eyes according to his needs, his feelings of the moment, affected by such transient things as the way she happens to look that day or the way they themselves happen to feel. The images they will have of her are quite changeable.

Even when they liked me, they could still get very angry with me, show disappointment, and treat me as if I were the last person in the world they wanted to see that day. To say they treated me as a mother image is to simplify. Sometimes that was so, but it is more important to realize that men deprived of women will, when one happens to be as close to them as in a therapeutic relationship, see her in as many ways as they can. It was my impression that the inmates who expressed extremely negative attitudes were, in a sense, the "weakest" persons. Their self-image was poor. They felt inadequate and their negative feelings were their defense mechanism, covering up their basic insecurity. It also made them look better — tougher in front of the other inmates. The healthier the man was, the more at ease he was with the female therapist and the better able to handle his transference feelings for her. Their attitude toward a female therapist also helped in our diagnostic assessment and treatment.

As more women work in jails, some are bound to fall for this idea of being the good, the ideal, woman who can save. Yet if women are to work in prisons, where they are badly needed, we will have to run the risk that some will be less trained, less competent, less intuitive and will learn by rather painful experience that to respond to these idealistic projections does not help anybody. Some men in correctional systems are afraid that prisoners might get too involved with members of the female staff. This has happened and it will happen again. It is something we have to foresee in training professional women to work in the field. However, it should be emphasized that involvement with a therapist in a therapeutic relationship is not restricted to a male-female one. It is largely a matter of dealing with the question of transference and counter-transference in therapeutic situations.

When a woman therapist becomes so involved in her work that she responds to the emotional feelings of the inmates and acts as an ideal or a savior, both the therapist and the recipient of therapy are in a false situation. These two people, if acting out their fantasies after the inmate terminates his sentence, will have to work out in real life problems that should have been worked out in the mind of the therapist as soon as such thoughts were entertained. The problem of

142

female staff marrying inmates has not often been encountered, but we do know a few instances and none has worked out well. Because a man is a persistent offender does not mean that he should not get married, nor, for that matter, to a woman of a higher educational or professional status than his own. This is not the only problem. The main problem is that we have to help these men deal with reality so that they can establish relationships with women that are real, encourage them not to pursue some "ideal" that has no relationship to any woman who has ever lived.

I believe women should work right inside the prison and not remain at the periphery because of the fear that they will become victims of being either idealized or the opposite. At the beginning, I worried about my students when they became involved in a world of fantasies and began to question themselves or believe that some of these men might have made the grade if they had encountered "me" before. But I found they could usually see their way clear. Later, I only worried when the phase lasted a little too long and they didn't sort their feelings out quickly enough; I felt simply they could put the days or weeks to better therapeutic use if they could understand a bit faster. My main concern with students was that, because of their need to feel successful and effective, they had a tendency to identify with the inmates and do too much for them. My goal was to help them to become more realistic and guard against overinvolvement.

Students must, of course, be closely supervised and selected on the basis of emotional stability, integrity and ability to handle the anxieties encountered in transference and counter-transference.

Among the many female students who have now passed through the Clinic, none ever became involved in a personal relationship with an inmate and many of them have continued to work in the correctional field. Looking at them now I feel their prison work was a true life experience.

One unequivocal effect the presence of women has on the atmosphere in the therapeutic community is the effect on morale. A significant change took place in the dress and appearance of the inmates. They corrected and watched each other in their manners, and developed more socially acceptable behavior such as being polite and considerate. They also attempted various manipulations to get attention

143

from both male and female therapists — but particularly the latter.

The real question, I suppose, is how to remain objective and uninstitutionalized in a prison. How can you keep your feelings of humanity and your belief in the dignity of life? This is the real challenge. We felt it was important to do part of our work in the prison itself and the rest at the Clinic, which is on the university campus, where we see ex-inmates and offenders on parole or probation, men whom we had seen in prison and some who, unfortunately, will return there. We see them in and out, so to say, and this was a sort of buffer against our becoming institutionalized. Prisons institutionalize their staff almost as quickly as they institutionalize the prisoners.

What male staff seem to fear most is that the presence of female staff will arouse in the prisoners feelings that are bound to be let down. This fear appears to us to be quite irrational, as in fact this is a normal occurrence in the everyday life of men and women. In expressing these fears, the male staff are simply projecting their own frustrations and concern. They may appear to be generous in wanting to spare prisoners heterosexual stimulation, but I believe they would react very badly if such "generosity" were likewise shown them. It was initially difficult for the correctional officers to accept the presence of the female therapist, and it became as important to win the officer's confidence in me as well as the inmate's ability to handle himself. Yet it should be stated that at no time was I in a situation where I felt unsafe or threatened.

Our daily life at the Center was conducted in such close proximity that we were often able to observe how far individual interviews could go toward involving not only the inmate in therapy but through him his peers as well. The case of *Roger T*. shows how discussion of a problem hitherto undisclosed influenced his life and his relations with others.

Roger was 32 years old, and during the many sentences he had served he had always succeeded in creating the impression of being a ladies' man, boasting about his sexual prowess, how great a lover he was, and so on. One day he opened up on the subject and revealed a picture of himself that was rather different from the image he had created. The truth was that he had never had a sexual relationship with any woman, nor had he been involved in any homosexual relationships. He had never talked

144

about this to anybody before and he almost cried when he first discussed it with me.

This revelation had a great influence on his behavior at the Center. He became friendly with *Biff*, who in his own way was a ladies' man — but I will talk about him later. The fact that *Biff* was a ladies' man and that he was also on my caseload probably influenced *Roger* to become his friend, and enabled him for the first time to discuss with another man his inability to have a relationship with a woman. It was somewhat of a relief for him to have a male friend know about his real self, not the false image that he was finding harder to maintain year after year. In his own way *Biff* became a second therapist for *Roger* and in discussing their views on women, I think these two ladies' men helped each other.

I followed *Roger* while he was at the Center and, as a result of the therapy and his friendship with *Biff* I was able to observe his progress. He was certainly more at ease with his real image but from there to becoming a real ladies' man was another matter. In his relationship to me he started from scratch and instead of expressing sexual feelings or fantasies, he was almost like a child around his mother or a schoolteacher and he got very upset if he felt I was showing more attention or devoting more time to other inmates. He even kept track of the length of time I spent interviewing other inmates.

While at the Center, his problems with women could not go much beyond this infantile level, but I have followed him after he left the Center. Outside the problem has become a lot more realistic. Much as he wanted to relate to women, he was shy and awkward, afraid that he would not do or say the right things, but in freedom, at least he could discuss these real difficulties rather than the question of how much or how little time I spent with him at the Center.

To ease the tension in his attempts to come to grips with his problems he resorted to drinking. As a result he became even more awkward and inadequate, and ended up being rejected in any courtship he started. He did succeed once in having a relationship with somebody he knew but this seemed to be far short of his expectations.

I feel that *Roger* is now able to live with himself rather than with the Don Juan image that he created for so long. I don't know if he will return to prison, but I feel that going to jail where he plays the part of the imaginary great seducer is less rewarding than struggling through the problem of the little he can get but which, at least, is real. When deprived of his liberty the only image he had of me was that of the mother or the schoolteacher who does not give him enough attention. During the two years I saw him in freedom I felt that he had a more realistic perception of me as a person who was there to try to give him the help he badly needed.

Roger, like *Biff* whom I have seen outside, illustrates how in prison the image that men have of people from the outside, particularly of the female therapists, is quite distorted by the psychological changes these men have to make in order to survive. Professionals in prisons will have to get out of their prisons and treat ex-prisoners in the community if they want to have a total image of themselves and those they treat. That is what we are doing at the Clinic.

Biff was quite a character when he first arrived at the Center. He was in his early twenties, younger than the others, and his relative youth showed itself quite aggressively in the first weeks. Right from the start at the community meetings he mounted the attack, using as many four-letter words as he could and as often as he could. He was possibly not aware that we were well equipped to handle such a situation and were neither shocked nor impressed by this; it was made clear to him when one of the staff members answered him in his own kind of language. In any case, his vocabulary was explicit, and he let everybody know how much of a ladies' man he was. I really don't know why at this stage *Biff* was assigned to a female therapist; anyway, after he realized that he could not impress me with his language, we were able to talk together as reasonable persons.

As already mentioned, through his friendship with *Roger* and others, *Biff* became quite involved in the therapeutic affairs of the community. In many ways, he was indeed a ladies' man, but he soon became aware that the number and extent of his conquests was probably due to his inability to stay with any one of them; his interest waned rapidly and he would move on to another. Later on, he had to admit to himself that his conquests were those who were easily come by.

As with many of the other inmates from the Center, I have seen *Biff* outside after his release. One of these occasions I shall certainly remember, and perhaps he will too. It was our first meeting after he left the Center.

Biff was a member of a large multi-problem family and some of his brothers were serving or had at one stage served prison sentences. I felt I knew them all because he had spoken of them during interviews. The Clinic was engaged in a research project dealing with multi-delinquent families at the time, and as part of my research I visited *Biff's* family when I was in New York after his release. I felt that *Biff* was pleased to see me and to have me meet his family but that he never really understood the purpose of my visit. I was quite astonished when he introduced me as his "girl," especially as he knew that I had already met his parents when they visited him at the Center, where I was introduced as his therapist. There was not much I could say at the time, and the visit proceeded as if *Biff's* girl was, indeed, quite welcome.

After the family visit terminated, *Biff* took me to a neighborhood bar for a friendly drink. Not much was discussed at that stage as I was to see him the following day and I planned to discuss this question of my being his "girl." The bar was a pretty seedy place, and it was easy to see that it was a happy hunting ground to get a girl if you wanted to do so. I must admit that I felt extremely uncomfortable in the shoddy atmosphere and I could understand how difficult it must be for *Biff* to fit into a milieu that I am accustomed to. It is difficult to change one's style and habits. He took me back to my hotel afterward, and there the line had to be drawn — and it was exactly where I imagined it would be — at the door of the elevator. There was no hassle; he left, and it was understood that we would meet the following day as planned for a more formal interview.

In that interview, his behavior on the preceding evening was, of course, discussed. He admitted he had not planned to introduce me to his family as his girlfriend; he simply could not bring himself to tell his brothers that I was a social worker, much less that I had been his therapist at Clinton. That would have spoiled his image. He also made the point that inmates as a rule reacted to female therapists first as women and second as therapists. Age didn't matter, even when I reminded him that I had sons who were older than he was. It should be noted that age has not the same importance for persistent offenders in general and most of the young inmates seemed to relate better to older women as this seems to be less threatening.

I don't know how he felt when a line was drawn between

us; a real line, not something that exists in words in a therapeutic setting.   But I do know he took it well.   Of course, I
had done only what I was professionally trained to do; but for
Biff it was, I think, an important experience in a therapeutic
relationship where he had to realize that you cannot see every
relationship with a woman as a romantic one, that he had to
learn to make a difference, even if he saw himself as a ladies'
man.

* *

Herman T. was among the first fifty inmates at the Center.
He was a likeable person in many ways: sensitive, well-mannered,
soft, but extremely dependent.   Although he opened himself up
to few people at the Center, once he accepted the therapeutic
relationship it was possible to get close to him and he would
respond.   He had been married several times and each of his
marriages had terminated when he served a major sentence.   It
may not be too far-fetched to say that perhaps one of the motivations for his crimes was to get a "divorce."   On each of his
prison sentences a wife divorced him, and that was the end of
that.

He was excessively demanding and had the ability to reach
his goals in prison, for example, the best job or the type of work
he wanted.   He was also one of the inmates who had a record
of the most sick leave, and nobody was annoyed by his
maneuvers, though perhaps we should have been.   I can recognize that our relationship was closer to a mother-son one, though
he objected vehemently to this interpretation.

I probably did play this role myself, as I must admit that
the correctional officers in particular would comment about my
being too motherly.   They would say, for example, that I treated
him like a child.   *Herman* did indeed seem to mobilize the
"mother" in me but even though he acted like a child and made
the same demands as a child does, he did not want to be treated
like one.

An incident during his stay at the Center showed the
rivalry that can exist between correctional officers and inmates
when there is female staff.   *Herman* had to go to a nearby
hospital for minor surgery and one of the officers, a nice looking
fellow who liked to think of himself as something of a ladies'
man, said that he would not let me make a hospital visit; he

148

even joked that he would try to keep *Herman* at the hospital
as long as possible to keep him away from me. *Herman* was the
type that an all-male correctional staff would have been pleased
to have out of the way for a while but, in fact, he remained at
the hospital only as long as he had to. The refusal to let me
visit him at the hospital however stood for many kinds of
feelings, more or less hidden, that can exist between the males
and females on the staff, and we were able to use the incident
to have a discussion on the issue of jealousy.

When *Herman* was discharged from the Center I was
working at Buffalo with Dr. Guyon Mersereau, a former
colleague at Clinton and the Clinic, in the newly established
forensic services there. It was quite natural for us to welcome
"graduates" from the Center, and *Herman* was one of the first
of these. Remembering well how demanding he had been, I
wondered how he would adjust to treatment on an out-patient
basis, and how I would handle the relationship. I needn't have
worried; he made it easy simply by being impossible. You
could never predict what he would come up with next. He
would get drunk and call me at one in the morning to come and
pick him up, or insist that I call his parole officer to come and
have him locked up. If he was having trouble at work, he
would call on me to help, but as time went on he became more
reasonable and manageable. He would still call me occasionally
at night when he was intoxicated, but he would remember to
ask me to apologize to my husband on his behalf.

Herman married again, has a child, and it is interesting that
just before the baby was born he was so anxious that he
developed physical symptoms to the point of having to be hos-
pitalized the day his wife delivered. Initially, his marital adjustment seemed to be satisfactory, but serious difficulties soon
developed. It is extremely important that he should work
through his marital problems as that would allow him to mature
and grow up. He is trying hard to keep the marriage.

The fact that he is fighting to maintain a marriage, instead
of returning to jail to bring it to an end, is one of the most
positive signs of success. Those who chided me for being too
motherly with *Herman* would probably reproach me now for
being too managing, but in the seven years that have passed
since I first became his therapist I like to believe that the change
in my attitude toward him is the result of his own changes,
though he still has a way to go. After seven years of working

with *Herman*, inside and outside prison, I have had the opportunity to observe the extreme difficulties that a man faces in
adapting to freedom and life outside. The problem of someone
having to grow up at the age of thirty-odd, under very dis-
advantageous circumstances, should make us all realize that
there are no miracle workers and there are no easy solutions
to the whole issue of rehabilitation in the field of corrections.

Ingrid Looks at Her Feelings.

During professional training and practice, I had been taught
about the phenomena of transference and counter-transference
in therapeutic relationships. Working in a prison therapeutic
community I discovered how this theoretical knowledge matched
the realities I encountered.

I think that any woman who chooses to go into the field of
corrections and work in a male environment must, at one time or
another, examine her motives. This I have done on various
occasions and was satisfied that I had not chosen this field as a
means of achieving recognition from men. I was human enough
to appreciate some of the flattery I received from time to time,
but I was well aware of why it came my way, just as hostility
also came my way at times. Men from a deprived environment
and background in a deprived situation are going to unload a
lot of feelings onto their therapists, male or female. Certainly,
there were times when I did take criticism and flattery personally,
but not for very long and never to a point where it interfered
with my functioning as a therapist.

When people from different settings, friends, relatives,
neighbors, would exclaim at the type of work I was doing, I
would often stop and wonder myself why I had chosen this
interesting, but demanding, job. It was precisely at such times
that I would feel thankful I had not become involved with any
of the men on a deeply personal level. That is not to say that
I did not like them or care about them, that I did not prefer
working with some inmates rather than others. But, up until
near the end of my stay and the incident I will describe, I did
not become emotionally involved with any of the men. I was
not naive enough to think that this could not happen. There
had been a case before I arrived, where one of the therapists

150

had left the Center and married one of the inmates. As a human being, I recognized that this could certainly happen. At the same time, I hoped that if it ever happened to me I would be able to handle it as my professional training had taught me.

There were certainly men in the community I would admit were physically attractive. There were others whom I found personally attractive, in that their personalities were more open and friendly and I enjoyed talking to them more than others. But in neither case was there a deep personal involvement. I remember being quite surprised after about six months of my stay there when I had an erotic dream involving one of the inmates who had just come on my caseload. What surprised me was that this particular inmate had never appealed to me at all in my conscious life. He was a tough-looking individual, a motor cycle gang type, who was always looking for a fight.

In the dream I was alone in a room with this inmate, surrounded by my colleagues who were observing our actions or involvements. My intense feeling in the dream was of being observed and criticized. Upon reflection, I realized that this dream reflected the concern at that time of both inmates and professionals as to what were the limits of a female therapist-inmate relationship, and would I become as involved with an inmate as Ms. M. had.

Near the end of my two years at the Center, however, I did begin to really like one of the inmates, *Eric J.* *Eric*, a man of about thirty-six, was one of Josh Zambrowsky's cases. Josh spent a great deal of time with him because he showed a lot of promise and was such a mature and interesting person to work with. He was held in high regard by both staff and inmates and it was generally thought by all the community members he was the least delinquent and had the best potential for complete rehabilitation. *Eric* had a long history of delinquency, but before his present incarceration he had been clear of crime for six years. It was apparent that his parole officer had done everything he could to keep him on the street but *Eric* violated so many conditions that he was returned to prison on a parole violation. He had some personal difficulties in relationship and, at some unconscious level, wanted to return to prison.

In trying to analyze why I grew to like this particular inmate so much, I concluded that, at least one of the reasons was that he was the most "normal" or "straight" inmate I had dealt with either in prison or out. When I say "straight"

I mean that he had qualities which would appeal to me if he were a chap I met in a social situation.

I became aware of the fact that I was reacting very personally to him early in our relationship. Josh had asked me on several occasions to speak with *Eric*, as I had been asked by other therapists to speak with some of their cases from time to time.

On a very irregular basis I would spend a few minutes talking to him about some of his problems. At one point I bought a painting from him; there was nothing unusual in this as I bought paintings from several of the inmates. We all did. When I bought the painting, *Eric* asked me if I would allow him to take a picture of me with the painting which he wanted to send home to his mother. There were no written rules about this sort of thing and it was more or less left up to the therapist's judgment. I can recall becoming rather flustered at his request, first saying no, and then, after discussing it realistically with Josh, changing my mind. Even this personal attention was not unusual as various inmates would, from time to time, make flattering remarks or do some little thing special. Nevertheless, the whole incident made me realize that I was responding as if *Eric's* personal attention to me was important. As I said, as soon as I became aware of my feelings I tried to analyze them, so that they would not interfere with the help I was able to give him. However, it certainly made my job much harder. I was always acutely aware of how I was acting in his presence and of what he said to me. I talked the situation over with Josh in order to reassure myself that I was handling it properly. I hoped that recognizing the problem was half the battle but I must say that I was thankful that I would not have to deal with the situation much longer, as in another two or three months we would be leaving the Center.

I felt quite bad the last day when Eric asked me to write in his diary, summarizing my impression of him. I did not comply, trying to explain by saying that I could not sum up who he was and my estimation of him in two or three words. Looking back on it, I think that had it been another inmate I would simply have scribbled something to the effect of "Best of luck, etc ... etc ..." but for me to describe *Eric* in his autograph book seemed to contain special significance. The rationale I gave myself at the time for not writing in the book was that we would be maintaining a correspondence, which he had requested and

which I did with several of the inmates.   Did I feel that by
signing the autograph book I was terminating the relationship
forever and I did not want to do so?   I wanted the hope of
maintaining some kind of communication, although it would
continue to be on a therapist-patient basis.   He left the Center
the month following our departure and he wrote once to Josh,
mentioning that he was going to drop me a line, but he never
did.   I must admit that I waited for his letter with some
anticipation which gradually dimmed.

I still don't think that I was deeply involved, but it was
nevertheless a therapeutic relationship that presented problems
for me.   It certainly taught me what transference and counter-
transference meant.

Looking back at it now from several years distance it
appears to me that I put a lot of my feelings on one particular
person as a part of the Center, a Center we loved and that we
were in the process of leaving.   We were all sad at that
particular period and leaving a part rather than a whole may
have appeared less difficult.   Today *Eric* and the Center are
fused again in my memory as they were once, except for the
short period when I had to look "professionally" at my own
feelings.

* *

Before arriving at Dannemora I had never heard of Ms.M.
but I was made aware of her existence on my very first day
and never allowed to forget it throughout the time I was there.
Her name was continually being brought up by the inmates in
a very casual manner. It was even mentioned by men who had
never known her. In other words, she had become a myth in
the community.

I asked my colleagues for information as I felt I should
be aware of what the inmates were referring to. From what
they told me I re-created a picture of a pathological situation
which the staff had recognized as serious but had apparently
been too paralyzed to deal with. She became over-involved in
her work with the inmates and because of this eventually left
the Center. This involvement had a disturbing effect on both
inmates and staff and this was still evident when I arrived.

Some of the professional staff who were close to her
attempted to help her sort out her behavior since it was
obviously a reflection of her own problems, but they had not

been able to do much. I noted that one of the senior officers who spoke of her as a person with problems, felt protective about her all the same. His attitude was typical of that of the rest of the staff. They neither condemned nor condoned, but they were very disappointed. Now when we discuss the problems we encountered during our six years at the Center, we look at it more dispassionately. If women are to "break in" to the prison world, it has to be accepted that a few will fail at it.

From the way the inmates talked about Ms. M. I got the feeling they also felt protective of her but did not quite know how to explain what had happened. Although I never heard her behavior condemned, I did get the message that I, as her replacement, should not behave as she did.

It was only towards the end of my two years at the Center that I began to hear direct comments from the inmates to the effect that Ms. M. had a lot of problems; this was stated in several of my group therapy sessions. I would simply listen and ask questions only when Ms. M.'s problems seemed to me to affect them personally. This was the case with *Milt R.* and *Neil F.* who had had her as their individual therapist. They were obviously attached to her and very hurt by the fact not only that she had left but also that she had married an inmate. *Neil* discussed in detail with me the sexual fantasies he had had regarding her, and *Milt* continually complained that I was not as warm or accepting of him as she was. On several occasions she had, in his words, "cried with me" concerning his condition and she had also talked about herself.

In spite of their sympathy for her, I had the feeling the inmates felt very threatened by what had happened. In other words, their fantasies about a possible relationship with a female therapist had actually occurred, and this made it very difficult for some of them to trust other women therapists. I don't know if it was my own illusion, but for a long time I felt that they were comparing me with her and that they were afraid I was going to act like her. Several of the inmates even told me they felt I looked like her, when in fact there was no resemblance at all.

* *

The men related to me as a female therapist in a variety of ways. In most instances, and this included those who were on my caseload as well as those in the community at large, the relationship was such that it provoked no difficulty either for the inmate or myself. These men, initially defensive and perhaps suspicious, soon relaxed and were able to relate in an open trusting manner. Some of them grew to like me a good deal and were able to express these feelings and view the relationship in its real perspective.

There was also a small group of inmates who, not being on my caseload, did not have to talk to me and they tended to avoid contact. I would usually approach them and begin a conversation. Knowing more about them later on, from these casual conversations and community meetings, I found that they were rather shy, out of feelings of hostility to women, or out of fear of being hurt by women. One expressed his particular shyness by saying, "I didn't want to talk to you as I didn't want to be considered another *Arnold F."*

Arnold F. came from a milieu of extreme deprivation and was unable to handle any feelings of closeness to a female therapist, either love or hate. He was a somewhat different case in the Center's inmate population in that he had experienced more early emotional deprivation than most and had physical handicaps to cope with as well. In his thirties, he had the appearance of an immature fifteen year old and his waif like, slightly odd appearance tended to evoke sympathetic and protective responses. The sympathy was increased by the fact that he had been more or less abandoned by his family and was, for all intents and purposes, alone in the world. A poorly managed hearing problem in childhood had resulted in his being treated as mentally retarded for several years. When he arrived at the Center he was beginning to overcome some of his defects as well as attempting to catch up on his elementary education.

Within the community, a system of relationships rather closely resembling those existing in a family had grown up around *Arnold.* He had already been a community member for approximately eighteen months when I arrived and had been more or less adopted by the whole community — both staff and inmates. I was assigned as *Arnold's* caseworker shortly after my arrival and the community seemed to view me as his "mother," i.e. as someone with whom they could share the parenting of this needy person. Even the way the case was transferred to me fed into this idea of shared parenting! The unit coordinator, who had been *Arnold's* worker since his arrival and who was

very fond of him, gave me the case, saying that he hoped I
would have more patience with him than he did, as it was
very difficult at times to understand him because of his speech
defect.   That the inmates perceived me as an equal partner in
the responsibility of taking care of *Arnold* was made clear to
me on several occasions when various community members
would approach me and ask how they could help him deal with
such and such a problem.   There was no doubt that they were
genuinely concerned about him and there was a whole series of
them on various occasions who played a special role in "guiding"
him.   I also became aware that at times they used this in order
to have extra time talking with me.   *Luke G.* a particularly
mistrustful inmate who kept most of the community at arm's
length, asked me quite seriously how much information about
sex I thought he should impart to *Arnold* as he felt he himself had
quite a bit of knowledge about this area of life whereas *Arnold* ,
according to him, had little or none.   On these occasions I was the
"good" mother while at other times I became the "bad" mother
when inmates would ask me what I was doing to *Arnold* to make
him so involved with me.   These questions usually came after one
of his explosions or temper tantrums that he gave vent to because
I had spent time with another inmate or had gone home without
seeing him.

    Arnold's intense feelings for me were difficult for both
himself and me.   He alternated between wanting to be very
close and expressing a desire to be my boyfriend or, when he
was feeling rejected, avoiding me by refusing to come to group
or, if he came, by refusing to talk.   At one point he kept a
record of how long I saw other inmates and would argue that I
saw so-and-so for an hour and a half and only saw him for
forty-five minutes.   On these occasions he would literally
haunt the corridor outside the interview room, peering inside,
crying and wailing.   Once, after I had left the unit for the day,
he tore down all the Christmas decorations on the upper floor.
Whole community meetings and many group meetings focused
on trying to help *Arnold* obtain a more realistic picture of his
relationship with me.

    It happened that my departure from the Center was
scheduled to take place just before *Arnold's* release.   As the
time approached, he demanded that I see him outside and that
he be allowed to date me.   When he began to realize that this
would be impossible, he made a sincere and pathetic request that

156

I take him home with me to be part of my family. He expressed
the feeling of how nice it would be to grow up with my daughter
and he was sure that my husband would take him fishing and on
trips — like in a real family.

After I left, the members of the staff, especially Gerry
Burke and Ray Casey, who knew *Arnold* well, helped him with
sympathy and reassurance. A great amount of work was done
to find a suitable place for him on his release where he might
further his development, a sort of sheltered place but in freedom and the last we heard he was adjusting well.

The most obvious factor in the inmates' perception of a
female therapist was that they put her on a pedestal. I can
recall that very early on I was given cues as to how I should
behave. It was apparent, for instance, that the female therapist
was not supposed to swear. I can recall the first time I used any
sort of profanity, which consisted of repeating a statement one
of my group members made in a session. The strong reaction
made it plain that they did not like this. I should add, though,
that one of my group members later told me that that was the
first time he really began to like me. Before then I was a rather
distant white girl from the north who they thought could not
understand their problems at all. According to him, they respected me because I was educated and understood people, but
until I fell off my pedestal they did not really trust me. I often
noticed at the unit that when someone took a woman therapist
off her pedestal, the emotional experience of this man seemed to
benefit the others in the unit in some fashion.

Homosexuality was never an obsession in our unit as it
seems to be in some prisons. In my group when it was discussed
it was often with a great deal of laughter and embarrassment,
both feelings expressing some uneasiness about the subject. A
few cases illustrate the range of attitudes.

Throughout the two years that I was at Dannemora there
was one inmate on Unit I, *Horace M.*, whom everybody recognized as the "resident homosexual" of our unit. He was a quiet,
extremely passive man who played a subservient role. He was
always on the housekeeping committee and kept the whole unit
in tip-top condition. I cannot recall a time when he was ever
asked to speak on the floor either by inmates or staff, and we
all accepted him the way he was. He was never ridiculed or

rejected by the other inmates, but simply accepted as a true homosexual.

On the other hand, I recall another case when the subject of homosexuality was brought up on the floor. A female type of homosexual arrived at the community, and he annoyed the other inmates by being overtly flirtatious. When the subject was discussed at the open meetings, the problem was not his homosexuality but his bothering those around him by teasing them and generally acting silly. He was eventually rejected by the "acceptance committee" as unsuitable for the program, again not because he was a homosexual but because he seemed incapable of adapting himself to the overall concept of the Center.

Three of my individual cases formed a close friendship and one of the members of this group was accused by other members of the community of having homosexual relations with the other two.

One of the men of this trio—*Ken W.*—had sufficient courage to confront the community with this, warning them to leave his friend alone and not make suggestive remarks to him about the nature of the relationship. *Ken* however, brought up the subject of his own homosexuality in individual therapy. It had been troubling him a great deal. During the fifteen years of his imprisonment he had, from time to time, become involved in homosexual activity although he did not see himself as a homosexual. He had always had relations with effeminate or passive types of homosexuals, he himself taking the role of the aggressor. When he came to the community he became involved with an aggressor who forced him to perform fellatio. The word "forced" was used advisedly, as *Ken* felt he was psychologically forced. He realized later he could have left the relationship, but stayed because he wanted the homosexual contact. He felt extremely guilty because he had accepted what he saw as an inferior position in the relationship. This was discussed over a period of several weeks and finally he managed to leave the relationship.

Certain of the individuals encountered among persistent offenders were referred to by some psychiatrists as "borderline" or "pre-psychotic." These terms "borderline" or "presomething" became an easy way out if one wanted labels, but I knew many such cases and in at least one of them, I felt the problem was determined by a deep-seated fixation, far more

158

serious than the definition "borderline" suggests. My relationship with *Dominic S.* went much more deeply than the feeling a man living in a world of men can have for a woman therapist. It has left me with a reluctance to give the easy interpretation suggested by acts and behavior and not look for their roots below the surface.

My first exposure to *Dominic* was before he was even on my caseload. It was at one of the anniversary parties where he insisted on sitting next to me and making a fuss over the fact that I was holding a sweater on my lap. When I finally placed it on the table, he began to pat it as if it were a kitten. I was unable to finish a dish of ice cream I had been served and he asked me if he could have it. When I agreed, he proceeded to eat it. Right then and there I felt that his actions contained much more than their overt meaning. Later on, when he was eventually placed on my caseload, I learned that he had a history of psychiatric hospitalization and aggressive violence towards women involving bodily harm.

In retrospect, I feel that it was a mistake for him to have been put on the caseload of a woman therapist because he was completely incapable of handling the relationship. I cannot say that I felt personally endangered by him, but he appeared at this stage too disturbed to deal with a woman in a therapeutic relationship. He was in my group therapy and he constantly tried to engage me in conversation after the meetings. On one such occasion, he was sitting on a table. When I made a move to leave the room he said he could not get up and when I asked why, he said he had had an orgasm and was extremely embarrassed and was unable to get up. I believe he was telling the truth.

In individual therapy he would tell me about how much he wanted to hold my hand, and how much I meant to him. He was constantly writing me letters and sending me cards. He was very jealous of the attention I gave to other inmates and had several outbursts where he knocked down a notice board in the foyer. He would follow me to the door at night when I left to go home, peering out through the window. He also followed me everywhere in the community, constantly begging for interviews. When he was aware that he could not achieve what he wanted, namely to have a close relationship, he became abusive and reached the point where he threatened to harm me as he had his girlfriend. On one occasion he went into the office where I had left my handbag and threw it on the floor. In itself,

what he was saying or doing was not so unusual; many other
inmates on my caseload or in group therapy displayed similar
fantasies or forms of acting out but in some way, somehow,
Dominic was living this reality at so deep a level you felt it
could only be either psychotic thinking or psychotic behavior
It is for this reason that I felt very uncomfortable with him.

Impulsive outbursts had been a pattern for him throughout
his stay at the community, even before I was his therapist. He
was finally sent back to prison because it was felt that he could
not cope with the therapeutic community. I recall a staff
meeting about this where I, for one, expressed the view that he
be allowed to stay. There was a good deal of feeling among
the inmates about this matter as they thought I had voted that
he should leave. I was made aware of the inmates' hostility
towards me; they felt I had got *Dominic* involved with me and
was now punishing him for it by having him evicted from the
community. Before leaving, *Dominic* became very repentant
and admitted to me and to other staff members that he had
been impulsive and childish.

Later on, after he was released from prison, he telephoned
me long distance at the Clinic in Montreal. He was very amiable,
told me how he was getting along, and also that he still thought
of me a lot. Some time after that he was picked up for carrying
a weapon and he was returned to the Center.

Some of the staff continued to believe that I would have
been in danger if *Dominic* had not been removed from the Center.
Although I have doubts about this, the few *Dominics* that one
has to deal with in a penitentiary make one realize how complex
are human thoughts and feelings, and how difficult these thoughts
and feelings are sometimes to understand. After all, *Dominic*
was doing things that many men do, feel or express in a relationship to a woman, should she be a therapist or not, but for *Dominic*
nothing was at the surface: everything emerged from deep in the
lower caves of the unconscious.

Betty and the Angry Men

What I remember about my first day at the Center, sometime in May 1970, was going through a maze of halls, being
presented to a lot of people, and having to rush upstairs to be on
time for the community meeting. Feeling a little ill at ease, I
did not want to sit in the first row of seats so, I sat in the second

row, thinking I would be less conspicuous. The meeting got started at once, I was introduced, someone immediately started off by discussing his problem; other members mentioned that it was parole day and that a number of inmates were not at the meeting because they were downstairs meeting the parole board. This had no sooner been mentioned than one of the potential parolees came into the meeting, plopped himself down beside me and seemed to be in a rather excited state. I was attending to what was going on in the meeting, but I could feel that the man beside me was giving me the once over. Within a few minutes, he remarked, "Hey, you've got some legs there." I tried to remain nonchalant and just said, "When you get out, you'll see many more like that," and went on listening to the meeting. He continued by saying, "Wow, not like that." I ignored the rest of his comments, and then someone asked him what had happened at the parole board hearing.

Each member of the professional staff had a caseload of eight to ten inmates, we also had weekly group therapy sessions of eight to ten inmates (not the same ones), as well as the daily community meetings, so that we were all pretty well acquainted with most of the inmates in the unit. My caseload comprised men with records ranging from crimes against the person, including sexual offenses, to crimes against property. My first difficult, and at times emotional, experience was in handling the case of *Linc V.* an inmate who was doing his second term at the Center, and consequently knew most of the therapists. He criticized me continually and made a point of doing so on the community floor. Only with time did his behavior toward me change. I particularly remember one incident soon after I started at the Center. I was interviewing him in an office off the shop area. Whenever I looked out the window that faced on the hall, I noticed that another inmate kept walking back and forth, kind of checking up on what was going on. This was *Perry F.* who was sort of the "social conscience" who tried to maintain peace in the community. I subsequently learned that at the time I was interviewing *Linc* the men were afraid he might get violent with me.

At the beginning *Linc* presented himself as a ladies' man who had no difficulty getting on with women. As I got to know him and learned more about him, he was no longer able to hide behind this facade. What was revealed was a man who was very hostile towards women, one who had suffered emotional rebuffs at their hands and who took offense readily. With the passing of time, his aggressive and hostile attitude towards me slowly changed to a protective and supportive one. On the community floor, this behavior would be dealt with by the other men and it became clear that these outburts were hiding what he felt to be a deep liking for me. Once this feeling was out in the open, it was no longer threatening to him. It was obvious to the community and he accepted it, and in fact could even take the community's ribbing. At times, however, he got jealous and would go around pouting or letting off steam.

He was one of the cases in an experimental project where we engaged in intensive therapy and I saw him every time I was at the Center, which was two days a week. The increased individual contact intensified the positive relationship that had developed and also increased his trust. As part of the experiment the men were asked to keep a diary and to write as much as they could about themselves. This was discussed in the interviews. More of the truth came out about *Linc's* problems.

Difficulties were again encountered when he was getting close to being released. He became aggressive again, and began criticizing me but not as much as in the beginning. He was even quite sensitive and perceptive about personal difficulties I was experiencing and showed considerable discretion. I was at the Center one day when my mother was critically ill following a heart attack a few days earlier. I was interviewing *Linc*, continuing in the normal way, but he cut me off and said he could tell something was wrong. I mentioned that my mother was seriously ill and that I was concerned about her. He did not press for further information and we continued with the interview, but he did make the comment, "Well, you're also human and have problems."

To get back to *Linc's* behavior towards me, I would like to mention that when Juanita Chandler, another therapist, was with our unit *Linc* underwent the same type of experiences with her. In fact he was much harder on her, probably because she was black, and as a black woman she was more threatening to him because of his past experiences with women. While she was there, the intensity of his feelings towards me were diffused on another woman which made it much easier.

Norman B. was another of my cases who was also aggressive, and hostile towards me, even more so than *Linc V.*

He had been involved in violent crimes. He had a tremendous animosity towards his mother, was violent and had acted out physically against her. He also had some previous psychiatric institutionalization. Over the two years that I knew *Norman*, a positive relationship did develop, although he remained jealous.

There were times when he could not tolerate my presence in the unit. For quite some time, whenever I would call him for interviews, his behavior was as follows: when I came to the shop he would walk away; he would pass me by and shout, "Don't call me today, because I'm not going to see you." Then he would avoid me. When I would call him, he would not come right away, then he would stalk into the office and say, "I told you I'm not going to see you today so why did you call me? " I had a great deal of difficulty with his case but after discussion with Dr. Angliker it smoothed out and I would deal with the situation by saying, "Well, *Norman*, I have you scheduled for an interview so I have the time set aside for it." Sometimes he would stay, at other times he would walk out, and when I would tell him, "Well, I have forty-five minutes or half an hour scheduled and it's your time," he would generally come back. It was a game he played and it took a long time to work it out. He always felt that I was controlling him and would declare that no woman was going to control him and tell him what to do. With time, this feeling increased. Sometimes when he could not see me, he would later tell me, "Well, I've done a lot of writing about you," referring to the diary he was keeping.

He was a violent individual, and his feelings were eventually expressed in violence. Once he came into the interview room with a knife. He was particularly angry at me that day. Either I had promised him an interview, and spoken to another inmate instead, or some such reason. It was known on the unit that *Norman* always had a knife on him or in his room, but he never had any incidents with inmates. I had seen another inmate and asked him to tell *Norman* that I'd like to see him. It was a time when he was frequently calling me a "bitch," a "whore" and other names. He came into the office rather smugly, saying that he was really "a bad guy" and placed the knife on the desk, saying to me, "now see what you're going to do about it." I just continued with the interview, ignoring the knife on the table, and a few minutes later another inmate knocked on the door, came in and said, "Could I have that please? " and *Norman* gave him the knife. I believe it was something he had set up and planned, or else he had told the other inmate about it and the latter was concerned and intervened. The other inmate was *Linc*.

There was another interview, which I think was the turning point. It centered on the fact that *Norman* felt that I was "controlling" him. He did not come to the interview when called, and I did not call anyone else and simply waited. About ten minutes later, he barged in. He was in a furor and began calling me all sorts of names. I managed to remain calm and greeted his tirade with the comment, *"Norman,* I don't know what's wrong but all I see is a very angry human being." This somehow took the wind out of his sails. He sat down, and told me that he was very fed up and angry, that he had such a long sentence to do. It did not matter whether he got more time, and he was ready to take the desk and turn it over on me.

Later there were times when he could not tolerate my sitting behind the desk with him opposite and would pull his chair around and put it beside me. All this worked out, but it did take time. When he called me names in front of the community the other men were very uncomfortable but they were afraid to tell him anything because he could be violent. When I finally got fed up with it, I decided to deal with this behavior in a group setting. When he called me names, I would involve the others by saying, "I think *Norman* knows how to handle the situation better. Do you really think he wants to call me this? " They got involved. *Norman* would smile, and eventually this behavior stopped. He was one of the men in the community who, particularly during leisure hours, liked to strut around shirtless, or with his chest bared, and make sure that he passed my way.

In his diary he eventually discussed quite openly his feelings about his homosexual relationships. He had so many problems that after a while I decided to deal with his behavior here and now and there was more than enough work at that level.

I didn't have only angry men in my caseload, but in thinking back on it, they are the ones who stand out. *Lionel N.*'s criminal offenses were aggressive assaults on women. One of the women he assaulted was his ex-wife, and he smashed her face. He also was involved in slashing incidents with men. It was sometime before *Lionel* attacked me openly on the community floor, but, during individual interviews, he generally challenged me on the level of my being a white woman, who thought no one was good enough for me, and why was I not married, was I a lesbian? Just because I had an education didn't mean that if he met me on the street he couldn't get me and so on.

Somehow, reflecting back on it now, I believe that perhaps the intensity of the aggressive lashing out verbally at a female therapist, whether Juanita or myself, could have fluctuated with the men's homosexual involvement at the time. What I am saying is that if a man was heterosexual in freedom and was involved in a homosexual experience at the Center, then in men so insecure in their sexual identity as *Lionel* it is at least logical to think that when involved in a homosexual experience in the community his aggressivity toward women would increase. I think this also happened in the case of *Roy H.* which I will discuss later.

There was another inmate, *Victor S.*, on my caseload. In terms of transference, he never saw me as a potential sex object. He always looked on me as a sister, or at least this is what he said. He was a homosexual in prison although he was more of a tease, who teased the men but did not "come through," as the expression goes. Men such as he, on the other hand, who are relatively secure in their homosexual identity never saw me as a potential sexual object.

Terry O. was another inmate who was very possessive about me and resented my speaking to other men. His history was that he started criminality at the age of eight or nine. He was extremely possessive of his mother, deeply in need of friendship, whether male or female, and exaggerated his attachments towards people. If someone spoke to him and was nice to him, he interpreted it as deep friendship. Consequently, my being nice to him, that is, saying hello and acknowledging him whenever he was around, was misinterpreted by him. It was only with time that this was worked out.

There was one incident where *Terry* was so fed up, and furious, whether it was with me or just in general, that he came to a group meeting drunk and it was obvious to everyone. I can't remember the content of the meeting, but I do remember that he **broke** down and cried. He was not so drunk that he did not know what he was doing; and I recall holding the others

back, and just letting *Terry* ventilate for a while. Then I asked
him whether he felt he was in control of his behavior, otherwise he should leave the group and go to his room to pull himself together, but he preferred to stay. There was considerable
discussion afterwards concerning his reasons for coming drunk
to the group and it was felt that this was his way of getting my
attention and holding it at the expense of the other members.
There was a series of meetings when he would come into the
group, go off to a corner, and speak only when I would say
something. This was particularly observed during the period
when Miles Mesic conducted the group with me. It was Miles
who would point out to *Terry* that when I was there he always
seemed to speak but when I was not there he did not speak.
Discussions with *Terry* on an individual basis, once he was able
to cope with his tense feelings towards me, revealed that when
he had lived with a woman on the outside he became so
possessive of her that he almost stabbed her.

The effect of being a woman at times indirectly brought
out some other problems that might not have been evident
otherwise. For example there was one black man from the
South who kept calling me Miss Malamud when the rest of us
were on a first-name basis. There were other black men in the
group and it was one of them who confronted him about this
and asked whether it was because he felt white women were
better than he was or had he never had a chance to talk with a
white woman on an equal basis.

There were incidents in group meetings, one in particular
that I recall, where one of the inmates sometimes tried to sit as
close beside me as he could. I was sitting at the end of the row
and he kept pushing over towards me and almost pushed me off
the chair so that after a while I had to say: "Can I either have
the whole chair or I'll have to move? " and this broke up the
whole meeting. It relaxed the tension and made a joke of the
situation and just brought into the open that he liked to get as
close as he could.

A theme that did predominate was that the men did not
like to be ruled by a woman. I had shared leadership of my
group with Art Rabideau who also experienced difficulties in
this line. It took some time for the two of us to discuss this
and work out the conflict, because at times when I was leading
the group, he would intervene.

166

Another incident revolved around *Roy H.* He was very emotional and had a psychiatric background. He was aloof, criticized me and held to himself. There was one meeting where he was extremely angry and he lashed out at me and called me the worst four letter word that there is. There was dead silence in the meeting and no one seemed to know what to do or say. It was Dr. Simons who intervened and said: "Roy, that was unnecessary." I recall not saying anything for the rest of the meeting. The community would not accept *Roy's* abusive behavior toward me and at the next community meeting there was a great deal of discussion and organizing, spearheaded by an affable black inmate who liked to keep the peace. The community got *Roy* to apologize to me on the community floor. It was not a direct apology, just "I am sorry" but it was an apology. He was extremely aggressive, had a high I.Q. and was a leader in the community, and to get him to apologize openly was quite a coup. I think his outburst at me that day in the community meeting was tied in with his homosexual involvement at the time.

About a month before he left, at the suggestion of Dr. Simons, his therapist, *Roy* asked if he could talk to me, and it came out that he really had a great liking towards me and hid behind it by acting very aggressively, criticizing me and trying to ridicule me in front of others. He also said that it reminded him of his previous experiences with women, and seemed to follow the same pattern. After he left, he maintained a steady correspondence for a while. I saw him later in New York, where he was doing quite well. He is someone who was previously rather deeply involved in the New York underworld, and it was rumored that he was a marked man. When I visited him in his office, he was pleasant, but he criticized me for being unemotional, acting the therapist and that sort of thing.

We always seem to spend a great deal of time dwelling on the inmates' behavior, and very little on our own behavior, attitudes and feelings towards them. As a female working with fifty inmates plus male officers and staff, it can be darned difficult. Someone is going to find your weaknesses, and it takes some time to feel at ease and not be threatened by the continual search for vulnerable spots. In addition there are sexual feelings that are revealed. This is something I discussed with Ingrid, and we agreed there are a few to whom you are

167

going to feel more attracted than others. This takes a great
deal of knowing and accepting, and not being frightened by it.
It's not always pleasant to go in to work and find that you are
being picked apart from head to toe. For example, *Norman B.*
would come up and say "Hey, you like wearing black slips" or
"you like black underwear." Or another inmate would come up
and say, "Why do you work in a male prison? You must like
attention, or else you must be pretty hard up." There were
times when you'd like to wash your hands of the whole
situation.

Things were always easier when there was another female
therapist on the unit. I'm talking about when Juanita was there.
Yet, because a large number of the community were black and
some of the white community had antiblack feelings, I think
that Juanita was put through a much more difficult time from
both sides than I was. She was the coordinator of Unit II and
at the beginning the men resisted her direction, but after a
while they accepted it and, in fact, supported her.

Inmates in the community felt quite differently towards
the female therapists than they did to other women who
happened to come to the Center, either as visiting students or
as guests on special occasions. They generally looked kindly
on these visitors and would build all sorts of fantasies. They
rather enjoyed the way they dressed and would comment
favorably on it. The more seductive the look, the better: but
this was not always their feeling about the women therapists.
I do not mean that they did not want us to dress well. In fact,
they were looking for this and would pass remarks, but in some
way they did not want the therapists to dress as freely as some
of the guests or visitors. In a way the female therapists were
seen as "their women." It was as if they wanted some control
over us. In that sense they behaved like many husbands or
boyfriends who want to be proud of their wives or girlfiends
and want them to fit the image they have of them and want
others to admire them as well, but when it comes to other
women they will look approvingly on behavior or style of dress
that they would not find suitable for their own wife or girlfriend.

If one asks whether the presence of women has any influence on the increase or decrease in homosexuality, this is difficult to answer. Perhaps at the beginning homosexual activity decreases a little and some men experience a feeling of uneasiness about their feelings and behavior. But once the women on the unit are accepted, my feeling is that the men's behavior adjusts to this. The continued presence of women may further decrease the amount of homosexuality as at least the men can talk to and be around women, living models rather than calendars and posters, and thus lend some reality to their world of fantasy. As one inmate said while we were discussing his homosexual practice, it was nice to be able to sit beside a woman and "smell" her. Maybe this "smell" in a therapeutic relationship did more for him than any experience he had had in the past in the many difficult relationships which gave him no great sensory feelings to remember.

While talking about homosexuality at the Center, I can recall now my own feelings at first on this subject. At the beginning it was difficult for me to represent in my own mind what homosexuality was, but my attitude to the question took a new turn soon after my arrival at the Center. I knew the textbook theories and had heard lectures and discussion of cases, but it was not until I heard an inmate on our unit actually speaking about it on a very emotional level that it really sank in that homosexuals experience deep feelings of love just like that between men and women. From then on I lost my uncomfortable feelings on the subject and I also had the impression that the inmates sensed this and seemed to feel a lot more free to talk to me about the subject after that. Learning through that sort of emotional experience makes you realize that intellectual knowledge sometimes isn't enough.

Were the inmates' attitudes and behavior with female therapists different from similar relationships they had in freedom?

At the beginning I thought so, but as time went by I saw many inmates in freedom similar to those I knew at the Center, and this first impression is now greatly shaded. Living in a deprived world has a great impact on how men relate to women and it changed their relationships with men also. Those who were very angry at me were also very angry with women on the outside. For some, the verbal abuse they hurled at me was only a pale expression of their aggression with women they met or had lived with for a time. There were also those who kept the same measured distance from women at the Center as they kept outside. How can you be any further away from a woman than when you place her on a pedestal? The reactions of the inmates who are angry with women, and the ones who idealize them instead, contribute to the knowledge not only of how they felt about women but how they felt about the world at large.

It is unfortunate that homosexuality in a prison appears to some as a simple matter that could easily be solved by the availability of women for the purpose of sexual gratification. This thought is somewhat simplistic as it does not take into account either the inmates or the women. Many inmates could in fact relate only to women who were freely and submissively accessible and one could think that if women were available in prison they would carry on their angry pattern without making any efforts to understand why they did so, nor to effect a change. As to those that already idealized women and put them on a pedestal, there is reason to believe that they would perpetuate this pattern in prison.

Then there is the question of just who would constitute this body of available women. One can only assume that they would not be unlike the old type of "camp followers," prostitutes who followed the armies in the campaigns and when the wars were over had to seek new grounds. Or they might be like one of the characters depicted in the writings of the Marquis de Sade, Justine, who in wanting to practice virtue ends up always being the victim of the worst sexual abuse.

CONCLUSIONS:

It is in freedom that one can feel love and share it. But even in freedom one can be imprisoned within one's self and struggle to get the few gratifications that are within reach. The persistent offender, whether he is an angry or a passive stranger in free society, has his problems of transference and counter-transference that he brings into prison with him. When he enters prison in his relationship to professionals and correctional officers, he traditionally faces men who think that they are objectively carrying out the duties delegated to them by society, ignoring that they too have their own problems of transference and counter-transference in a man's world. They feel they are well protected against any homosexual feelings and drives or more or less conscious involvement, and most of them would be surprised that it was a subject even worth raising. These feelings exist whether professionals, correctional officers and administrators admit it or not.

Male staff in penal institutions are very keen to see how men react to women. Sometimes the women in our group had to remind us that as men we too had feelings to be looked at. For the male staff of our clinic this did not appear unusual as it was first part of our training and later part of our work to train others how to look at their motivations and feelings. But to suggest to men who have worked in prisons all their life that the strong dehumanizing forces in prisons are related to their own more or less conscious homosexual feelings may appear repugnant to some and can arouse hostility.

Among ourselves, Miriam, Lydia, Betty, Ingrid and other female colleagues were somewhat more alert and possibly had greater need to describe their own feelings in a man's world. They suggested that had their work been in a female prison, in a woman's world, so to speak, they would have had to look at quite another set of relationships and emotional experiences. Very few staffs have ever described what it means to live in a man's world for most of their life. Most live and think like "outsiders" when in fact they are very much inside the ring. The day the watchers will look for their hidden feelings, the hidden part that they will discover is the part the watched are ready to like. Notwithstanding what has been said about inmates' feelings towards their guardians, the strongest walls that prisons have are the psychological and emotional ones that the guardians have built around themselves. The real walls are within the prisons, not around them.

4. Work I

*The greater the aversion to work, the more
evident is other pathology in the personality.*

The habitual criminal's inability to hold a steady job, even
when he wants to, is one of his greatest handicaps and any
serious attempt at reeducation must take this into account.

Work is more than an economic necessity: it implies
active participation and the means of achieving status. The
difficulty of the persistent offender in accommodating to work
is therefore a matter of no small concern.

The history of prison labor shows that inmates traditionally
have been forced to work, and, in the past, it was customary to
treat convicts as a slave labor force. In more modern penology,
work combined punishment and penance. It was believed that
through hard work the inmate would not only pay his debt to
society, but would also correct himself and leave prison a re-
formed man. Work and isolation were the harsh philosophy of
the early penal system. Now, however, work is seen as a means
of resocialization and of bringing a man into contact with his
community. The emphasis has, therefore, been placed on
education and vocational training, the idea being that if a man
were skilled and had a trade he would not need to steal.

We need to explore what work means to persistent
criminals and why they are so unstable at work. The refusal
can be so total that the question has been raised whether
inability to work is a cause of criminality. The difficulty
encountered in an essential function like work, however, is
only one aspect of a complex pathology, a symptom, among
others, that includes criminality.

The greater the aversion to work, the more evident is other

172

pathology in the personality. Maladjustment to work shows up in various forms depending on the type of personality deviation and the neurotic conflict of the individual offender. Some have almost never worked in their lives. This attitude is found not only among very severe offenders, but among petty criminals, vagrants and derelicts who make up part of the jail population. Others have had too many jobs. They have a compulsive personality, great motivation but little tolerance for frustration. The constant leaving and finding of jobs is as much of a compulsive repetition as their compulsive criminality. It is an alternating symptom.

Neurotic conflicts about work are also shown in poor job performance. This is expressed as failure in personal relationships at every level: with authority and employers, with coworkers, in work associations and in unions, in recreational activities. The neuroses are further enhanced by an inability to derive satisfaction from accomplished work and by a sense of alienation that we have found in varying degree among all persistent offenders. They cannot tolerate work frustration, just as they cannot tolerate other frustrations in life.

Work records of an inmate in prison seldom correspond with those he had on the outside. A persistent offender frequently becomes a good worker in prison. The reason for this difference is that work in prison and in open society have different meanings. On the outside work requires self-discipline as well as motivation. It demands qualities in which he is particularly lacking: responsibility, regularity and attention to the job, and a willingness to work with other people. The prison system itself does not foster the development of these qualities. The persistent offender continues to feel that work is either a form of punishment or a means of passing time.

The pattern is not immutable, however. In the face of repeated sentences and accumulated time in prison, the older persistent offender begins to equate his consistent reappearance in prison with his work failure. He begins to realize that one of his greatest problems is that he has not come to terms with work.

Before discussing our experience at the Center, it might be useful to summarize the main patterns of behavior and attitudes toward work common to persistent offenders. These patterns

173

are not mutually exclusive and an individual can display a number of them at the same time. Also, patterns can change in the same individual and one that was prevalent five or ten years earlier may no longer exist. It should especially be noted that individual work histories are important and should not be dismissed by a routine statement such as, "Unstable work record Could not hold a job," without further investigation.

Most persistent offenders have actually acquired more than one skill sufficiently well to earn a living on the outside. Hence, their problems with finding and holding jobs are not usually due to lack of knowledge or training.

Many are good workers in prison and get better as time goes on. This improved adjustment does not necessarily mean they have acquired good work habits, merely that they have adjusted to prison life. It ensures that no privileges are lost and that a prisoner can get along with "management" without at the same time antagonizing fellow inmates.

Others display no interest in work, no matter what the inducement. Such offenders show their restlessness by frequent requests for job changes or changes of operation, constant griping and complaints. Changing jobs is thus another means of varying the monotony of prison life. In prison, change of work is often necessitated by special prison situations such as transfers of prisoners, overcrowded workshops or insufficient work, and some persistent offenders know how to take advantage of these opportunities. This work pattern inside is very different from the one outside where work diversity usually does not exist, especially for unskilled and semi-skilled workers. Most men do the same job or the same kind of work year in and year out, and when a worker changes either his job or his type of work he usually does so to improve his situation. Change of work in prison is not necessarily synonymous with improvement.

There are a number who, while in prison, are remarkably steady, remain in the one shop or even on one operation comfortably and without stress and establish good relations with instructors and fellow workers, but they are seldom able to transfer this quality to the outside. These are men who give every outward indication that they enjoy work as work. Unfortunately their good work qualities seem to exist only in an authoritarian setting. When they are able to transfer a genuinely good quality of work acquired inside to the outside, then criminological prognosis is greatly improved.

Some inmates, for whom work in the shop has little significance, are able to occupy their time in their cell with hobbies, with reading and educational courses, and the work they do on their own is often of high quality. One reason for this is that they have no boss telling them what to do, but their good work is far removed from the reality of earning a living in the outer world. "Self-employment" is a means of avoiding conflict with authority, and although few people can assure their livelihood by these means, some offenders are able to use these self-taught skills to better advantage than those required in a prison shop or training program.

Another pattern is that of the sporadic worker who has periods of enthusiasm and good work followed by lack of interest, dejection and work of poor quality. This pattern can be observed through the years in many different types of work and usually indicates that the work record outside has the same swings.

Although some persistent offenders acquire certain skills, knowledge and self-education that could be used for more challenging jobs in the prison, they seek easy jobs, deluding themselves that they will use their skills after release.

Others become deeply absorbed in prison "gimmicks" such as gambling and petty rackets, and work often becomes a field of operation for their gimmicks. They may even go so far as to show a good work adaptation in a particular area which they consider an advantage to them.

Some offenders reach the point where they pride themselves on a particular skill. This may be realistic or an overestimation. Inflated views are common and some men boast of their work as they boast of their criminality. On the other hand, some men minimize both. Even when the self view is realistic, failure may arise outside the prison from a personality defect that appears when they have to be responsible for themselves. For example, an alcoholic or a drug addict who does not appear to suffer from deprivation while serving a sentence will resort to drugs or alcohol as soon as he is free. For such men prison can lessen anxiety, but the anxiety rises rapidly when they are released.

While serving a sentence, an inmate often also expresses the conviction that he will have no trouble in finding a job and that the job will be equally easy to hold. Toward the end of his sentence, this conviction can reach near delusional proportions. He will state with absolute sincerity that he will work and stay out of trouble. Yet on release, he seems to create much of his own difficulty in finding work. He will, for instance, apply for jobs that he can neither secure nor hold. He will blame the exterior situation, especially his prison record. Difficulty in finding work because of a prison record is undoubtedly a real problem, but it is also greatly exaggerated and many persistent offenders convince themselves of this obstacle, even though they may have been working when their last offense was committed. Sometimes they work and steal at the same time. The fact is that most persistent offenders find some work between sentences but it is usually ended for reasons other than their criminal record.

When taking the case histories of persistent offenders, therapists often observe a tendency to greatly overestimate the length of work periods on the outside in the face of direct evidence to the contrary. For instance, they will claim with confidence that they are extremely good workers and have never been fired and then go on to state that they have held as many as twelve to twenty jobs in the one year.

A contrary attitude is the absolute certainty felt by some persistent offenders that it will be impossible to find work. They speak of their record as if it were a form of invalidism, like an accident that incapacitates one for work. This justifies them in soliciting welfare and other types of social compensation; they may not even look for work but spend much of their energy trying to get social welfare assistance. This attitude of persistent offenders is similar to that of workers who develop a compensation neurosis after an accident.

Many offenders try to bargain with society by putting a price on work and services. They say that they will be law abiding provided society pays them, and they expect to be very well paid, invariably mentioning sums beyond the value of their work and in excess of the current maximums for such work.

A variation of this attitude, frequently encountered among young offenders, is their decision to take only jobs they like, jobs that are "interesting," or jobs that "suit" them. This amounts to a daydream of a life where there is no such thing as frustration or boredom. Since such fantasies of an easy and enjoyable activity rather than work are so far removed from reality, this must be seen as merely another way of saying they will not work.

The opposite reaction, an earnest intention to take any

kind of job at any wage, often proves to be just as unrealistic .
When they attempt such work, they find they cannot use it as
a point of departure toward bettering themselves, and they
become disappointed and leave. An unsatisfactory job can
have value only if it is seen as a stopgap, a temporary measure
to tide them over.

Another fantasy is that of finding some place far removed
from their present whereabouts or from the place where they
got into trouble. They believe that in such circumstances
they could work normally. Sometimes they follow these plans
to go to out-of-the-way places and even succeed for a while.
What follows is that they get into trouble wherever they happen
to go or, more likely, they are impelled to return to their
original setting where they get into trouble again. The extreme
"traveling" type is the one that moves about from one locality
to another until he eventually gets into trouble.

In stating these various points on work patterns and
attitudes, we have used a stereotype style that may seem rather
remote from the life history of the men we had in mind.   The
reader should remember that these statements are based on our
reviews of the life history of individual offenders encompassing
many years from the time the man made his first attempt to
work until well into adulthood.

Beyond the different points made here, the clinician will
have to look for the complex dynamics behind work adjustment
and behavior. We have said that play and games were the fore-
runners of future work adaptation. It would have been logical
to investigate offenders' play habits and behavior at games when
they were children but this was somewhat beyond our scope,
since most of our subjects were well into adulthood and,
realistically, we had to think about the present. We were
satisfied, however, that childhood play was probably no more
rewarding for these men than their work activities when they
grew up.

It is our impression that the way children behave at play
has been undervalued as a possible preventive measure for
delinquency and adult criminality. It has often been pointed
out that severely delinquent children are frequently restless and
agitated. We suggest that if we were to look at the reason why
these children are not able to enjoy games we might get closer
to the root of the problem. If we were to succeed in helping
children who are unable to play by themselves or with others,

177

we might be able to prevent them from developing into persons who are unable to work either by themselves or with their peers.

Any program which aims at effecting important changes in the personality and behavior of persistent offenders must take this work defect seriously, and a somewhat new approach was worked out for the Center. The establishment of a shop was not seen, as in the past, in terms of vocational training, as the inmates, persistent offenders with many previous sentences, had already learned a variety of skills and trades. Indeed, not one had fewer than two ways of earning a living. The accent was on work habits and attitudes, and the program was presented to the inmates as a means of reeducation. It was also a lesson in responsibility.

We set up only one shop because we believed that no matter how much choice was given the men, there would be dissatis- faction and a wish to change. (The inmates themselves conceded this point.) Work proceeded for five hours a day with sufficient volume to keep the men fully occupied, a condition not always achieved in prison where there are often more men than available work. The shop, which was next to the men's living quarters, opened at 7.50 a.m. and work started at 8.00. The men were not paraded to work: it was their responsibility to be in the shop by 8.00. When they were late, they had to account at the community or group meeting or to their counselor. Lateness was treated as a symptom and we attempted to solve it through therapeutic means. The ideal policy would have been to tolerate no more infractions than would be allowed on the out- side, but this was unrealistic; these men had a psychological handicap regarding work. Normal procedures would have been too stringent and would have inhibited reeducation.

A therapeutic community involves a great deal of group and individual counseling but this part of the program was carefully arranged so that it would not infringe on the work pattern. Community meetings, group therapy and other thera- peutic sessions involved ten to eleven hours per week. These, along with education and recreation, took place outside working hours. The one exception was the individual therapeutic interview for which a man was allowed to leave his work. The interviews were by appointment and as the interview rooms were next to the shop, the absence of a man from work was for the exact time of the interview only.

Many therapeutic communities, from the description of their program, seem to overlook faulty work habits as a symptom and the use of work as a tool for treatment. In the Clinton program we recognized bad work habits as symptomatic behavior in persistent criminality. Work itself was used therapeutically as part of the treatment process, and work problems were dealt with in this spirit. We took this approach because, for the type of persistent offenders treated at Clinton, exposure to many vocational programs during past sentences had failed. It was necessary to consider work not as adding more know-how but as part of the climate which would remove psychological barriers to work and all related attitudes, conflicts and symptoms.

5. Work II

While we agree that work should be part of the prison regime, we cannot automatically conclude that it is in itself therapeutic.

We believe that prison labor should be an integral part of the national economy and paid for on par with salaries paid in free society.

This idea has been repeatedly expressed in United Nations meetings on the prevention of crime and treatment of offenders and in papers by many writers in the field. It would mean that offenders within a correctional system would 1) be responsible for their own upkeep; 2) be able to shoulder some of the responsibilities they had at the time of their arrest; and 3) be able to set something aside in preparation for their release and reintegration into society. We need not point out that no matter how forcefully these principles are advocated, there are few penal institutions in the western world where they are put into practice. One exception is the van der Hoeven Clinic in Holland where they have long been in operation. Recently, the Canadian Penitentiary Service began a pilot work in British Columbia where a number of inmates, during the latter part of their sentence, work in construction and are paid the federal minimum wage. They are covered by unemployment insurance and social security and work side by side with civilian employees. Hopes are high that such an experiment will lead to radical changes in prison labor and its payment.

Though these reforms are badly needed, we must nevertheless recognize that the work attitude of some offenders is such that normal incentives like adequate pay and work opportunities are not enough to overcome their antipathy. Their difficulties in the labor market are so great that they

180

amount to a form of social invalidism which has its roots in
their personality and character development. In a reeducation
program we must look at the psychological factors that prevent
them from using existing opportunities.

At Clinton the first fifty subjects admitted included twenty-
seven white Americans, twenty-one black Americans and two
Puerto Ricans. The racial or ethnic origin will not be mentioned
again because we found no difference in their work behavioral
patterns which could be attributed to their origin. The age
spread of the subjects was from twenty-four to forty-seven,
the average age being 29.9. The majority ranged in age from
twenty-five to thirty-four. (See Table 2)

* *

A man's work record can be seen as an extension of his
school record and, earlier still, of his family relationships.

One of our fundamental premises is that the inability to
work steadily, to withstand the frustration of work and its
relationships is a symptom in persistent offenders. From childhood they have had difficulty relating normally. Play and
games at home and at school are pre-experiences to work. Most
persistent offenders, particularly those with a history of childhood and/or adolescent delinquency, are school dropouts first
and work dropouts later.

Table 1 shows the level of formal education prior to
imprisonment. The IQ level of fifty subjects is listed in
columns three and four. As we were aware that the earliest
difficulties might be characterized by school problems such as
truancy, misconduct, stealing, etc., we obtained from probation
reports the age at which behavioral difficulties began. In
certain cases we noted that the difficulties were obvious even
prior to school age and were included in statements made by
parents or guardians to children's services or mental hygiene
clinics. When available these sources of information provided
material that the subjects may not have remembered, and com-
plemented the case history obtained from each subject. In fact,
because of early personal difficulties or family problems in
general, half of the sample of fifty men had been reared by
people other than their parents at some time in their lives before
reaching the age of sixteen.

Some of the headings in this table were designed to show

181

how much time each inmate had, in fact, been employed outside prison. In order to arrive at this, we used a coefficient of incarceration. This was defined as the percentage of time from the age of sixteen on that a man had been confined in a penal institution. The time he had spent in freedom was also tabulated and from this we calculated a coefficient of work, which was the percentage of time that the subject actually worked while in freedom. For example, a man who was free for twenty-four months between sentences and worked twelve months would have a work coefficient of 50 per cent. In cases where this applied, the work coefficient was shown. It included time spent in the armed forces as well as an index calculated on the basis of civilian jobs only. As a further characteristic of the man's history, we attempted to assess the number of jobs he held in the time he was free as well as the longest term of employment in any single job. Where this was impossible to estimate correctly, the figure was marked with an asterisk. We were also interested in finding out how many skills a man acquired in prison and how many of them he used while outside.

Looking at their school performance, we see that twenty-one did not go beyond elementary school, twenty-seven did not go beyond junior high school, and only two attended high school. (See Table 3) This poor school achievement is partly explained by the high incidence of serious behavioral problems during and even before school age. In thirty-two cases we were able to document that behavioral difficulties were present even before the age of twelve; in thirteen the onset was noticed between ages twelve and sixteen. Only for the five remaining subjects did their history of difficulties begin after age seventeen. This means that forty-five of the fifty subjects had behavioral disorders that could be traced back to childhood or adolescence. (See Table 4) The seriousness of behavioral disorders during childhood and adolescence is further emphasized by the fact that twenty-six of the fifty subjects had been put in an institution before the age of seven. (See Table 5)

The highest IQ recorded was 122; none was lower than 90. It was noted that in some cases there was a great discrepancy between their present ratings and those given them as children or adolescents. So great was this difference that some had been thought to be of low intelligence and even mentally retarded when young. These low childhood and adolescence ratings can be seen as one aspect of a disturbed development in which potential flourished only later in life.

The data on the childhood and adolescence of fifty adult offenders did not replace dynamic case histories dealing with relationships, motivations, and psychosocial development, but it did show that early behavior disorders had interfered with schooling and resulted in court appearances or placement in youth services and institutions.

Such data confirmed our premise that serious work difficulties in the life of adult persistent offenders found their antecedents in their behavior at home, in the neighborhood and in school. They had serious handicaps in adapting to work situations just as they had had in their adaptation to school. Their work record was as poor as their school record.

Our detailed examination of the inmates' work record outside prison was carried out by a personal interview with every man, and by the examination of prison files and of reports by probation and parole officers. The inmates were aware of this research and appeared to take considerable interest in it. Gaps in the written reports were filled in by information given by the inmates and we had no reason to assume that it was inaccurate or designed to mislead. Furthermore, about twenty-four inmates participated actively in the collection of the data. They worked in groups of three, two proceeding to interview the third one about his prison and work histories, and using the same indicators as we did. When the investigation of one inmate was ended, the second was investigated by the other two, and so on, until the investigation of all three was completed. At the end, these groups of three were interviewed by one of us and their findings were discussed in relation to our own. This direct involvement of the inmates in the research created a very favorable climate.

In general, we could see (as indicated by the coefficient of incarceration) that in most cases we were facing men who had spent much of their adult life in prison: thirty-four of the fifty had a coefficient above 40 per cent; of these twenty-one had a coefficient of incarceration of 60 per cent or higher. (See Table 6)

We made a comparison between school performance and achievement and the coefficient of incarceration. The twenty-one who had not gone beyond elementary school had an average coefficient of incarceration of 59 per cent; the twenty-seven who attended junior high school had an average of 48 per cent;

and the two who went to high school had an average of 29 per cent. This comparison indicated that those who achieved less at school also spent less time in freedom.

It was not surprising therefore, that those with a poor school achievement had the lowest coefficient of work. The twenty-one who did not go beyond elementary school had an average work coefficient of 45 per cent; the twenty-seven who attended junior high school had an average of 58 per cent; and the two who attended high school had an average of 72 per cent.

We also found that seventeen worked less than 40 per cent of the time while in freedom, thirteen worked between 40 per cent and 60 per cent of the time, while twenty worked 60 per cent of the time or more. The work coefficient here did not include the time spent in the armed forces. (See Table 7)

The coefficient of work had to be seen in function of the number of jobs held by these individuals in the period spent in freedom between sentences. These fifty men held a great number of jobs, as shown by the fact that twelve of them held one to four jobs, twenty-three held five to nine jobs, eight held ten to fourteen jobs, four held fifteen to nineteen jobs, and two held more than twenty-five jobs, so many in fact, that we could not assess their exact number. (See Table 8) The great number of jobs was not explained by the fact that these men were in and out of jail. In fact, a high coefficient of incarceration usually stemmed from two or three long sentences rather than a series of short ones. Thus, the numerous jobs held were interesting to study in comparison to the longest time spent in any given job.

The shortest job held by one man was less than a month; for nine the longest job was held from one to four months; for nineteen the period was five to nine months; for six it was ten to fourteen months; nine men held jobs fifteen months or more, and six could not be assessed. (See Table 9) The number of civilian jobs, as well as the length of time these jobs were held, illustrated that these men were unable to stay at a job for any length of time. Both the holding of too many jobs and the holding of too few indicated restlessness and not being able to stay long at one place. For some the short time at a given job was because they could not stick it out; for others work was ended either by arrest or by dismissal.

At the Center we attempted to measure work habits just as employers would outside by simple quantifiable indicators, such as absenteeism with or without excuse, sick calls, and lateness. Lateness or absenteeism was dealt with as a symptom and discussed at the community meetings.

A detailed record of workshop attendance was kept and the figures for the months of September, October and November 1967 are shown in Table 12. Of the fifty-one men accounted for in this table, thirty-nine were subjects also described in Table 1 so that for these thirty-nine men their work history inside and outside prison was documented by the indicators we selected for these studies and the data in Tables 1 and 12 could be combined.

Absenteeism with or without excuse was considered as true absenteeism since in most cases the excuses were weak and would not have been accepted in a free work enterprise. Lost time at work was caused by walking off the job, intolerance of being given orders, difficulty with other inmates, trouble in coping with a particular task, or, very important, in coping with the shop atmosphere itself.

All the men were in good physical health and their complaints were similar to those regularly found in a penitentiary sick parade, that is headache, tension, hypochondriacal and somatic complaints. In September 1967, almost two-thirds of the men had sick calls, the figure dropping to just over one-half for October, but rising again to nearly two-thirds in November. It will be seen that in each of the three months there was a considerable spread ranging from thirteen times for one man to once for eleven men, but the number of sick calls was strikingly large considering that these inmates were among the healthiest of the general prison population.

The improvement in absenteeism figures from September to October to November could be explained by the fact that while this research was going on much emphasis was placed on these figures at the community meetings. At times absenteeism figures were brought up more than once in a week. We were certain that confronting the men with their unmotivated absence or weak excuses for absenteeism would produce an improvement in the overall rate of shop attendance. At the same time, a factor that should not be minimized was the number of new arrivals in October and November, as seen in Table 12. The newcomers tended to be as conformist as they had been in the institutions from which they came. They found it hard to believe that no disciplinary report was written for absenteeism and that going to the shop was their responsibility just as it was their re-

sponsibility to be at work when they were in free society.
Generally speaking, it took them a few weeks to accept that they
could choose to be "delinquent" and actually became so in the
work area. No figures or indicators showed better than the
absenteeism rate how regimentation in a prison suppresses
symptoms rather than allows them to come into the open where
they may be dealt with.

It was interesting to note that inmates with the highest
rate of absenteeism were also those with the greatest number
of sick calls. We selected ten offenders who were absent without
good reason fifteen times or more and compared them with ten
who were absent less than five times without having given any
excuse. These ten best workers did not include those with no
absenteeism at all. As a matter of fact, there were only three
with no history of absence without excuse and all were relatively
new arrivals at the Center. The tabulation of absence with or
without excuse, sick calls and lateness showed that those who
were more frequently absent without excuse were also absent
most with excuse. (See details Table 13)

The amount of data collected on the work habits of the
men would have been an exercise in futility had it not been used
to try to understand each as an individual. We will briefly outline six cases selected from the best and the worst workers at
the Center's shop because they illustrate the variety of reactions
to work and even the differences of work habits inside and outside prison.

Sid C., age thirty-five, was one of the best workers at the
Center, but he had an incarceration coefficient of 42 per cent.
Between sentences, he had spent 137.5 months in freedom
and had worked for forty-nine months, giving him a work
coefficient of 36 per cent. He had held twelve jobs, the longest
for twelve months. He had a remarkably good record at the
Center, being absent only two half-days without excuse and two
half-days with excuse. He was never late, nor had he had any
sick calls. He showed pride in his work and one of his most
rewarding experiences was a promotion for achievement and
sense of responsibility. He derived great pleasure from two
other activities which were also achievements for him: bowling
and painting. Bowling was an especially good experience since
he had never before taken part in group sports nor in a social
atmosphere such as that in which the game is played. He also
started painting for the first time and did remarkably well for

one who had never thought of or attempted such an endeavor.

On the other hand, his actual participation in the program was minimal. He had great difficulty in taking an active part in therapeutic and group meetings. Outside the shop he appeared so detached that he gave the impression he was either deeply depressed or was off in a world of his own. When we became better acquainted with him we could see that he needed to communicate. However, he was shy and withdrawn and had difficulty in doing so. One of his ways of dealing with this problem on the outside was to seek refuge in heavy drinking. When he was drunk he usually became belligerent and aggressive. At the Center, however, he was quiet and never presented any disciplinary problem.

From the number of jobs he held on the outside, it was evident that his record was far from good. He generally worked as unskilled labor at various seasonal jobs. If one compared his work achievement inside and outside, it was evident that this man could do remarkably well in a protective milieu. When unprotected on the outside he was unable to work steadily or responsibly. He benefited through passive rather than active participation in the program, that is, he silently absorbed what was going on around him rather than express his thoughts and views in group meetings. It should be noted that he had spent nearly ten years in freedom between 1951 and 1961, though there were numerous charges and arrests for drunkenness and misdemeanors related to drinking.

Another good worker in the Center was *Bert V.* aged thirty-two. He had an incarceration coefficient of 69 per cent. Out of sixty-three months of freedom, twelve were spent in the armed forces, and twenty-four working at various jobs. His work coefficient, including time in the forces, was 57 per cent. Excluding this it was 38 per cent. He had held nine civilian jobs, the longest for five months. At the Center he was well rated by the instructor, but the report we had of his work adjustment outside was very unfavorable. Most of his offenses were crimes against property committed when he was working. More often than not, his jobs were ended by his arrest.

This was a well-meaning man with a background of great deprivation. He tried to do well but was unable to build a solid relationship. He failed in his attempts and was eventually brought back to the criminal milieu where he was accepted. No meaningful relationship or friendship had ever been established in the work situation so that work had never really had a motivating meaning for him. On the outside he was bored by work but in prison he was a reliable worker who could be trusted to do a difficult job well.

Rick M. was also rated a good and steady worker at the Center being absent from the shop for only three and a half days without excuse and three and a half days with excuse. He was late only once. Age thirty-one, he had an incarceration coefficient of 78 per cent. Out of the forty and a half months spent in freedom he had worked for seventeen months, his work coefficient being 42 per cent. Of the five jobs he held, the longest was for six months.

In other prisons his work and adjustment were considered to be fair. At the Center they were considered to be poor, because of his lack of participation in the program other than in the work area during the three months he was observed. He would follow the routine as required and was all right in circumstances not requiring initiative, but in any situation that did require initiative he rated poorly. While absenteeism from the shop was low, it was very high for group therapy and community meetings.

Once when he was praised in the community for his good work habits, he was most upset and expressed this vehemently. To be known as a good worker in a regular prison was far from being valued by one's peer group. At the Center such recognition in a community meeting was usually well regarded by both inmates and staff but he reacted as he would have in any other prison.

He quit two of the five jobs he held outside and three were ended by his arrest. One of his employers reported that he was a "conscientious, hard-working, reliable, good, substantial employee..." from which we concluded that his work outside was good while it lasted. He seemed able to withstand the frustration of work within the protected and well-guarded atmosphere of the prison. Outside he was unable to remain long at a job without reverting to crime, because he gave up easily, whereas inside he had no choice and simply conformed.

Max W., age thirty-four, had a very poor work record at the Center; he was absent without excuse nineteen times and with excuse twelve times. His incarceration coefficient was 65 per cent. He spent eighty months in freedom, but his work coefficient was difficult to assess because he had held at least thirty-two seasonal jobs. The longest time spent on any one job had been thirty-six months; this was prior to his first imprisonment at the age of twenty.

The instructor described him as courteous, calm, studious, neat, except when he was depressed. Then he was irritable, impatient and inclined to blow up verbally: "Well, if you know so much about all this, you goddam hack, why aren't you a doctor or something like that? " At such times he stayed away from work, but eventually he would come back and discuss his feelings, his problems, his moods. Despite his moods, he was generally well liked by his therapists.

When he was outside prison, the pressure of difficult situations was alleviated by drinking or by getting into trouble. His record included many minor offenses having to do with drinking. His recorded IQ of 91 was decidedly inaccurate. Clinically, we would have said that he was bright average.

The number of jobs held outside corresponded well with his recurrent depressive states inside the Center. When he left a job due to boredom or depression, he became more depressed and in fact was in a state of real need. Depression and criminality were very closely linked as shown by the fact that his criminal record revealed offenses such as stealing goods, alcohol and food. His depression and explosive behavior became increasingly marked with age. Although he was considered among the poor workers, he was far from being so. In actual fact he was a man who was struggling with his problems. However, in the free labor market, one cannot expect an employer to be a therapist.

Nick G., age thirty, had an incarceration coefficient of 40 per cent. He spent 102 months in freedom, was employed for seventy-two months and spent eight months in the armed forces. His work coefficient was 70 per cent including armed service, and 67 per cent excluding it. He had held no less than thirty-six civilian jobs, the longest for seven months.

During the period under study he missed thirty-four half-days of work at the Center. Otherwise, his work record was fair. However, he was moody, had difficulty accepting orders, and did not work well under authority. He was somewhat unpredictable. When asked why he wasn't attending shop he replied, "I don't have to go if I don't feel like it." His appearance varied from neat to sloppy and he could be well-mannered or cocky. He had episodes of recurring depressive states of short duration.

This unpredictability was also in evidence when he worked outside. Many of his civilian jobs were as a waiter in restaurants. He left these jobs because he would get angry with his employer, another worker, or a customer. In many of the jobs he stayed no more than a few days. In others he was asked to leave or he was dismissed. His work record at the Center was somewhat similar to that outside. When depressed or moody he would simply go his own way just as he did outside. At the Center, when his outbursts of temper, his moodiness or his depression passed, he was welcomed back at work. An employer could hardly be expected to display such forbearance and understanding When free, he had never had the opportunity to return to any of his jobs following his depressive episodes.

Bryan L., age twenty-seven, had an incarceration coefficient of 53 per cent. He spent sixty-two months in freedom, during which he worked for thirty-four months and was in the armed forces for ten months. His work coefficient was 71 per cent including his armed service and 55 per cent excluding this. He held fourteen civilian jobs, the longest for six months. During the period studied, he was absent from the shop twenty-seven half days without excuse, nine half-days with excuse, and had twelve sick calls.

At other penal institutions his adjustment was considered poor and most of his disciplinary problems related to his refusal to go to work. His numerous absences at the Center would obviously have justified a poor disciplinary record had his absenteeism not been dealt with as a symptom. Despite this, his overall adaptation at the Center was fair. He tended to be moody, impatient and somewhat compulsive. At times he presented psychosomatic symptoms including neurovegetative ones, with accompanying states of tension and anxiety. Impulsiveness and acting out seemed to alternate with a neurotic and hypochondriacal state.

All his outside jobs were menial ones and he could be considered as an individual who would not be able to support himself. He was highly dependent on his mother, a woman who was even more in need of help than he was. Had we summed up his work record inside and outside, the results would have been the same. In both situations the employment would have come to an end because the subject was impulsive and tended to act out. At the Center, his behavior was dealt with on its own merits. It was interesting to note that as the subject dwelt more upon the cause of his trouble he became more anxious. When he left the Center there was marked anxiety as he was now more conscious of the meaning of his personal difficulties rather than simply being bored with the particular type of occupation he happened to be in at the time.

* *

These short histories demonstrate the value of knowing the early behavior of every inmate. Good work records inside and outside sometimes coincide. At other times we see good records inside and poor ones outside, or vice versa. These histories illustrate that a good or bad work record does not necessarily provide a sure source of knowledge of the inmate, as it could also be a symptom involving the total personality.

What is important is that work in prison exposes all of a man's assets and problems. At one extreme, good work habits can be a way of dulling the pain of serving time rather than preparing for life in freedom. The six cases selected had a lot in common but they also differed in many respects. They illustrated the need for clearly evaluating work habits.

No one inmate could be treated as a stereotype. Despite the passivity or aggressiveness of some and the passive-aggressive attitude of others, the fate of these six offenders was relatively good some seven years later. *Sid C.*, *Rick M.*, *Nick G.* and *Bryan L.* had neither returned to crime nor violated their parole. *Bert V.* had violated his parole and was returned to the Center, but parole was restored. *Max W.* was convicted of a minor offense, served his sentence, and parole was again restored. In view of the many patterns, symptoms and habits projected in the work area, it is valid to ask whether work in a prison can be considered a therapeutic activity.

* *

To the extent that the penitentiary rules allowed, work at the Center was seen as an activity that a man is expected to undertake freely. Conditions of work were far removed from the ideal of integrating prison labor into the national economy and remunerating a prisoner for his work so that he can be self-sufficient and thus responsible for himself.

Our experience with free attendance at the workshop

made us feel that the cost of living in prison could be determined by some convention which would make it possible to fix wages so that, without necessarily being on a scale with those paid outside, the inmate would feel he was paying his own way.

This could not be envisaged while this experiment was going on at the Center because the per diem pay of thirty cents was too low. Also, inmates were allowed to receive so many extras from their relatives or approved visitors that they did not have to rely on their earnings to make purchases at the canteen.

Almost all institutional activities such as work, recreation, music, art and the like are lumped under "therapy." In the world of freedom these activities are not called therapeutic, and the fact that they take place in prison does not automatically transform them into treatment.

Enforced idleness is no longer advocated and work is universally accepted. While we agree that work should be part of the prison regime, we cannot automatically conclude that it is in itself therapeutic. The meaning of work and its role in the resocialization of prisoners, particularly persistent offenders, is far from being understood well enough for a consistent policy to be adopted.

Incapacity or inability to work must be approached from a number of angles. Being unable to work, whatever the cause, is a social handicap. It leads to a state of dependency where social assistance must eventually be resorted to in order to obtain the essentials of life. When the reason and the cause for the inability to work have been established, the incapacity becomes a symptom, rather than a handicap in itself.

Some work incapacity, for instance a physical handicap, can be corrected by remedial training. Such training includes learning, apprenticeship and work. While work can to a certain extent be considered as treatment in remedial training, it is basically part of a learning process. No one speaks of work as a treatment in the training of the blind and the deaf, though the work involved undoubtedly has social and human implications. For most physically handicapped people education and training are techniques for learning rather than a form of treatment. Once motivation is present for the physically handicapped (except where the medical state precludes training), invalidism is often reduced to a minimum through education and training. A main cause for inability to work is to be found in the personality of the persistent offender. In general people who are not motivated to work find other solutions. Social assistance, begging, vagrancy, accommodation and willingness to adopt less than conventional standards, being a non-conformist and a work drop-out are all among non-delinquent solutions. When the incapacity to work is psychological, as it is with persistent offenders, it is only logical to ask whether compulsory work eventually leads to a "symptom cure." Our first answer tends to be no. It has been observed that in certain chronic states, such as in phobic and obsessional neurosis, symptoms tend to change or to become extinct with time even without treatment. One of the premises of the Center was that persistent criminality abates with age but we feel that time alone is not the healer; it is what goes on in time. The complex interplay of experiences and relationships changes man's adaptation as he proceeds from one stage of life to another.

Looking at the persistent offender's chronic incapacity to work and his exposure to compulsory penal work, our view is neither to deny therapeutic gain nor to make positive claims for it. We do say that under enforced exposure to work, an individual who is psychologically refractory may eventually find certain satisfactions and rewards, or acquire a certain tolerance which was previously non-existent. This is not enough to justify considering compulsory work as a treatment, but it can be compared to other learning experiences acquired in spite of a negative attitude.

What gave us greater knowledge of the offender and his work habits was the wealth of information we secured. Work for the persistent offender is at times so irrational and apparently meaningless that at first glance there seems little to talk about. However, when his work habits are seen as symptoms, there is a great deal to investigate. There are many types of persistent offenders and there are also many different types of poor adaptation to work. If we want to use work as a therapeutic technique in the treatment of persistent offenders, we have to look at what work means for each one and be ready to look at the many symptoms that manifest themselves in a work situation. Work is not just performing a task, but a part of living, of being with others. We must take for granted that in placing a persistent offender in a work situation that is non-authoritarian and non-compulsory he will not only reveal his incapacity to work, but all the flaws in his personality. Observing a persistent offender in a working milieu gives us clues not only regarding his work habits, but also his reactions as a person in a complex situation which is a part of daily life. Work in a prison workshop is part of a program and we are looking at it as behavior, side by side with relationships, moods and thoughts. In fact, we are looking at a living situation of which work is a part of the whole. Work can thus be part of a treatment program, but it would be an abuse of words to call work alone a treatment.

Our approach to work was probably best summed up by a former inmate, one of the first fifty to be admitted to the program. When the Center had its sixth anniversary party, he returned as a guest for the first time since his release:

> Man, I hated that machine when I came to the D.T.C.,
> but I made up my mind — that machine was either
> gonna beat me or I was gonna beat it. So, even though
> I hated every minute of it, I really busted my ass over
> it and, square business, I got so qualified on that
> machine that I even thought about opening my own
> tailor shop on the street. As it turned out, man, I
> never looked at another sewing machine after I left
> the joint, but the discipline that I developed is re-
> sponsible for me being able to succeed at the kind of
> jobs I've had since my release.

6. Acting Out

*Acting out on the part of inmates must be seen not
as a problem but rather as a function of the program.*

In a conventional prison setting, prisoners are confronted
with a highly artificial milieu characterized by rigid controls and
strict rules governing conduct. The objective is to maintain a
peaceful and orderly institution rather than to equip the inmate
with behavior patterns translatable to open society. The behavior most condemned and punished is that most likely to
provoke disturbance within the institution: refusal to accept
orders from officers, aggressiveness toward officers and staff,
and fighting among themselves.

In the traditional prison setting many inmates are able to
conform to the rules and accept the behavior patterns of their
environment. Their lives are so structured and regulated, they
actually experience a reduction in anxiety. The ever-present
threat of punitive action acts as a further spur to conformity.
In this setting, the inmates successfully suppress symptomatic
responses, but they gain little insight into their basic problems.
Voluntary self-control, however, is what an open society requires
of its citizens.

This is why a therapeutic community in the prison milieu
attempts to provide an atmosphere as similar as possible to the
one found in open society. Rather than having strict rules, we
try to promote an atmosphere of open interaction among inmates and between inmates and staff.

Such freedom of action inevitably leads to interpersonal
conflicts, but we believe that the acting out on the part of the
inmates must be seen not as a problem but rather as a function
of the program. To attempt to suppress it by punitive means

or authoritarian approaches would be to frustrate our objectives. The inmates must be allowed some latitude to display their symptoms if we hope to diagnose and treat them.

In conventional prisons even basically non-delinquent acting out is dealt with as an offense: "missing" or "being late" for shop, questioning orders, talking back to officers and similar non-violent displays of aggression. In a therapeutic community such behavior is considered "normal" or "problem" depending on the situation. We are more concerned with determining why an inmate has trouble in going to work rather than with forcing him to go or punishing him for failing to do so. We are more concerned that an inmate be able to express his hostility, than that he may become somewhat abusive while doing so. It is through the process of his behaving "naturally" that the unacceptable facets of his conduct can be interpreted to him by fellow inmates and staff, and thus help him to develop some understanding of his actions and their effect on others.

Three predominant forms of acting out are 1) stealing, 2) the making and drinking of home-brew, and 3) physical violence, mainly fighting. These three areas are important also because they are prison problems that correspond to offenses the inmates commit in open society.

Stealing can take three distinct forms: stealing another inmate's property; stealing property belonging to the state; and organized stealing characterized by its visibility and the implied involvement of more than one inmate. Visibility adds a dimension of great significance here.

Stealing by one inmate from another may be motivated by a simple desire for material goods and/or envy of the one who possesses them.

Theft of property belonging to the state or institution, however, is motivated by the desire to achieve as much comfort as possible inside the prison. These thefts usually are objects such as lamps, chairs, or paint. This type of stealing is considered acceptable by many inmates and it is frequently condoned by staff and administration unless it becomes epidemic.

The third type of stealing, the organized and undisguised type, should be the easiest to deal with. However, we know that when inmates steal in an open, obvious and organized fashion over a relatively extended period they are experiencing a high level of anxiety, and trying to convey some message to the staff. This open acting out can be a cry for help, a way of asking the staff to deal with conflict in the community, insecurity over lack of direction, or some other serious problem. The staff has the dual function of helping the community explore the roots of the disturbance and of dealing with the problem caused by the acting out. The phrase "helping the community" is of prime importance, for it is basic to a therapeutic community that the inmates themselves assume the responsibility for coping with their own problems.

Stealing in any form in any prison is a serious matter for it is a reversion to — or a continuation of — the type of behavior that brought most of the inmates to prison. Theft is all the more serious in a therapeutic community because each member theoretically has access to the same number of material objects. Minimizing the importance of thefts because the stolen objects are small is a mistake. A carton of cigarettes stolen in prison is equivalent to the theft of a rather valuable commodity on the street.

Where a community spirit has successfully been instilled there is strong group pressure against stealing. When this does not exist a great deal of ambivalence occurs among community members and this can be greatly magnified if the staff overlook the offense. They can seem to condone it simply by failing to insist it is important enough to warrant the community's full examination. Knowing that such behavior is to some degree inevitable inside a prison, the staff may default because it does not have the resources to withstand inmate pressure to overlook the incident.

Further conflict is created when the staff verbalize certain attitudes about acting out, but pursue a contrary course of action. Positive peer group pressure which is indispensable yet difficult to achieve, in a therapeutic community becomes all the more elusive when the staff's own vacillation causes the inmates to revert to the prison code of each man for himself. Though this makes them feel more secure, the reaction is only temporary. Ultimately their guilt feelings increase, paving the way for a vicious circle of behavior repetition.

When the principles of confrontation and community discussion are not followed, the inmate feels deprived of any effective instrument to deal with stealing or any other acting out. In the traditional prison the mode accepted by the inmate is to use violence against a thief. As this is known to be an unacceptable alternative in the therapeutic setting, many inmates choose either to cast a blind eye on stealing or to turn the stealing to their own advantage.

In a session held with the inmates to discuss their attitudes on the matter, we found that they did not want to know who was stealing, because if they did they would want to deal with it in the way they know best — the use of force. In this way inmates confine their concern to themselves and their friends. If an unpopular inmate is caught stealing the others are more likely to try to make a deal for a share of the loot rather than to confront the guilty party on the community floor. If the staff, through its own avoidance of the problem or through inconsistent behavior, fails to sustain peer group values, the community will quickly regress to traditional prison values where one inmate confronting another on the community floor is considered "ratting."

The very question of what constitutes "ratting" is of fundamental importance in the therapeutic milieu. In the traditional prison the revelation of an inmate's activity or behavior to other inmates and, particularly, to staff and administration is tantamount to treason. It is the greatest crime which one inmate can commit against another. An inmate who is branded as a "rat" is ostracized by his peers and is often severely punished by them in other ways as well.

The therapeutic community, on the other hand, functions largely on the basis of open verbal confrontation between inmates and between inmates and staff. The newly arrived prisoner is both surprised and threatened by this type of interaction. In order to gain his cooperation in this approach, he must be assured that the reason for this type of confrontation is not malicious but geared, rather, to help peer group members to communicate so that they can give each other insight, and deal with conflicts and personal problems. The only really effective means of transmitting this value to the inmate population is by example. This implies that professional staff and officers must accept open confrontation themselves. If this does not occur, inmates justifiably complain about different standards of conduct for staff and inmates on the community floor. It is only by providing examples and by disapproving of vindictive confrontation that an open climate can be created. It is unrealistic to expect inmates to drop their defenses until staff and officers have dropped theirs.

One particular occurrence at the Center will serve to illustrate the dynamics of stealing and the staff management of it.

A rash of open stealing occurred with inmates from the two units stealing from each other. The property belonged to the prison but it also represented some of the most valuable amenities available to the inmates, including hot-plates on which they could prepare their own food and the highly valuable shop radio. It was obvious, however, that several inmates were involved and that the objects were missing and not just borrowed. Since these objects were community property, the only concealment was the identity of who actually took the objects, but the fact that the loss constituted self-deprivation indicated that the thefts represented a deep disturbance within the community.

Briefly this was the order in which the events took place: some Unit II inmates apparently went to Unit I (there is free access to each unit) and stole the shop radio. Retaliating, Unit I inmates stole two hot-plates from Unit II. Then Unit II inmates stole a third hot-plate and a toaster from Unit I. There was yet another, though this time unsuccessful, raid by Unit I inmates which was detected by Unit II members.

Despite its negative character, this situation provided an unusual chance for the inmates to take responsibility both for dealing with offenses in their own midst and for working through the problem of anxiety which had precipitated it. From the outset, it appeared that the situation would hinge on how the group responded to the problem. As for the staff, it could have attempted to mobilize peer group pressure to deal with the problem by insisting that the situation be discussed at community meetings and group therapy sessions; it could have directly intervened in a regulatory and punitive manner; or could have been simply placating in order to reduce tension. Some staff members who feared loss of control wanted to intervene directly to show authority. Heated debates took place as to which of these courses to follow.

We describe what happened in order to demonstrate what we felt was a poorly managed situation. The clinical director's first reaction was that this issue should not be dealt with on the community floor because of the high level of tension then existing. He preferred that the staff conduct their own investigation into the affair and take the needed steps to restore normalcy to the community. Some staff members asserted, however, that the daily community meetings were ideally suited for discussing this type of community problem. Indeed this very type of predicament was the *raison d'être* for these daily sessions.

Initially, this group prevailed and the matter was brought to the community floor. Predictably, the community was strongly displeased at being confronted with the problem. Pressure came from some inmates for the staff to "solve the problem," although such a solution was not possible since the acting out came from within the community and was precipitated by the inmates' own anxiety and disturbance. This effort to throw responsibility onto the staff represented the classical response of inmates when faced with a question requiring that they not only examine the root of the problem, but also attempt a solution other than recourse to the prison code of keeping silent about other inmates.

In response to this pressure and to the hostility of the inmates, the director chose to tell the community that the question of the missing goods was a closed issue, that it had already been dealt with. A particularly heated staff meeting followed. Some staff members felt that this approach directly contradicted the therapeutic community philosophy in that it removed personal responsibility from the inmates. It was finally decided to toss the situation back at the inmates, and explain that they were the most affected in the community by this type of behavior and, therefore, they must be the ones responsible for defining the community they wanted and what behavior they were prepared to accept.

Considerable anxiety continued to exist in the community and it became evident through conversations with inmates during that day that concern was developing about the effect this type of behavior could have on the program. There appeared to emerge a favorable consensus that those responsible, whether or not they were known individually, should be pressed to return the stolen goods. The community also began to realize that there was a need to discuss openly their feelings regarding the incidents and the possible causes.

Late in the afternoon, a joint community meeting of both units was called for this purpose. Two serious tactical errors were made in conducting this particular meeting. The director, again apparently seeking to pacify, started off, not by asking the inmates what they felt was behind the particular behavior, but by providing the community with various ready-made interpretations for it. He said that it could have been because of anxiety in the community about some professional staff who were leaving, or because of a shortage of staff, or some similar reason. Predictably enough, this provoked a positive response from the more threatened community members who were eager to accept this rationale. They developed an air as if to say, "Oh, well, now they've told us why we've done it, they're going to tell us what they're going to do about it and everything will be forgotten." Fortunately, other community members pointed out that staff members frequently changed without evoking this type of acting out. The group then discussed inmate responsibility and the destructive forms of behavior which could endanger the program, as well as other related problems.

The director concluded the meeting with the open-end ultimatum: "The missing goods had better be returned by four o'clock today." Until this statement was made the staff had been trying to make the community sensitive to the problems, and the community, in turn, seemed to be ready to undertake the problem of dealing with the situation. The ultimatum, however, altered the complexion of the staff's message. It implied that the inmates were not called on to resolve the problem simply because it affected them and their lives in the community, but rather to prevent some undefined punishment. In later conversation it appeared that the members who seemed most disposed to acting on the problem began to be cynical about the ultimatum. They felt that the staff wasn't confident that the community would deal with the situation without making an underlying threat.

At four o'clock that afternoon, an unidentifiable inner part of a radio was handed to an officer. Its origin was impossible to determine. It could have been the inside of any radio. The other missing items were not returned.

At the next staff meeting, there was again much disagreement about the ultimatum. The director finally conceded that perhaps he had erred, but that as far as basic policy was concerned, there would be no change. The ultimatum would be forgotten and the community would continue to be reminded of its responsibility to deal with its own offenses. It will be clear to the reader by now that the staff had already mishandled the situation due to disagreement, ambivalence, and frequent changes in policy. The staff were impeding rather than helping the inmates.

The next day, many of the consulting staff members being absent, the resident staff again told the inmates that the situation *had* been dealt with and that the administration would order two new hot-plates and a new shop radio to replace the ones that had been stolen. This reversal can only be explained as the staff's inability to deal with the anxiety provoked by the situation itself and the hostility it evoked from some of the less mature community members, or their belief that they had already messed up the situation and therefore could not put the onus on the community members to contend with it realistically. The first interpretation is probably more accurate, as there was from the outset evidence of a good deal of staff insecurity.

This, unfortunately, is where the issue remained. It was considered "solved," amid great sighs of relief from the administration. However, it constituted a massive failure on the part of the staff because the two major objectives were not achieved: the inmate population was not stimulated to deal effectively with the problem, nor did we learn the underlying causes of the anxiety. Moreover, there emerged a rather serious split between the resident and consulting staff concerning basic therapeutic community policy.

We didn't deal so maladroitly with all our stealing situations, as the following example shows. It involved two inmates who participated in the hobby of photography. *Bill W.*, a particularly level-headed, responsible member of the community, was in charge of the photographic paper. One day he found *Jack C.* in the act of stealing some of this paper for his own use. *Jack* was superficially popular with the other inmates, though he had difficulty in forming close relationships. *Bill* confronted *Jack* and told him that he would bring the matter up on the community floor.

Inmates often express the fear that such a confrontation will result in the accused inmate being blamed not only for his current misdemeanor but also for various other unsolved thefts, and *Jack C.* was not the type to become a scapegoat. Sure enough, when the confrontation on the community floor took place some inmates commented on things missing from their rooms and implied that perhaps *Jack C.* was responsible for those thefts as well. Neither the majority of inmates nor the staff allowed this attitude to prevail. The inmates' view was, "Well, look man, this guy admitted that he was stealing, so he admits that he's got the problem and it's up to us to try and find out why he did it and try and help him with it. There's no point in bringing up any other things that happened before." What followed was a rather sympathetic yet probing investigation of *Jack C.'s* motives that yielded a fair amount of insight into his personality. Most important, it provided an example of an interest in the inmate's stealing merely as a symptom rather than with a view to punishment. The episode also instilled in the other inmates the confidence to deal with these sensitive situations at community meetings.

During the discussions it became clear that in a matter of two weeks or so *Jack* would have had enough money to buy the paper he had stolen, and that there was no rush involved in the work he wanted to do. His problem was that he simply could not defer gratification for even such a short period of time. Furthermore, *Bill* stated he would certainly have given *Jack* the paper out of his own resources had he but asked.

What had taken place was typical of the deprived personality of the persistent offender. He found it easier to steal than to ask for the object in question, because asking would have put him under obligation. It would also have raised the possibility of having to deal with a rejection had he been refused. He was emotionally unable to cope with either situation.

These points were discussed at the community meeting and the entire group seemed to have benefited from the discussion. As mentioned, envy and retaliation are among the main reasons for stealing in the therapeutic milieu and the case of *Mark L.*, discussed earlier in this book, is an example.

Another form of acting out which essentially is meant to go undetected is drinking, or making home-brew. This is often motivated by a desire to ease depression, to retreat from the reality of imprisonment, and, occasionally, to celebrate the impending departure of a friend. In short, it is used for many of the same reasons for which alcohol is used in open society. Occasionally, however, there are cases where its use and manufacture are so overt that those involved really seem engaged in attention-seeking activity. In such cases it is then necessary to deal with both the reasons for the activity and the symptom itself.

Similar problems exist in handling drinking as in coping with stealing. One difference, however, is that because drinking in moderation is socially acceptable in open society, inmates attempt to justify their use of alcohol on the same basis. This often makes it difficult for the staff in a therapeutic community to take a strong position on drinking. Again here, an inconsistent or ambivalent attitude by staff will be reflected in the inmates' attitudes. We do not insist that staff attitudes must always be rigid or unanimous. We do insist, however, that their approach be as realistic as that expected from the inmate group. In this situation, the Department of Corrections Regulations were the reality with which we must live and which in turn must be interpreted to the inmates.

It was, therefore, decided that the inmates must be informed that while they were perfectly entitled to have their own opinions about the acceptability of social drinking, they were in an institution which did not allow it and they must learn to accept this reality. Life in a therapeutic community is unstructured by comparison with other prison life and allows a great deal of personal freedom. This should make the members more willing to adhere to the few rigid rules which do exist. It is expected therefore that they be able to develop some control in not drinking and failure to do so becomes an offense within the milieu. (It is important to note that as far as the acceptability of social drinking was concerned, many of the persistent offenders in the Center were not social drinkers but rather persons for whom drinking was a symptom of their social pathology which created extra problems for them.)

Because of this it would have been irresponsible for the staff to decide that since drinking will always occur in institutions, it should, by and large, be overlooked. To do so would simply reinforce the inmates' desire to make their own rules — behavior which leads them into difficulties on the street. Also, to punish drinking only when it is flagrant and a possible embarrassment to the institution, and to ignore it when it is relatively discreet, is to uphold a traditional delinquent value: that the important thing is not to get caught.

The following incident illustrates how failure to be consistent about drinking can result in rapid escalation of the problem, cause an over-reaction from the staff, and yield negative results in the long term.

Incidents of drinking had been observed by officers in both units over several weeks. Because of uncertainty as to how to deal with it, they either ignored the drinking or made very mild remarks to the inmates in question. By not bringing the problem to the attention of the staff or the community as a whole, a form of staff complicity developed which became a problem in itself.

Consequently, drinking reached such an extent that some

inmates were actually drunk during community celebrations to which outside guests were invited. While this might not have become visible to the guests, the fact remained that there existed a potential for serious incidents. There was also a marked increase of drinking in the evenings.

Finally, forced to take some kind of action, the staff resorted first to threats and then withdrawing commissary privileges for all inmates. This was both a punishment and prevention; preventative in that certain items used for the making of home-brew whisky were available in the commissary. This evoked a great deal of inmate hostility. There were protests that many were being punished for the crimes of the few and accusations that the values of a traditional prison were being imposed on the therapeutic community. The action succeeded in suppressing the symptoms only; the long-term effect was that inmates refused to confront others about drinking for fear of further restrictions being applied to the whole community. They considered drinking not as a problem which was theirs to deal with or be concerned about, but rather one for administrative regulation and punishment.

Recourse to punishment becomes extremely destructive in a setting where the objective is to achieve adherence to rules through agreement and cooperation of a community as a whole. It undermines the integrity and efficacy of the program itself and the resulting loss of confidence on the part of the inmates is something that takes a long while to restore. Had the staff taken a more consistent and firmer attitude from the outset, it is unlikely that the situation would have deteriorated to the extent it did.

Most drinking in a therapeutic milieu is done as a means of escape and is arranged in such a way as to make detection very difficult, but this is not always the case. Earlier we discussed how open stealing can represent a cry for help on the part of the community. The same applies to drinking.

Don R. was a seemingly self-assured, cocky inmate who was well liked by most of the community members and staff. He was by no means a model prisoner, but with the development of insight into his own problems and those of his fellow community members, his immature and sometimes irrational behavior seemed gradually to be replaced by more responsible patterns.

As the time approached for him to meet the parole board, he became increasingly irritable. He continued to maintain that

he was fully confident of his ability to succeed on the street and
that he had no major problems which he could not handle.
Then three days prior to his appearance before the parole board,
he was found, roaring drunk, wandering through the corridors
of Unit I. "Found" is certainly an understatement as he practically waltzed right into the arms of one of the officers on duty.

He was confronted with this on the community floor the
following day. After initial truculence and refusal to respond,
he was asked whether he was really afraid to go home and
whether he felt he had problems out on the street that he could
not cope with. He finally admitted that this was exactly the
case, that despite the bluster and the facade of self-assurance, he
really had grave doubts about his ability to make it outside. By
getting himself into trouble within the institution, he hoped his
parole would be denied, giving him more time to work on his
problems. He explained that he just could not bring himself to
come to staff members or other inmates and say, "Look, I'm just
not ready to go." He had even refused to admit to himself that
this was the way he felt about his possible release. Acting out
to bring attention to himself was the only way in which *Don*
was able to summon help. The incident precipitated an examination of his fears and anxieties, most of them genuine but some
caused by last-minute panic. It was hoped that through interpretation it would become easier for him in later circumstances
to admit his doubts and shortcomings and to seek help more
directly and simply.

We mentioned earlier that inmates sometimes drink in
order to celebrate an event such as the departure of a friend.
Our experience is that most of the inmates who use this reasoning have a history of drinking in prison and have abused alcohol
prior to arriving there. We are well aware that even in the rather
depressing existence of prison life there are occasions for joy
and celebration that seem to call for "a drink." However, in
view of the aims of a therapeutic community, we felt we had to
help the inmates express their joy in more moderate ways.

Physical violence, another major kind of acting out
usually appears as a fist fight between inmates, but, at times, it
takes on more serious proportions: an inmate will attack another
with a lead pipe or similar weapon; he may even —although this
is rare — attack or threaten an officer or staff member.
Physical violence is the form of acting out that occurs

least frequently in a therapeutic community and is probably the most satisfactorily dealt with by the community. Fighting between two inmates is such a visible form of acting out and the danger is so obvious that both inmates and staff tend to deal with it directly and consistently. The possible consequences of letting it escalate seem to be realized much more readily than the potential dangers of stealing or drinking.

Of the three basic types of acting out, only violence was singled out for mention to new inmates when they arrived at the Center. Not only would it not be tolerated, but indulgence in it might result in their being returned to the prison from which they came. When a fight or other physical violence did occur, it was immediately taken up at a community meeting where the combatants were encouraged to discuss the reasons for their conflict and helped to resolve it. It is interesting that although inmates may feel ambivalent about intervening in other forms of acting out, such as stealing, they readily intervened when physical violence occurred. They recognized its threat to the Center, but at the same time they do not consider physical conflict and fighting as an act of delinquency, but as something arising out of a personality clash or the participants' immaturity. Even inmates serving sentences for violent acts that may have resulted in death do not consider their behavior an offense. They see it more as human conflict than an infringement of rules, they feel less bound by the traditional prison code of silence, and they will feel freer to bring the participants to the community floor for open discussion.

The inmate attitude toward fighting is significant and should provide an important awareness to the staff. Of course, inmates and staff may differ as to what degree and circumstances of physical violence constitute a delinquent act. Nevertheless, if the staff could correctly and consistently interpret other kinds of behavior problems as easily as they can physical violence, inmates might come to regard these other forms of acting out also as "problems," rather than as clashes of divergent value systems held by the staff and themselves.

Although acting out by inmates could result in their transfer back to the penitentiary, this did not occur when the situation was simply one of a flare-up between two inmates, but only where an inmate was frequently physically aggressive and unable to respond to non-punitive forms of intervention.

Frank M. was a Unit I inmate with a long history of

breaking and entering, and sexual offenses, including rape. It was obvious when he entered the community that he was extremely threatened by the "bombardment" of therapy, by the concerted attempt to bring him out of his shell, to have him talk about his problems and to come to know himself better. As he became involved in the therapeutic process and began to verbalize some of his conflict, his anxiety level rose. He had reached the stage where awareness was having its initial unsettling effects on him, but he had not yet sufficiently incorporated this awareness. As a result he became quite surly. It was now necessary for those dealing with him to proceed cautiously. One afternoon when he and a few other inmates were returning from the gymnasium to their living quarters, he took exception to the manner in which an officer spoke to him and threw a punch at him. Though the officer was not injured, this nevertheless constituted an unprovoked attack on *Frank's* part.

At a staff meeting to discuss the problem, there was a great deal of officer pressure to have *Frank* removed from the community — the traditional response when such an act occurs. Understandably, since the officers were trained to act in a therapeutic way and the "club" had been removed from their hands, it seemed intolerable for them to be subjected to any kind of physical attack by the inmates. However, some of the staff felt that the attack was a direct result of the anxiety of a rather disturbed inmate becoming involved in a therapeutic process for the first time. They urged that *Frank* be kept on at the Center to determine whether he would calm down as his anxiety diminished, or whether he really did lack the control necessary to live in such a community. This approach was unacceptable to the officers, and rather than create friction it was decided to return *Frank* to prison.

From a clinical standpoint this was unfortunate because it was unlikely that *Frank* could begin this tremendously difficult process of therapy for a second time. It was hoped that a slightly less rigid attitude regarding violence could be developed, along with more understanding on the part of some officers as to its cause and clinical significance in the therapy of a particular inmate.

When discussing aggressive behavior, we must not overlook verbal aggression. As long as it remained verbal, it was accepted and by no means discouraged, but there were instances when it assumed rather important proportions. Many inmates know no outlet other than physical assault when they

208

are angry or anxious. Others feel that the verbal expression
of anger has no end product other than physical assault. With
the first type of inmate, our aim was to have them learn to
express their anger without a corresponding need to hurt
somebody, and not bottle it up until it explodes. With the
second type of inmate, we were anxious that they learn not
to fear anger and to realize that it need not result in physical
confrontation. The only way they could learn this was by
practice, so we tried to interpret the reasons for their verbal
aggression rather than punish them for it.

One incident demonstrates the thin line which sometimes
exists between verbal and physical aggression. It also shows
how difficult it can be for the staff to deal with one without
provoking the other. *Bob J.*, a man in his late forties, was one
of the more angry members of the community, a man whose
hostility toward society was not diminished by his years in
prison. He was a rather paranoid individual who had to be
handled carefully, for he interpreted negatively most interventions concerning his behavior.

On one occasion he was confronted by a shop officer for
not going to work. He was very upset by this as he considered
himself (and rightly so) one of the best workers at the Center.
Nonetheless, there was cause for concern. *Bob* had threatened
that if the officer so much as spoke to him again he would beat
him up.

At the community meeting, *Bob* refused to discuss the
matter at all. It was obvious that his anger was intense and very
near the surface. When another officer attempted to pursue
the subject, *Bob* jumped up out of his seat, stood over him
threateningly, and dared him to say another word about it,
obviously implying violent consequences.

The chairman of the meeting was somewhat at a loss as to
how to proceed. The threat of imminent violence had long
been part of *Bob's* method of keeping staff and inmates at bay.
This intimidation was partly successful because he was indeed
serving a sentence for murder. It had worked several times
before in community meetings, but now the chairman's feeling
was that, as *Bob* was nearing the end of his sentence and the
community hadn't really gotten to him in a positive way, his
behavior should be challenged. He was, therefore, confronted
both on his previous threatening behavior and his immediate
gestures toward the officer. The outcome was that *Bob* picked

up a chair and threw it in the chairman's direction. He then came up and stood in front of him in a challenging and menacing way. The situation remained thus, with neither one moving. The inmates swiftly intervened and ushered *Bob* back to his seat.

The issues involved were plain. *Bob* had been getting away with intimidating and threatening behavior, and he had used this instrument as a means of refusing to deal with himself. It was clear that he was very distraught on this particular day. Yet he was being pushed, perhaps too far, by the staff. Had he actually thrown a punch or committed some other aggressive act, he would have had to pay all of the consequences: he would have been shipped back to prison, perhaps charged with assault. Yet he would have been justified in thinking, "They knew I was hot — why did they keep pushing me?   They should've known better."

The therapist involved later came to feel that the wiser course of action might have been to let *Bob* get away with his threatening behavior for one more day and then confront him with it the following day when he would probably have been much calmer. The same end would have been served, that of letting him know that he couldn't get away with threatening the community, but it would have been done at a time when he could have accepted it more easily.

These incidents bring to mind that the inmates are the ones who pay for the mistakes made by therapists, officers and administration. When one considers what is at stake for the inmate, it makes it absolutely mandatory that everybody involved improve their techniques and skills so that errors and inconsistencies occur less frequently.

The success of a therapeutic community depends upon the creation of a milieu where the inmate feels secure enough to renounce behavior patterns and values which he formerly saw as necessary to his survival. It is therefore policy to have inmates attempt to deal with problems with as little direct interference as possible. The principal role of the staff is to direct the attention of the community toward the particular problem and to help interpret the behavior.

Most inmates are used to dealing with difficult situations in one of two ways: by spontaneous reactions geared to achieving immediate gratification, or by avoidance. Well thought out, progressive and long-term approaches to problem solving seem impossible to many persistent offenders because they cannot stand to be frustrated and since sustained involvement with an anxiety-provoking situation is so difficult for them, they exert great pressure on the staff to "Deal with this situation — what the hell are you paid for? " Because of the great amount of time spent with inmates daily, and because of the level of verbal aggression permitted, it often becomes just as difficult for staff members to cope with existing tension as it is for the inmates. When the staff yields to pressure and assumes responsibility for restoring equilibrium, the result is the immediate gratification which the inmates so vigorously seek. It also represents a backward step in developing the ability of inmates to solve their own problems. Furthermore, it reinforces the inmates' delinquent technique of either "muscling" or manipulating the staff in order to get what they want.

In a community operating at a low ebb, these mechanisms can become so strong as to represent a reversal of roles between staff and inmates. When this happens, the staff no longer defines what inmates will deal with, but rather inmates define what the staff will deal with. This situation can be avoided only by consistency in staff behavior. The inmates should not get the feeling that the amount of responsibility they will be asked to shoulder will vary according to the amount of pressure they apply to the staff. Once an inmate population believes that it can intimidate and manipulate, the therapeutic community ceases to exist. Inmates adapt their delinquency to a new milieu rather than the staff creating a milieu where delinquent behavior is immediately recognized and interpreted as unacceptable.

7.   Breaking Down the Codes

Little by little relationships developed between inmates and officers and the open schism which usually exists between the two groups in a prison faded away.

We have always believed that the officer-inmate relationship is the most important factor in defining the atmosphere of a prison.   It is basic in a therapeutic community that there be a positive interaction between these two groups if a humanizing and rehabilitative atmosphere is to be formed.   Hence it was important to find out exactly what officers and inmates thought of each other and what the relationships were both prior to coming to the Center and afterward.   Accordingly, we made a videotape film of three discussion groups in November 1971. One group was composed solely of officers, another solely of inmates and the third comprised both officers and inmates. Before coming together for the joint session, each group had seen the tape made by the other so that everyone was well acquainted with the attitudes expressed by each group.

Each of the sessions lasted an hour and a half.   The following are selections of representative comments from each group regarding the others, and about issues of common interest and importance.   Since the comments were selected from various segments of the tapings, there will be only a few instances of continuing interaction between the participants regarding a particular issue.   Most of the comments were chosen to illustrate points of prime importance, and our interpretation attempts to summarize the overall impressions gleaned from the four and a half hours of sessions we observed.

212

I. OFFICERS' SESSION

Attitude Toward Inmates Before Coming to the Center

Art Rabideau. Actually, to keep them there (in prison) you had to look down on them. You had to look at them as creeps — you didn't accept them as your equal. You had to look down at them a little because you were in control of an awful mass of bodies and being in control of this mass of bodies, what you had to do was put them through their paces and have them do what you wanted them to with as little trouble as possible.

John Coffey. I would say that in my experience of the past nine years, it was strictly a military system and you couldn't buck the system. You went along with the system, or you didn't work there. Whether you liked inmates or you didn't, the point was that you did what you were told.

Charlie Hayden. I think you'll find in every institution there's a small nucleus of officers at all levels that are highly displeased with the prison setting *per se*, where the inmate is always wrong and has no rights. There is a small nucleus that would like to help the inmate in some way, to rehabilitate him, but the point is in an institution of two thousand men it's impossible, so all you could wind up doing was keeping order.

Bob Racette. When I came here I had worked nights for eleven years. My attitudes were more or less formed through association with the people I was working with at that time. I changed a lot of my attitudes since then, in fact almost completely. Art was right when he said we looked down on them. I think in all fairness, though ... I felt I did look down on them, but I wasn't conscious at the time that I was doing it. It just seemed like the way to be, the thing to do, because everybody else was doing the same.

Denny Champagne. I used to think those guys should be punished. Not any more, but at the time that's exactly how I felt.

Changes of Attitudes After Coming to the Center

Hayden. Well, numbers is certainly a good place to start.

The ratio of officers to inmates here is much higher. It makes it much easier for you to have time, and to find time, to communicate with them as individuals and to find out how they feel.

Racette. Yeah, and when you find out how a guy feels you readjust your own attitudes. You feel a little empathy and you can put yourself in his shoes, so to speak. You can understand him as a human being, it is much easier to accept him.

Hayden. I think the difference is in terms of what the institution is trying to do. In prisons they're interested in developing the ideal inmate, the kind who will follow orders, who won't make any disturbances, and so on, so we treat them that way. Here, in a sense, we're trying to develop the type of person who will be able to live out on the street, so we've got to treat him very differently, we've got to give him a lot more respect.

Attitudes Toward Crimes

Champagne. I used to think that if a guy committed a crime against a child or something, you know, I would agree with the man on the street that this guy ought to be hung up by the balls, but when you get to know the guy as a person, you start to realize the type of problems that he's got. You begin to see how he got this way, that he had no other choice but to get that way. This makes your attitude become different for him. My own feeling is that they should still be in jail but should be treated humanly and (we should) try to make them understand how they got this way.

Security and Therapy: Possible Conflict in Dual Role

Champagne. When we started, it was something like 75 per cent security, 25 per cent therapy, but as we progressed over the six years I've seen the security as not being so important. It's a human relationship you're forming here. The security really isn't needed.

Rabideau. I think the best security in an institution is a good treatment program. This may be the crux of the whole thing, that you have a good treatment program. When you have something like that going, security will take care of itself.

214

Champagne. It's a bit confusing at first, but I think after
a while most officers get into the scheme of the program and
figure security will look after itself. There are always some,
though, who still think the other way and put security first.
They treat the guys differently than they would in prison but
they're still fairly traditional in their attitudes.

Officer and Inmate Codes

Rabideau. Well, there's an inmate code that has to do
with ratting. In prison, nobody talks about anybody . . . .
Personally, I don't believe in rats. If a guy rats to me, I don't
want him around. Although I feel that there is a difference —
I may be wrong — but I think there's a difference between a
guy who rats for the sake of ratting and the guy who's going to
tell you something to help someone. There's a helluva big
difference. You have to learn how to distinguish the two. I
think there's confusion on the inmates' part as well as our own
as to what constitutes ratting. When they first come here and
they come out of a group session, they say, "Well, that's just a
rat session." After all, all they can see from their point of view
is guys squealing on each other. After they're here for two or
three months, though, they understand that what's really going
on is people trying to help each other and they learn to make the
distinction between what's ratting and what's confrontation and
therapy.
    . . . there's an officer code as well. We were brought up
in a kind of officer culture where the officer was never wrong —
you know — I don't care what the officer did, but he was never
really wrong. Sometimes you'd tell him later, "Don't do it like
that again, you were wrong that time," but at the point it was
happening, he was always right and the inmate was wrong.

Hayden. We were sort of trained in the system to think
that we were "holier than thou," and we found out many times
that we were quite unreasonable. We'd make statements and
give orders with very little thought to the repercussions and
we'd make demands that sometimes weren't reasonable. We
think, though, that in this program, by explaining why we do
what we do and why it's necessary, letting the inmate know what
our job is and what is expected of us, they understand better
what we're trying to do.

II. INMATES' SESSION

Attitudes Toward Officers

Ken W. I've been in jail since 1946 and in some of the institutions the officers were terrible. They didn't believe in ever putting their hands on you — they just hit you with a club. For seventeen years I worked in a block where they broke in the officers and I'd say 80 to 85 per cent of the officers coming into prison work were reasonably decent dudes and usually the guy who would break them in was somebody who was known to be, you know, con-wise or jail-wise, and he would break them in to all the games that we played and that they played and if they get a bum breaking them in, they become a bum too. No matter what kind of a decent dude they were when they started, if a bum broke them in, then they treated us like garbage.

Ross P. I was considered a troublemaker ever since I've been in prison. I've never been able to establish a meaningful relationship with an officer. Maybe some of it was my fault. I could never trust him, not even when I came over here. I knew it was supposed to be different, you know, but my attitude was that I couldn't even use the officer. This would be bending my principles. When I first came here, I jumped on an officer every opportunity I could. You know, this was a privilege to me. For eleven years I couldn't say nothing back. I just said to myself, "accept that shit." So, every time I thought they were wrong, or I was justified, I would jump on them. Recently my attitude started to change. You know, I used to deal in absolutes — all cops were pigs and I really believed it. Just recently I started to realize that they're doing the same thing to us — all convicts are animals. I still don't like all of them, but I'm beginning to see that some of them have their good ways.

William O. I think the officer is an instrument of the system and in times gone by the system has used him to keep us, the inmates, in check, so that's what the officer did. He did just what he was told and a whole lot of them enjoyed their job. Now the system's changed a little bit and they start lightening up more on inmates. They started in this direction, and so you see the general overall attitude of the officers changed. I think the reason we see such a large change in officers here at the Center is because this is an entirely different system. The system

216

here, the authorities here, the people in power here — they want the inmates treated different, so even some of the same dudes who banged heads next door in Clinton, they come over here and they change up their techniques over here. I think the majority, if you take them up there and put them back over the wall into prison, well they'll go right back to their "clubs as trumps."

Well, I feel like this particular job of a prison officer calls for a man with almost no ambition; doesn't have to have too much mentality. All you have to do is be able to count up to thirty-five or forty and turn the key. But the man gets a helluva lot of compensation from that. Back in the days — and this is not too long ago — when you were a prison officer, he came in, he was automatically better than 2,000 men, and you had people who had gone through college—doctors and lawyers in jail — and there you took one of these slobs who couldn't do nothing but count and turn the key and he automatically got to be better than you. I think that's why a whole lot of people got into the field of being a prison guard, cause he got to be superior just because he locked you in every night.

I think we're gonna see here a stereotype officer just like we have in the prison, only this is going to be a therapeutic officer and he'll have his stock answer about how he goes home every night, and that's why his way is the right way, etc. But you know the qualities that make a good officer, say, are the same qualities that make a good inmate, which is, you do what you're told. Now, once you get a police who will question his sergeant or his captain, he generally makes a good police as far as the inmates are concerned. But a good police as far as the inmates are concerned is a lousy police as far as the authorities are concerned. But the man who will question orders, who will attempt to look at himself every now and then and act like a human being rather than a robot — well, good officers are robots. Good inmates are robots too.

Question: Can you ever forget that this man is an officer?

Ken W. I could never be a friend or try to be a friend to somebody that I always got to ask and can't give. Put me in the position where I'm a beggar, no matter what you say, if I need a pair of pants I've got to beg for it; a pair of shoes, or anything in that line. If I want to go through the door, I got no key.

Peter B. But hold it now — individualize a little. I dis-

217

agree. There's this man here who's completely different than any other man that I've met before. This man treated me like a brother — you know, like another con, and I treat him like a con, you understand? I don't see him as an officer; I see him as another guy.

Freddie H. I wouldn't dislike this guy because he's an officer, but I must respect him because he is an officer. Now, that's what he is. I'm an inmate — he's an officer, and at least once a day that distinction is made. At least once every day you see the difference between the officer and the inmate and that's when he locks you in.

Billy M. Yeah, I can see what you're saying — that you can trust this man with anything; you can tell him anything and treat him man-to-man and he treats you man-to-man, but still, I don't see where you could forget he's an officer.

Peter B. I just don't see him as a cop.

Billy M. But he is one.

Peter B. Well, that's just his job, man. Everybody makes his living doing something!

Inmates' Code: Ratting

William O. What constitutes ratting and what doesn't constitute ratting? Well, I'll tell you. We had an incident over in our community meeting — I won't mention any names. One inmate complained to another on the floor about his going up against the food committee and disagreeing with them, causing them problems. Then this other guy got up and said, "Well, hey, what about the wine that you had to sell the other day?" Well, that first guy, he was confronting a guy about something that was going on in the community, but the second guy, he was only ratting. And you know there's got to be a distinction between trying to tell a guy why he's not functioning in this or that area, and you know that's what we call a therapeutic move, not ratting. What we call ratting is when you get personal with a guy like that wine incident, or "Why did you bring that book in here?" — "Why did you do that?" — that's when it becomes ratting. I guess the difference is when it doesn't seem to be done in order to do anybody any good but just to get a malicious thing off.

Ken W. When I first came here and I'd see a dude snitch, I felt like saying, "Man, you ain't doin' nothing but ratting, man,

you know that — you ain't nothing but rats." But I've learned to distinguish what is a rat and what isn't. I mean a lot of times if something is brought up to try and better the guy involved, then that's not ratting, and if it's told to him — even if it's in front of other people — you're talking right to him without problem, then that's not ratting. But don't mistake, man, there's still a lot of ratting going on in this place.

III. OFFICERS AND INMATES TOGETHER: GROUP SESSION

What Constitutes a Good Officer

Freddie H. A good officer — well, ten years ago I might have said that the only good officer is a dead officer, but now I think that a good officer is somebody who's gonna tell you what he thinks; that he's not going to be telling you one thing and then talk behind your back saying another thing.

William O. I guess the qualities of a good officer would be the qualities of a good human being, one of the first being that regardless of his present position here — he realizes his own faults and admits to them as well as mine.

Question: What do you consider a bad officer?

Bob Parker. Just the opposite - a guy who harasses inmates, may be a guy who isn't too honest with them.

(At this stage, the inmate group put the questions to the officers as to whether there were bad officers in the Center. The officer group grudgingly admitted that there might be a few but found it difficult to take this position.)

Question: Can you forget that a man is an inmate?

Miles Mesic. Yes, I can because I look at him as an individual.

Freddie H. Yeah, but, say you're looking at him as an individual, you know, maybe you can accept him as a man, but how can you for one moment forget his position?

Mesic. It's not that conscious a thing.

Ross P. How can you do it without any reservations? Like, I'd always imagined that you say to yourself, "Well, this

guy — he's a criminal; he's gotten himself into trouble before, he could probably do it again," and so you've got to have a reservation like this.

Mesic. On a personal level, I actually try to take him as a friend, with no reservations.

Rabideau. Why do you have to have any feelings either way? Can't a man walk in on one of the units and exist for eight hours, deal with the people there and intermingle with them, whether they're inmates or officers, and not have this feeling?

William O. I don't see how you could forget it because you're overlooking two basic things: why the inmate is here and why the officer is here. The inmate is here for breaking the law and the officer is here to keep the inmate here and that's the two basic reasons why you're here, and therapy and everything else comes a little later on.

The Possibility of Officers "Going Back to the Clubs".

Ross P. I always got this little fear that if I do something wrong, even if it's a little bullshit rule that I'm breaking, that I'll be disciplined for it. I can never get it out of my mind that some day the other shoe is going to fall.

Freddie H. Say one day someone comes down from Albany because there's a little tension here and the program wasn't going the way they like it and they say, "We're gonna go right on back to the sticks" — could you do that?

Rabideau. I never carried one.

Freddie H. O.K. You never carried one, but there are officers here who did, and I want to know if they would use them if they were told.

Coffey. What do you mean? If there was a riot or something? In that type of situation, as a last resort I probably would.

(At this point, there was much cross talk. Most of the officers stated that they would not use clubs, but were constantly trying to get the inmates to qualify and be more precise about the question. They seemed to want to have it far more clearly defined before they were ready to answer. Only Coffey, the officer quoted, came right out and said that as a last resort he would. The other officers would not take a firm position in response.)

220

Hank S. Well, look — how do you feel about the fact, man, that we've got these reservations about you?

Parker.   I can understand that. In fact I feel the same way too. I mean, if I'd been kicked around, say by the police, and put myself in a situation to get manhandled and beat up and went through the prison system for ten or fifteen years and all — you know, beat up by blueshirts — it would be hard for me to accept. I'd always have it with me — I'd never lose it.

Attitudes Toward Sexual Offenders

Question: *Do you think the type of crime committed in the past affects the way in which officers relate to you?*

Sid A. Sex crimes — I think they're the only real ones — sexual offenses. But one time I was rapping with an officer, you know, and I got busted for selling drugs and I don't think he knew it at the time. But he made the statement, "I would kill all the drug pushers," and I said, "Well, you know, I sold drugs," and he stopped rapping with me.   Like in prison, you know, there's this hierarchy by the type of crime you commit — like robbery, murder, assault, you know, and all the way down to sex offenders. I mean, here the officers don't seem to have that kind of viewpoint — they don't see sex offenders as being low-down degenerates. They see them as (having) a sick mind.

John E. Well, that goes the same for inmates too. When I was in prison, I used to look at somebody who was in for a sex offense as being a piece of scum. Here I don't. . Here I've learnt to look at them as somebody with a problem. I think that the sad thing is that despite all this insight we've acquired and everything, if we were to go back to prison today we'd resort back to the old attitude toward sex offenders. If we were to associate with a sex offender, we'd be outcasts. We'd be the same kind of outcast which he is in prison, which is a lousy thing to be in prison. You know, in prison you've got to go along with the tide of public opinion — (cross talk: denial from some inmates) Well, maybe you don't have to, but I do because I know that if I go back to prison I'm not going to associate with a sex offender because I know that you, you, you and you would ostracize me because of it.

Ross P. ` You're worried about the negative values of your peers. In other words, you'd be a hypocrite. What you're

221

saying is the same thing — you're down on the officers because we say that if they go back to prison they'd pick up the club — well, you're saying the same thing . . . . If you would go back there, you would put down the sex offender, you would ostracize him. If you were a guy's friend, you know, and you're sitting next to him and he was a sex offender, if you would have to go back to prison, you'd put him down because you would succumb to this negative pressure. You're saying that you would . . .

John E. No, I'm not saying that — what I'm doing is trying to be truthful.

* *

One of the striking points in conducting these sessions was the contrast between the relative ease with which the inmates were able to talk compared with the officers who needed to be prodded quite frequently. We asked them many more questions in trying to elicit some of their past and present emotions and experiences. Because their imprisonment was the dominant feature of their lives, the inmates were able to respond with more emotion and more spontaneously than the officers. For the latter, conscientious and involved though they were, it remained that they were talking about their jobs and were more prone to intellectualize about the type of work they did rather than express, as the inmates did, deeper basic feelings about the type of life which they were leading. There appeared also to be more interaction within the inmates' group because of the bonds they shared. Although it was pointed out that there was an "officer culture" and an "officer code" there seemed to be a closer and more uniformly experienced bond among the inmate group.

The difficulty in expressing themselves was heightened during the combined officer-inmate group where the officers seemed even more reluctant to express themselves. This seemed to have been caused somewhat by the gulf between the sharply differing officer and inmate realities. When the officers were asked in their own group whether they could forget that they were dealing with the inmates and whether the relationship could be simply man-to-man, the answer most frequently given was that they could. In the inmate group, it was quite obvious that there were great reservations as to whether the officer could be seen as a man distinct from being an officer. In the common group, the officer-reality as such was somewhat modified when confronted with the inmate-

reality. In fact, the officers withdrew from the position they had taken in their own session. They began to realize that what they had really been saying earlier was: "I can learn to like a lot of these men, I can learn to respect them but perhaps I really can't lose this reservation about them as inmates as if the barrier didn't exist." In terms of implications for treatment, it is probably healthier that this reservation did exist in the minds of officers and staff.

Another area where officer and inmate attitudes conflicted somewhat was regarding the role of the officers as both guards and therapists. It seemed to be a bit jarring for the officers when the inmates' reality was thrown at them: "Sure, we know that some of you are really good guys, you're sincere, you're interested in us and all that, but you are officers and we can never forget that." It stands to reason that it is easier for officers to "forget" that they are dealing with inmates. The inmates, on the other hand, are constantly reminded no matter how permissive the atmosphere or how good their relationship with the officers, that they are indeed inmates. This is demonstrated by the fact that they are locked in every night.

For an officer coming from another prison where he was used to being quite rigid and allowing little or no mobility, he can perceive a tremendously liberated atmosphere. However, from the inmates' point of view they tend to focus more on the limitations which remain rather than on the freedoms which are given through this type of program.

On the other hand, it must be pointed out that all of the officers involved in these sessions had been at the Center from its inception six years earlier. Their memories of oppressiveness were not so fresh as that of inmates who had recently arrived from a traditional prison environment.

What was evident in the officers' group, however, was that while we generally perceived this type of program as being humanizing for the inmate, it also acted in this way on the officers. This was apparent in their changed attitude toward inmates and toward crime since being in the Center. They also stated that they wouldn't feel comfortable in the rigid and oppressive role they had had to play in the conventional prison.

While the inmates verbalized more ambivalence toward the officers than the officers did toward them, it seemed that beneath the surface the officers themselves really felt greater ambivalence regarding their role. We became aware of this in the third session.

The inmates placed the officers in a rather difficult situation by asking them whether, in an Attica-type crisis, they would obey orders to pick up a club and attack the inmates. It was significant that only one officer could bring himself to say that yes, as a last resort he would indeed use physical means. There seemed to be considerable indecision and qualification among the officers. Evidently they had a great deal of difficulty in seeing themselves in that type of situation, that is, going back to their former role with all that it implied. In reality, they couldn't say that they would, or would not, respond in terms of their former training.

When the same situation was posed to the inmates, on the other hand, they stated that despite the close relationships they had developed toward the officers, they would certainly do what they had to physically in order to further their aims. Whether they would indeed act thus is open to speculation, but they had a far clearer conception of what they might do than the officers.

Another striking element in the third group was the fact that the inmates were on the offensive much of the time while the officers were on the defensive. It was as if the inmates felt that the officers still had to live up to certain stereotypes and were attempting to make them admit that this was indeed the case. The officers had begun to perceive their role as essentially therapeutic, as they should, given the setting in which they worked. It was, therefore, unsettling for them to have the inmates tell them: "There are two reasons for all of us being here — we're here because we committed a crime, and you're here to keep us here." This was a very clear vision of the situation from the inmates' point of view. The officers tended to deny that this clear-cut reality existed, pointing out that, "It isn't really like that here because of the therapeutic program. Our reason for being here is to play our role, which is mainly to help you."

Significantly, each group was essentially correct in viewing things from its own perspective. It was evident, of course, that the inmates had only one role to play, that of inmate. The officers, with their dual role of security and therapy, had a certain ambivalence forced on them in attempting to function in both respects. While it was not particularly remarked on in the session, we had observed that when the inmates vigorously confronted the officers the latter tended to back off and became more the guard and less the human being, whereas in other situations this was reversed.

As clinicians, we did not have to experience this ambiva-

lence and confusion in our roles, and it was important to realize the particular dilemma that faced the officers in this setting. The officers seldom, if ever, had to act in the stereotyped officer role at the Center. Where the program had perhaps been the most successful was in making it totally unnecessary for an officer to use the controlling or punitive techniques that have always been necessary in a prison. This was largely because they had built a rapport with the inmates so that even when the latter were agitated there was enough of a relationship to allow for a dialogue and cooling of tensions through discussion.

This interaction between officers and inmates was referred to on another occasion when an inmate pointed out that he found it to be a rare privilege to attack officers verbally when he first came to the Center and that he took advantage of it. While this naturally made the officer defensive, the inmate realized that there was no retribution against him and his own aggressiveness diminished considerably. Little by little relationships developed between inmates and officers and the open schism which usually exists between the two groups in a prison faded away. The officers learned to live with the reality of being confronted, instead of their accustomed role of confronting the inmates. Through this experience they learned to understand the reactions of others when being confronted. This tended to modify their technique of how to confront. They learned to do so in a progressively more human and reasonable fashion, thus obtaining better results when confrontation was needed.

At one point the inmates expressed fear of having to return to conventional prisons where the officers still used clubs and physical violence. This was interesting, however, since they themselves had pointed out that they would probably revert to their old ways despite the understanding they had gained at the Center regarding the ostracism of sexual offenders. It became clear that each group was largely victimized by the code which it developed: the inmate code, with its hierarchy based on the type of offenses committed and its fear of open communication, often construed as ratting, and the officer code, with its need of looking down on inmates and constantly putting them in the position of being wrong.

At the Center, the tradition of both the inmates' and the officers' code was broken down, if not completely, then at least to a good extent, allowing both the inmate and the officer groups to function more as equals and interested human beings

interacting profitably with each other. When these codes are broken down to the extent that they were at Dannemora, it is then difficult to use a term such as "the watchers and the watched" for, despite the situation in which both groups find themselves, it becomes more a case of people interacting on an equal basis, where each has the chance to confront the other for errors, misbehavior or incompetence. They react to one another in emotional ways due to slights or insults, real or imagined, and personal conflicts which develop in any day-to-day situation. The stereotypes tend very rapidly to fall by the wayside in this situation, and it is largely through this disavowal of stereotyped thinking that the therapeutic process becomes possible, for in reality, therapy can only proceed from a human relationship.

8. Black versus White

*Through the subjective experience of our black
and white prisoners and our white staff, we became
clinically involved in what it meant to be black or
white: living together in or out of jail, reaching out
for, avoiding, or simply tolerating one another.*

People who are segregated by ways of thinking, living and
feeling are not necessarily induced to live together in a spirit of
brotherly love by the kind of integration found in the New York
State Correctional Service. The Clinton Diagnostic and Treatment Center was, of course, an integrated institution and when
we use the word segregation we refer to white or black inmates
separating themselves out of psychological need, not because of
enforcement.

We had to accept as a reality the black and white situation
in American society, particularly as it existed in New York State,
and we could not concern ourselves with the political and social
aspects of the problem. That there is a problem of black and
white in American society, that this problem affects all members
of that society, social institutions as well as individual life, is
taken for granted. (The reader can obtain first-hand information
from the numerous American studies on this subject.) It would
be unrealistic to think that the black and white problem as it
exists in New York State would not be reflected in its prisons,
all the more pointedly since the ratio of inmates is considerably
higher for the black than for the white population. But the
problem is not peculiar to New York State; hence we refer to
it as an existing reality to be lived with by inmates and staff.

The Center was located in a predominantly rural area
where the population is mostly white. The staff of the penal
institutions at Dannemora is drawn from among these people.
For some of these white correctional officers, it is almost a
traditional family occupation (Clinton Prison was opened in

1845 and Dannemora State Hospital in 1898). The question always raised by visitors, and even by members of the McGill staff before they became aware of the historical and geographical background, is why were there no black members on staff when there were so many black inmates. The answer is simply that since there was no pool of black manpower in the region, there were no black candidates to choose from. Furthermore, it is difficult to attract black correctional officers from metropolitan areas to come to live and work in a very small city in a relatively remote area.

We worked with the situation as we found it but we believed that black staff at all levels, professional and correctional, would have been very desirable in the project, even though we were aware that this would have created other problems — namely that of the white correctional officers learning to work with black colleagues. Throughout our six years we had only one black staff member — a female social worker who worked as a clinician at the Center for almost a year, then left when her husband was transferred elsewhere.

The real problem of relationships between black and white can be discussed objectively, just as other social issues can be discussed when there are no conscious underlying motives or when the issues are not distorted by prejudice. From the start of the Center, the problem existed as to what extent the black and white issue would be talked about. There was no intellectual opposition on the part of the staff toward discussing the problem. However, a few expressed fear that unrestricted discussion of black and white relationships might lead to the sort of chaos which at that time prevailed in different parts of the country and had led to a number of riots. Some went so far as to say that we should "let sleeping dogs lie." Also, awareness of the difficulty and magnitude of the general problem tempted staff to shy away from it.

Fortunately, common sense prevailed and the all-white staff realized that such an undeniable problem would ultimately reveal itself in an institution where the inmate population was split between the two races. Personal problems give a special tone to the racial issues, on the one hand, and, on the other hand, the racial issues sometimes affect personal problems.

Through the subjective experiences of our black and white prisoners and our white staff we became clinically involved in what it meant to be black or white: living together in and out

of jail, reaching out for, avoiding, or simply tolerating one another.

Before setting up the therapeutic center at Dannemora, we had no firsthand experience of racial discrimination in the New York State Correctional Services. From information obtained from administrative and correctional staff we concluded that there was some separation between blacks and whites despite the fact that they lived under a racially integrated regime. Many examples provided proof: for instance, blacks and whites worked closely together in the shops but during their free time in the yard they clustered according to color, to the point that an uninformed observer might believe the cleavage between the two groups was enforced segregation. Since this was not so, the behavior is a good example of psychological segregation.

Persistent offenders nearly all come from socio-economic ghettos, black, white or mixed, but black inmates usually come from the very poorest areas. The racial separation in prison reflects what is found in large metropolitan areas. White and black, especially the latter, tend to live in segregated areas of large cities in America. This "togetherness" of the ghettos is part of what Oscar Lewis describes as the culture of poverty. Further, blacks are kept together by outside forces, including the resistance of skilled, middle and upper class whites who do not want their neighborhoods integrated.

When the Center was established, we made no arrangements or allowances for differences of color. The very nature of the program made it inevitable that all would live and work closely together, sharing the same quarters, some the same dormitories, and participating in groups and in social therapy together. Since most of our inmates came from conventional prisons, black and white inmate relationships showed themselves in individual and group relationships. The clinicians used these as they presented themselves and interpreted them in the same manner as other relationships. It was hoped they would be learning experiences — whether their content had racial overtones or not.

In this report we will deal first with the racial issues experienced by individuals, then with problems arising from black and white inmates living together as a group. In trying to understand individual relationships we selected examples which show how neurotically conflicted persons with character disorders can distort real social problems while

believing that they have an objective view. These observations were collected during the first twelve months of the Center when we were possibly more aware of individual problems. Later, we were on the lookout for group behavior expressing individual conflicts.

Our basic approach was clinical. In other words, we tried to look at what was going on immediately around us, to analyze what we saw, and to make as objective an assessment as possible. Although we interviewed inmates, correctional officers and members of the staff at large, this approach did not yield as much material as we obtained through observation. Direct questioning yielded "appropriate" answers rather than answers expressing true feelings. Informal conversation and discussion about racial and other problems corresponded more to reality. We also had free staff discussions. Here are some of our observations.

Alfred E. gave a good example of how one individual can express hatred for another in a black-white relationship that was actually the displacement of a social problem. *Alfred* was a likeable character with an ebullient personality and he had a very good relationship with his therapist Abraham Ferstman. In general he was an aggressive but resourceful inmate to deal with.

During one interview with Abe, *Alfred* shouted, "I hate white men." The discussion went on about his hatred of whites up to the point where the therapist asked him, "What about me?" To this came the usual rejoinder, "Oh, you're different." Then *Alfred* went on to express his hatred of white men throughout the world as if he had not already made one exception. At the end of the interview, having ventilated his feelings against white men, he left the room with a big smile, exulting, "I feel good — I feel good — I feel good."

This episode of aggressive outburst against white men was, of course, not disturbing to the therapist, but it released additional aggression from *Alfred* against the Center. He began to question all rules and regulations, and whenever he met with opposition or refusal he interpreted it as racial discrimination. He was generally well liked by his fellow inmates and he was able to organize a clique around himself. But gradually both black and white inmates took a rather passive attitude toward him because his irrational interpretation of everything as anti-black was so obviously unjustified.

230

His rebelliousness continued to increase, however, and it became necessary to remove him from the Center. When told of his impending removal he made a sharp return to proper assessment of reality. The reaction of both his black and white fellow inmates was somewhat mixed; they felt relieved at the prospect of the lessening tension his departure meant but also sorry because they had liked him. They were reassured when we told them that *Alfred* could return to the Center later if he wished — and there was genuine pleasure all around when that happened. By then he was able to discuss racial issues with objectivity and good judgment.

It is interesting to note that *Alfred* established a very close friendship at the Center with a Catholic padre, and that friendship is still maintained. Whenever Father Walsh goes to New York he is a welcome visitor; he often stays at *Alfred's* home and is treated as a member of the family.

Although *Alfred's* behavior undoubtedly was connected with his being black and relating to white people, it would have been a mistake on the part of the therapist to regard his racial statements as objective. What he really was after was a reason to express himself forcefully, and eventually, as he felt more security within himself, his aggressive outbursts and acting out subsided. He no longer needed to attack white people indiscriminately.

Just how completely confused on racial matters it is possible for someone to be is illustrated by another interesting case, that of *Joe L.* A note in the minutes of a staff meeting in November 1967 should have forewarned the staff of his problem. During an informal conversation in the corridor between *Joe L.* and a white female clinician, Susan Waters, *Joe* mentioned that his male therapist had told him he had problems with women. The therapist had made no distinction as to whether the problems were with white or black women but *Joe* went on to say how he disliked white women, mentioning some experiences he had with them while working in a cabaret. As the conversation went on, he asked if he could be interviewed by one of the white female therapists on the staff. Such a request, after he had expressed feelings against white women, was unexpected. But even more unexpected was his next remark to the effect that there were enough black people on the staff at the Center, when in fact there were none.

This was later discussed with Susan in a staff meeting.

What *Joe* meant by his request for a white female therapist was not immediately apparent, nor was his remark about there being "enough" black people already on the staff. It turned out that he was referring to the presence of Dr. M., a resident in psychiatry at the Clinic who, as part of his psychiatric training, went regularly to the Center with the McGill staff. Around the same time, the Wednesday evening program had also, for the first time, invited a black professor as a guest speaker. *Joe* decided that Dr. M. must be an Uncle Tom, a friend of white Americans, when, in fact, he was a militant who had been so actively involved in the liberation movement in his native Caribbean country that he could no longer return there. But, in *Joe's* eyes, any black professional coming to the Center must necessarily be an Uncle Tom who had sold out to white power.

Blacks who have integrated themselves in the white establishment may often be viewed with contempt by black inmates. *Joe's* reaction to Dr. M. was certainly an aspect of his tendency to treat any black therapist as a sellout. Although white inmates can also feel that their therapists are too much a part of the establishment, the problem is more complex for a black inmate who may see the black professional as having sold out to whites in general and the white establishment in particular.

The white inmates in the first group of fifty to be admitted to the Center appeared not so much unprejudiced as uninterested where racial questions were concerned. As individuals they seemed to take the attitude that there might be a problem, but it was not a white problem. This detachment in the face of such a serious and undeniable issue could only be seen as a front that an individual puts up to avoid looking at something unpleasant.

The attitudes of four white inmates toward black-white issues illustrate how closely they reflected the range of attitudes encountered in American society at large.

Gil H. was a quiet, serious individual with genuine talent as a painter. He was a self-taught artist who derived considerable benefit from the help he received from the art department of Plattsburgh College during his stay at the Center. He was well liked and rather objective in his outlook. During a discussion touching on racial relationships, he quietly made the point that the United States Government should "spend less on the war in Viet Nam and more on creating opportunities for equality for colored people." This statement was made calmly but forcefully as a plain political appraisal of the present policy of his country.

232

Nick G. was also a talented painter and one could wonder why he had not somehow been able to make his way as an artist. He was simultaneously dramatic and compulsive; he was capable of great enthusiasm for short periods of intensive production, then he would suddenly go to the other extreme and drop everything. As a painter, as an inmate and in the labor market he was therefore quite unpredictable. He wanted to show himself as being a rather progressive, liberal individual. In discussion he stated that, although he was very sympathetic to the black cause, he wondered if black people might not have come to ask too much. He said that he was not worried about this for the present, but that if they carried on this way their demands might become too great. One could detect behind his ideas and feelings a liberalism hedged by apprehension.

Mike K., like *Nick*, was quite dramatic in character. In his own way he too was an artist. He was a compulsive talker. Some of his tirades or interventions in discussions almost took the tone of a preacher. In the shows put on while he was at the Center, he took an active part either as an actor or a monologist, and derived great pleasure from the opportunity to show off. *Mike* reinforced what *Nick* said but pushed it further. "The black doesn't contribute enough — they'd get more from society if they contributed more." This statement was meant to be objective and unprejudiced.

It was interesting that these three inmates reflected the views likely to be met in one form or another when discussing racial issues with the average citizen.

Tim R., on the other hand, expressed outright dislike of black people. He stated quite openly that he disliked Negroes, that he was born that way and would never change. This blatant avowal aroused a brief heated discussion involving both black and white inmates. Such crude expressions on the part of persons who never acted out their hatred beyond vocal outbursts were usually taken for what they were — irrational and gratuitous sentiments. In the case of *Tim*, his therapist pointed out that a week or so later he was observed in the community meeting sitting for the first time between two black inmates.

Another example of how an inmate with personal conflict can distort a social situation along racial lines is provided by the case of *Max W.*

Max, a black inmate, was well into his thirties; he was

generally well regarded by the staff and his fellow inmates. His rather solemn expression covered a lot of anxiety and depression; this was usually under control but could sometimes rise to a dangerous level. His danger level seemed to be reached when his individual problem became entangled with social pathology involving white and black relationships.

He lived in a common-law relationship with a white woman by whom he had three children, a relationship he felt was approved by neither black nor white. *Max* was originally from the south, and his need to relate to a white woman seemed so deeply rooted in his makeup that we were not fully acquainted with all the dynamics involved in the selection.

Max also said that he found it difficult to relate to male therapists. In retrospect, we feel this was a means of obtaining a female therapist. When Lydia Keitner, a research associate at the McGill Clinic, was assigned to him as therapist, the transference relationship rapidly took on a racial content. He vehemently reproached Dr. Cormier for not hiring any black staff, and, by extension, accused McGill University of being racially prejudiced. He refused to consider the fact that there was no black staff on the New York side and argued that McGill and Dr. Cormier were more guilty since Canada was less prejudiced than the United States. Although he said this not hiring of black people was outright discrimination, he did not include his white therapist, Lydia, in his unfavorable judgment.

Having lost touch with his family and his children, *Max* felt rather isolated and lonely. He asked Lydia if she could find a woman with whom he could correspond, specifying that it should not be a black woman. His transference toward the white female therapist became increasingly apparent. On the days she was at the Center, *Max* wore an ironed shirt and was all slicked up in his best clothes.

Within this situation, *Max* developed an intense hatred toward the shop foreman, even though the latter had a special liking for him because of his ability to execute fine work, and to rise to the challenge of difficult jobs. *Max* told his therapist that he was obsessed with thoughts of killing the foreman and even threatened that he might do so. As the situation evolved it became evident that *Max* was very jealous of the foreman. He kept an eye on his whereabouts, watched his comings and goings and voiced the thought that when the foreman left the shop it was to meet "the girls" ("the girls" here refers to the four

234

female therapists who were attached to the Center at the time). This accusation was displaced later on by the statement that the foreman was prejudiced against the black inmates. *Max's* intense hatred for the foreman, supposedly on account of racial prejudice, was in fact a near-delusional belief that the foreman was having an affair with his female therapist.

Because of both the depressive and the paranoid intensity of his feelings within the transference situation it was felt that this should be dealt with not by the therapist alone but within the total social setting in which it occurred. The positive transference of *Max* for Lydia was apparent to all. Since his intense dislike of the foreman, Ray Casey, was also known, it was agreed that his feelings toward these two people would in all likelihood be stripped of the delusional proportions when the individual problem and its social manifestation were put in proper perspective. How to do it? *Max* had never made any of his accusations against Ray on the floor, but he had made them privately and so often that he had actually convinced other inmates that Ray was "chasing" Lydia. Dr. Cormier, Ray and Lydia discussed the case and it was agreed that Ray would take the initiative in bringing the matter up on the floor at a community meeting, stating that he and other officers had heard the inmates claim he was chasing the female therapists.

The discussion did not take on great proportions. *Max* was silent throughout, but those who were aware of his feelings came away with the impression that a lot had gone through his mind during this meeting. Soon after the meeting, *Max* had an interview with his therapist. Every aspect of the problem then fell into its proper perspective. He asked her if he should apologize to the foreman as he realized that his hating this white man had been based on a triangular relationship between himself, the therapist and the foreman.

The important thing to stress here is how it took a social dimension within the therapeutic community to help *Max* solve his personal problem. *Max* had no further crisis of this nature. He received his discharge from the Center in 1968 and has since managed to struggle through on his own.

* *

The individual problem was emphasized in the clinical

examples because when these individual problems are surrounded by prejudices, it is the prejudices that get emphasized at the expense of the individual problem. There is also the danger that behavior interpretation could be subjected to individual and social bias. Much has been written about the scapegoat on whom a group places its individual responsibilities, but there is also a contrary means where a group is used by an individual to justify his own problems or failures. Either means permits an individual to put responsibility outside himself. White as well as black inmates use this mechanism of displaced responsibilities. It is easier to use such mechanisms when society provides many objective "proofs" of prejudice. Unfortunately, when the responsibility is fully projected outside, all doors to insight are closed. Max's case shows the plight of a black man coming from the south to the "Promised Land" of the north only to feel more conscious than ever of being a black man and a black inmate. In such a case we see how difficult it is to maintain a balance between personal and social problems.

When the Center first opened the black inmates tended to be subdued, silent, and somewhat ill at ease dealing with an all-white staff and with living so closely to white inmates. The white inmates dominated these early discussions in community meetings and in groups, but the black inmates soon asserted themselves and when their initial shock reaction was overcome, they became even more active participants than their white counterparts.

The two groups of inmates interacted with little or no visible conflict. However, each inmate related more to those of his own race, spent more time with them and chose his friends from among them. This was not considered a racial problem since there was no discernible malicious or hostile exclusion of the other race.

One of the difficulties of the white staff was to distinguish between a natural grouping and a clique among black inmates. In prison, a "clique" is a group of prisoners who operate within the prison world as they did in the criminal milieu. It was relatively easy to distinguish natural groupings from cliques in the case of white inmates, but either because of difficulties related to cultural differences or because of latent prejudice, some staff members tended to see all black inmate groups as cliques. At the same time white staff members were more prone to tolerate black cliques because they were afraid of

being considered racist if they confronted them either on the floor or individually with behavior not compatible with the therapeutic project.

As a group, the black inmates tended to be more social and gregarious, and were generally more active in the program. They were very much aware of their racial background and expressed it in a variety of ways: by wearing colorful shirts with African motifs and Afro hairstyles. It was also projected in the decoration of their cells which were as colorful as they could manage. White inmates were more conventional in their style of dress and their cells were less colorful and more prosaic. These differences became more marked as time went on because restrictions on the way inmates dressed were lifted and each was encouraged to follow his own bent in decorating his cell. While white inmates did not initiate special festivities other than the usual ones in which all inmates participated, the black inmates felt the need to organize at least two special days which they celebrated during the year: Martin Luther King Day and Black Nationalist Day.

As there was no precedent, the organization of the first Martin Luther King Day celebration aroused some friction between the staff and the black inmates. After much — and sometimes heated —discussion, the first celebration took the form of a study session on Dr. King, his work and his message to American society, but before reaching that point, the staff and the black inmates had traveled a bumpy road.

The black inmates who initiated the celebration formed a committee without informing either the community or the staff, making the day an exclusively black inmate operation. The organizing committee was not actually secretive, but they were not exactly communicative either. The white inmates had no part in the preparations and were probably indifferent in any case. This was not so with the staff who responded variously. As it became increasingly evident that a celebration was being planned, some staff members did not seem very concerned while others, who were more therapeutically minded, refused to accept the fact that any one group could organize something of this nature without either informing the community or having their program sanctioned by it and approved by the director, particularly since the plan meant closing the Center for a day. (As far as the white inmates were concerned, a day off was a day off, even in prison.)

Some of the staff took the initiative of bringing the whole question to the community meeting and stated quite openly that it was unacceptable to them that one group should proceed on such a venture without appropriate notice or consultation. No group, minority or majority, they argued, should make the decision of declaring a day to be a holiday without community agreement, and, ultimately, without the permission of its director. They insisted that there was no objection to the Martin Luther King Day as such; in fact, many of the professional staff and some of the correctional officers were even pleased about it.

Other staff members were fearful that the confrontation would result in a dispute over racial issues since it had all the necessary ingredients. The discussion that ensued was typical of many others and so was the outcome. Black inmates, particularly those on the committee to organize the celebration, took strong issue with the white staff for raising the question, and slogans such as "white imperialists," "white oppressors," and "anti-black" were trotted out.

In the face of this reaction, the staff was more determined than ever to keep the issue on the floor until the real problem was discussed. Despite several intense community meetings where a lot of angry feelings were expressed, they continued to maintain their view and to insist that the proposed celebration be considered as a community project and be sanctioned by it. Those members of the professional staff who felt most strongly about it clearly stated that if such a day were to take place they did not want to be excluded. Finally, one of the spokesmen for the black members of the community admitted, "Yes, you're right . . . we didn't organize it properly. But what we were really trying to do was to be hosts to the white members . . . We're proud of Martin Luther King and we felt that it was our day and we wanted to show what he stood for."

As a result, the overall community took a favorable view of the celebration, the day was officially approved by the authorities and the organization ran smoothly. Quite understandably, initiative was left to the black members to define the shape of the program. Appropriately, it took the form of a a study session, followed by the special repast that is part of any celebration at the Center. There was total participation of the community, black and white inmates and staff, in the study session.

By the time of the second Martin Luther King Day about half the inmates present at the first one had been released. Thus for many inmates it was their first acquaintance with this day at the Center. The organization took much the same pattern as the first one. However, this time the staff was more alert and the matter was fully discussed in a staff meeting. The consensus was that it would be appropriate if Juanita, the only black clinician, were to be the staff representative in the organization of the second Day, but this was taking the easy way out as by that time no one could ignore that she did not necessarily have an easy relationship with the black inmates simply because she too was black. As spokesman for the staff in the second celebration, she was considered by some of the black inmates to be a sellout, a delegate of white imperialists. Looking back, we feel that it would have been much wiser had the staff delegated a white member to work along with her.

The second celebration was far from being the outright success that the first one was. There was not the full partici-pation of the first occasion. Even some of the black inmates abstained. The emphasis had definitely shifted and the Day was devoid of the healthy, spontaneous, emotional and political significance of the first one.

In discussion afterward, the abstention of some black in-mates was particularly noted. One of the spokesmen for the absentees simply said, "Well, you white men don't have a special day for John Kennedy."

* *

Although "politicization," or "to be politicized," are terms commonly used on the campus, in labor unions and in citizen's action committees, they have lately even been used regarding in-mates, particularly in American prisons where many disturbances have had a racial tone. But we must ask if the persistent offen-ders treated at the Center were, in fact, politicized. To be pol-iticized is to be aware of the political and social realities in the state or community in which one lives. It also means taking a stand on these political and social issues. Conversely, it does not necessarily involve belonging to or actively supporting a political party though the politicized sooner or later usually affiliate themselves with a party.

Most of the black persistent offenders at the Center were very much aware of the fact that the black in American society

239

is in a state of change, but this does not mean they were politicized in the sense in which the term was defined above. They followed what was going on in society and they spoke up on the problem of the black in America. There is no doubt that they had a genuine concern about being black and about what was happening to the black people. In their case, "politicization" would be better described as awareness and pride and a search for identity.

The black persistent offenders were no more "politicized" in the strict sense of the term than were their white counterparts. They were certainly in rebellion against their milieu, as were the whites, but at no time did we find in their history a genuine concern about real social and political issues nor an active participation to achieve political goals of whatever nature.

We cannot, however, discard the meaning of black awareness or pride as having no political implications whatsoever. It is our feeling that there are now more black persistent inmates who are in the process of becoming politicized. As persistent offenders, they are more conscious than their white counterparts of the social factors that have contributed to their delinquency. In other words, because of his history — ghetto existence and segregation — we feel that the black persistent offender can trace the roots of his criminality more closely to social factors than the white criminal can. Though the white persistent offender may come from a similar social background and may be a victim of, or a rebel against, the affluent white society, nonetheless he remains a part of it. He does not have to struggle to overcome the disadvantage of having inherited a background of slavery and segregation.

Politicization, as we define it, arouses anxieties and fears in American correctional services, but it is highly desirable for both black and white inmates. Taking responsibility for society is not characteristic of persistent offenders, but it is a possible path toward their reintegration into society. We believe that ultimately politicization would reduce the disproportionate number of black inmates in American penitentiaries.

What should be feared is not politicization but the borrowing of political activist slogans and techniques to achieve private ends. The problem is to distinguish between what is really politicization and what are the activities and state of mind that hide behind that mask.

Can politicization be achieved in prison, particularly among persistent offenders?

240

In prison the black inmate is the one most likely to become politicized. One means by which prison authorities can avoid fears and anxieties regarding politicization is to foster it positively by programs that make prisoners aware of social problems and responsibilities regardless of race.

Under these conditions inmates will discover that to be politicized is not an easy path, that it involves not only their problems with society and society's problems with them, but also an awareness of problems that have no direct bearing on their criminality. A persistent offender who wishes to be politicized will discover that it is as difficult as achieving his objective to withdraw from persistent criminality, which in a way is a symptom of his non-politicization.

* *

Though a black inmate may argue vehemently in community meetings that he is in jail because he is black, such a statement is usually not pursued in individual discussion where it is apparent he was sentenced for murder, rape, armed robbery or the like. When an inmate uses this statement to draw attention to the black problem in American society and cites the high prevalence and incidence of black inmates in prisons, such statements aid discussion of the interaction between social and individual factors contributing to crime. To be poor, to live in a ghetto and to be discriminated against are certainly potent social factors in delinquency and criminality. However, some inmates maintain with great conviction both in group as well as in individual relationships, that they are in prison only because they are black. Some even go so far as to claim the status of political prisoner. When such a belief is held by an inmate in the face of direct confrontation with a criminal record that contains all his offenses, he must make a severe rationalization to avoid taking personal responsibility for his criminality. Such a line of defense that prevents a full investigation of personal problems is commonly found in severely disturbed persons. It closes the door to both insight into personal problems and to an objective discussion of the social factors contributing to delinquency and criminality, factors that are undoubtedly more important in the delinquency and criminality of blacks than of whites.

No white would claim outright that he is in prison because he is white. This does not mean that in group discussions a

241

white inmate will not use similar mechanisms. He will claim
and argue vehemently that he is in prison because he is poor,
because he is unlucky, or because someone is out to get him. In
individual discussions, most white inmates, like their black
counterparts, take a more realistic attitude and discuss the
meaning of being poor, unlucky, or why someone is after them.

9. Ripples from Attica

These men proved that if given the chance, they were well able to deduce things for themselves and behave in an intelligent and mature way.

In September 1971 a riot occurred in Attica Prison. Personnel were seized and held for several days. Eventually the National Guard was called in to deal with the situation. They stormed the prison and in the ensuing debacle several of the insurgent inmates and some of the hostages were shot and killed. This tragic episode gave rise to both national and international alarm. Its effect, particularly on other prisons in New York State, was notable.

The Center at Clinton had at that time been operating for just over five years. Most of the inmates were intelligent, reasonably well read, and aware of what was happening in the outside world. When the riot occurred at Attica staff and inmates were familiar with the blow-by-blow descriptions given by the various news media. The effect was quite enlightening.

Very few of the "old guard" day officers had worked in a regular prison. If they had, it had only been for a short time prior to being sent to the State Hospital. These men were undoubtedly upset about the events, but their response to the riot appeared to be quite mature. Many said that they could not "identify" too closely with the prison guard hostages whose work was totally different from their own. However, one of the hostages, Capt. Wald, had worked at the Center and was well known to both staff and inmates. Naturally the officers were concerned for him, but they were able to discuss freely their feelings regarding the riot both with professional staff and with the inmates.

After the disaster, when other prison personnel, the unions, and others were clamoring for stricter security measures, more

training in the art of self-defense, more maximum security prisons and less emphasis on human relationships between the two groups, some of the day shift officers at the Center were dismayed at this approach. None of them felt that tighter security measures should be taken at the Center. In fact most felt quite at ease with their routine. As a result, the riot did not seem to have had an alarming effect on the running of the Center.

On the other hand, reaction of the evening shift was totally different. Many of the officers were comparatively new to the program. A high proportion of them had been trained and had worked in maximum security prisons, one or two in Attica itself. They identified very strongly with the hostages and were extremely upset when some of them were killed after the troops were brought in.

Because of the difference in routine, the evening shift officers had less contact with the professional staff than the day shift.. They were more or less left on their own to relate to the inmates until the latter went to bed about 11 p.m. They played cards or table tennis with the inmates or they had discussion groups which varied in number and size depending on the circumstances. All this practically disappeared during and after the crisis. Although before the riots they had occasionally felt isolated and not part of the total program, during the crisis their anxiety became quite apparent: interaction with the inmates diminished; the officers kept to themselves, went around in pairs, and carried out only their required duties. They also requested more help and support from the professional staff in order that they might air their grievances. One other interesting feature was noted: they became, much more so than the day shift, over-involved in union activities.

The manner in which the inmates reacted to the crisis was partly predictable. Since these men had been extensively involved in crime and had spent many years in prison, it was to be expected that over the years they would develop many set ideas about guards. One of the main aims of our program was to encourage the inmate to develop more meaningful interpersonal relationships. This involved not only building relationships among themselves, but also between themselves and officers, other persons attached to the Center, and visitors. Needless to say, they were more prone to identifying with the "oppressed." Therefore it was not surprising that some showed a certain amount of relief that it was not one or some of their own who

had killed the hostages but rather the "aggressors" who had done so.   A few of the inmates even expressed some glee over the outcome.   They behaved very much as if at a football game or a wrestling match, cheering and yelling each time they heard that an aggressive act had been committed.   One or two made innuendoes that the guards in the Center had better watch out.

However, at no time did any of the inmates act out in any way and the impression given, as already mentioned, was that they were spectators at a game where the home team was fighting back against a far better equipped opponent.   Some men feared for the lives of inmates they knew were in Attica at the time, but there was also a sizeable number of men who could not have cared less what happened to individuals.

What did concern the men as a whole, one unit in particular, was the marked change in attitude of the evening shift officers toward them.   This gave rise to some apprehension and dismay.   In the community meetings they noted the fact that the officers would pair off, refuse to play table tennis, cards or chess, and to take part in activities with them.   They asked what they could do to ease the situation.   This is a typical example of reversed roles in which those who are supposedly being helped become the helpers.

During this time there was much discussion among the staff as to what could be done.   The senior professional staff held that they should meet with the officers and give them encouragement.   Some of the other clinical staff felt that joint meetings between the staff and inmates should be held, but there was no clear agreement on the best line of approach in dealing with the ripple effect from Attica.   The inmates, on the other hand, rallied around and called their own community meeting without professional staff being present.   They discussed the problem among themselves in a very concrete and mature manner and requested that some of the officers attend their meeting. They openly discussed the situation as they saw it and some of the more vocal officers were able to express their feelings. They said they were not concerned just about the effects of Attica, but that they were also very preoccupied with problems within their union, and this had caused them to isolate themselves from the inmates.   This appeared to be a highly defensive maneuver from the officers and the inmates saw through it, but the meeting did cause some of the tension to lessen and the relationship between the inmates and the evening shift officers gradually improved over the ensuing days.

The senior executive was less experienced in the therapeutic community approach than the first group of officers. It is interesting to note one particular incident. The screen windows in each of the cells were ordered closed. The excuse given was that this would keep out insects. However, the screens had previously been left open throughout the height of the insect season. It was apparent to everyone, particularly the inmates, that the reasons given were false. They challenged those concerned who eventually had to admit that security was the real reason why the screens were closed.

This case illustrates clearly that it is better to discuss rather than to suppress unpleasant matters. After an initial bout of hostility, anger, frustration or futility, these men proved that if given the chance they are well able to deduce things for themselves and behave in an intelligent and mature way rather than in an impulsive, destructive or overly dramatic manner.

10. The Professional Staff Talks about Race

*We can relate to the black inmates, at least we feel
we can, and when they can relate to a white person
and that white person can understand them, then
this is an education for both.*

Staff discussion is a very useful tool for evaluation and
analysis in milieu therapy. Spontaneous interaction among the
members often leads to fresh insights and listening to the tape
playbacks allows errors and faulty reasoning to be picked out.
This was especially apparent in a discussion which took place
among the McGill staff on the topic of racial relationships.
The following is an edited version of the discussion; repetitions
and extraneous matters have been omitted, but an attempt has
been made to keep the conversational tone and to include over-
statements and/or strong terms as expressed.

The twenty present at the gathering included staff and
student field workers but only the following actually participated in the conversation according to the tapes:

Bruno M. Cormier

Ingrid Cooper

Harold Finkler

Judith Princz

Madeleine St. Germain

Josh Zambrowsky

Harold Finkler opened the discussion: We decided not to adopt
a predetermined definition of a racial problem but to study the
relationship between black and white inmates as we saw it and
were part of it. An overall impression is that in the preceding
few years there had been a polarization of relationships, black

with black, white with white. We saw this in community meetings and in the program's recreational and cultural activities. Ingrid and I, who had been at the Center for only a year, certainly noticed this polarization of relationships. We tended to look at it as a natural phenomenon in the sense that perhaps the staff felt more comfortable with white inmates, white inmates with white inmates, and black inmates with black inmates. We did note some difficulty on the part of white staff to deal with the black inmates in certain situations. As for the inmates, there did not seem to be any deliberate mutual exclusion of blacks from whites.

St. Germain: Are there any black professional or correctional officers at the Center?

Cooper: There was only one black professional, Juanita Chandler, and she left the Center recently. We have some examples of how black and white inmates reacted to her. The absence of black professional and correctional officers is a major problem.

Finkler: We must differentiate between what is actually a racial problem and what is *seen* as a racial problem. The latter is really a rationalization, a defense mechanism, a means of hiding delinquency on the part of black and white instead of really dealing with the delinquent behavior. We think that the staff tend to overreact to polarization and to read more into it than there is. It could be dangerous to misinterpret black awareness as a plot instead of as a growing process, a natural polarization in the present context of American society. Black awareness can be used for many purposes, but we do not feel that racism was an important feature at the Center.

Cooper: We found that the two inmate groups, black and white, interact quite well on an informal basis, but naturally, as we would expect, each interacts more with its own kind. They form their friendships and spend more of their time with members of their own group. On the whole, the black inmate seems to be more sociable and outgoing, more gregarious, than his white counterpart. He is more active in the program. This may be our own bias, but we feel as therapists that the black inmate is generally healthier psychologically than the white one. Their awareness of being black seems to be a great happening for them. They show a lot of initiative in programs related to black problems. I remember last year, the first time they had a Martin Luther King Day. At first they excluded white inmates.

248

We confronted them about it in a community meeting and they said to us, "You're just trying to run our show — you're being white imperialists, you're coming down on us blacks."

Of course, there are exceptions and friendships do form outside of the groups. These inter-racial relationships are often resented by other inmates. One white inmate claims he has friends among both black and white inmates and he definitely states that he is ostracized by many white members of the community. This feeling may be nothing more than a reflection of his own attitude, uneasiness, or prejudice. But in another case ostracism was overt. Perhaps this case should be summed up to see what we can learn. *Bob H.* is white and he had two black friends. There was a lot of hostility from the white members of the community and it was hinted that there was a homosexual relationship between these men. There were verbal attacks against *Bob* and his black friends, but mostly against *Bob*. The whites seemed to have deep feelings about this relationship.

Black and white sexual relationships seem to arouse all the taboos and prejudices that are prevalent in society. This was never said in so many words, but *Bob H.* took a lot of verbal abuse referring to homosexuality. One day in the community, his two black friends said, "Look, you leave us alone. Leave *Bob* alone or there's going to be trouble." It finally resulted in a fist fight on the baseball field when an inmate made a crack with sexual connotations and *Bob* punched him pretty hard. In spite of everything he retained his friendship with his black friends to the end. He didn't give in to ostracism or pressure. It was known in the community that *Bob* had a black girl friend. He talked like a black man and seemed to identify with them.

Cormier: My feeling is that whether or not there was a homosexual element in the relationship is not relevant. Inmates are used to witnessing such relationships. The ostracism is probably related to deepseated prejudice against sexual relationships between black and white. As staff we may have missed an opportunity to discuss this question of prejudice in interracial sexual relationships. One could also wonder if it is the suspicion of homosexuality or if it was the fact of a white man going with a black woman that mobilized so much hostility on the part of the white inmates. If a similar case came up again we would attempt to get to the root of ostracism. *Bob H.'s* reaction of punching his aggressor was in many ways understandable. Despite the ostracism he continued to maintain his relationship with his black friends. In other words, he got some good reality testing in the community, in not giving in to their pressure.

Cooper: If you talk to the black inmates, most of them are politically conscious. They are concerned about the position of the black man in America and are quite angry about it, but very few of them use this as a defense for being in jail. I had two who did, and they were rather disturbed individuals. One was *Jim W.*, who maintained that he was in jail because he was black and he would never look further into his criminal behavior. He was so disturbed that at one stage there was talk of sending him to a mental hospital, but the staff as a whole finally agreed that he needed this defense. It was decided to go along with his near-delusional explanation of his persistent criminality. This way of dealing with one's criminal career is one of the most difficult defenses to break down when it reaches a delusional intensity and is no longer just a façade for the preservation of self-esteem.

The second case was that of a very anxious and restless individual. The only subject he could discuss was that he was black, that this was the reason he was in prison and that he was going to join the Black Nationalists when he got out.

Many black inmates will use this kind of rationale, but only when they are anxious.

An incident occurred in my group the other day with two black inmates who, whenever they got upset, insisted they were in jail because they were black. The group as a whole, blacks as well as whites, completely refused to deal with their rationalization. I finally asked them why everyone was so quiet. One of the men said, "Well, I can't really help this man because I'm not black." I tried to point out that they both had a lot in common, in that they both came from poor families and that they both had problems of interpersonal relationships. But there still wasn't much response. White members of the group came to me afterward and they were angry. They asked me: "Why did you put us on the spot like that? You know that what that guy was saying was a lot of bullshit, but we can't tell him that because we're not black."

Cormier: If a man says, "I am in jail because I am black" or "poor," one can immediately detect by his tone of voice whether he really means specifically that or if he is referring to

the social conditions in which the black and the poor live that
are very conducive to criminality.   If he really believes that he
is in prison because he is black or poor and cannot go further
then I quite understand Ingrid's remark that such offenders are
usually very passively or aggressively disturbed.   Clinically, it
is quite understandable that he would be very angry at North
American society, or for that matter at white civilization which
is responsible for his being there.   The same reasoning would
apply to the person who says that he is there because he is poor
and is unable to go beyond this.   He too is living in the abstraction
that he is a victim of the whole psychosocial, economic and
political system that results in putting him in jail.   It is interesting to note that inmates themselves make a clear distinction.
For example, such rationalizations will commonly be used in
groups.   But in individual contacts or personal relationships the
individual will admit that he has his own problems and will try
to find what his specific problems are as opposed to those of
society.   The combination of individual therapy and group discussion permit us to see more clearly how a person reacts to
personal relationships and to group relationship.

St. Germain: Are there any political prisoners among
them?

Zambrowsky: Political prisoners?   No, but there are
some who perceive themselves as such.   However, these few are
among the ones that everybody agrees are very disturbed individuals.   In serious therapy we have come across hardly anyone who would attempt to fall back on this status of political
prisoner and refuse to go beyond it in studying his problems.
Jim W., whom Ingrid mentioned, is the only individual who
would consistently fall back on this defense.

Cormier: When a black inmate uses the term "political
prisoner" he is really borrowing from the radical groups, be
they black or white.   Because of the social conditions under
which the black lives in the USA, there are historical and
political factors involved, but the fact of being a persistent
criminal does not automatically make you a political prisoner
in the usual sense of the terminology.

Regarding persistent criminality, there is not much difference between black and white inmates.   The disparity arises
from the same individual and social factors that find their roots
far back in the process of socialization or lack of socialization.
Since we will see more and more prisoners claim the status of

political prisoner, we must have a very clear picture in mind of what a "political prisoner" is as distinct from a persistent offender. It is often only at a certain stage of his criminal career that the delinquent begins to claim that his actions are politically motivated. How can he be a political prisoner when he was a delinquent all his life and for the greater part of it not interested in politics.

Princz: When at least half of the prisoners are black, as in Dannemora, wouldn't it make it easier to deal with this problem if there were black therapists and officers?

Zambrowsky: I think Juanita's experience as a black therapist and the problems she had with members of the black inmate community illustrate the fact that the presence of black therapists does not necessarily solve the problems. What they really want is not a black therapist but a black delinquent who will tell them that they are right when they say that they are in jail because they are black. In that sense, black and white delinquents are similar in the use of their rationalizations. They do not want a therapist who will identify with their color, they want a therapist who will identify with their delinquency. Therefore a black therapist, who essentially holds the same type of non-delinquent values as a white therapist, becomes an Uncle Tom, or some other pejorative term for a Negro who sold out to the white power structure.

Princz: It seems to me that what you are saying is that there should be no black therapists . . .

Zambrowsky: No, all I am saying is that if anybody believes that having black officers and black therapists would solve the problem of black inmates who are incarcerated, they are mistaken.

Cormier: We all wish that there could have been black staff and correctional officers. In group discussion, the black inmate can forcefully convince you that the Center will not function because there is no black staff. In realistic discussion, he recognizes, as we do, that the situation is unfortunate but unavoidable. Black correctional officers and black therapists are not seen by black inmates as the solution to their problems. Indeed, many of them come from institutions where black staff was available and it didn't solve their problems. At the same time an exclusively white staff presents problems and we should not shy away from them.

One of the black inmates came to me after a community meeting where there had been angry discussion about Martin

252

Luther King Day celebration. He said to me, "When you designed the Center's overall program, you didn't have black people in mind." I insisted that he say what he meant. "Well," he said, "exactly what I said. You didn't have black people in mind." As I knew him very well, I said, "Listen," and enumerated very rapidly his criminal record. I finally said to him, "There's not much difference between your criminal record and that of a white guy sitting there beside you." We went on to discuss that a black or white inmate who spends most of his life in jail is not really being very useful to the blacks or whites who are oppressed by society. The conclusion of our discussion was that he could derive a great deal from using the Center to deal with his emotional and personal problems so that he could do something for his people when he hit the street.

A similar incident occurred a few years ago when there was a research conference at the Center to which the inmates contributed. The inmates put forth their view that social factors were responsible for their criminality. When one of the guest professionals, who was considered a radical, heard the discussion of persistent offenders using the vocabulary of radicals, he responded to them very directly, more or less stating that they should solve the problems that put them in jail before they could hope to do anything about the problems of the street. In other words, this white radical was condemning both black and white inmates for using social clichés to avoid responsibility for their own behavior.

Zambrowsky: I think black inmates do a lot more testing of white therapists because of the intense feeling of nationalism that pervades the black community than, say, white inmates do. I can say without reservation that our group from McGill did not have a hangup about black inmates. We have not had problems in dealing with black inmates. But I think that some of the resident staff have been influenced by their American experience. They are more wary of blacks in general, and tend to react in a passive-aggressive way to blacks asserting their nationalism. On the one hand they back down and won't confront them on delinquency, but on the other hand they turn around and chop them down on other things such as the Wednesday night program which was often a black cultural program.

What the Dannemora staff sometimes fail to do is lay it on the line, to say, "O.K. —we know a lot of the stuff you're saying about black oppression is true, but what are you going to do about *your own* behavior, *your own* life that's going to make it more acceptable for you than it has been."

The staff often let blacks get away with verbalizing that they are victims of white exploitation, then they use other excuses to control them and black political activities within the prison, excuses that the inmates can see through. This leads the inmates to distrust the staff and makes a lot of black inmates very uncomfortable with some of the white staff.

Princz: I still think that Dr. Cormier's statement to the inmate about the program being designed for persistent offenders, black or white, would have had greater impact if it had come from a black therapist.

Zambrowsky: It is the validity of the comment rather than the color of the skin of the interpreter that is important. This is something that the black inmate has to work out for himself.

Of course, there should be black therapists, but you don't need black therapists to interpret and understand the delinquent behavior of black inmates. Once you get into an inmate's real problems, the color of his skin is irrelevant unless the therapist or inmate has a definite hangup in that area, in which case you direct yourself to that problem first.

Cooper: We can relate to the black inmates, at least we feel we can, and when they can relate to a white person and that white person can understand them, then this is an education for both.

Princz: In this context, I feel that the absence of black staff has a greater impact than you make it out to be.

Editor's note: It is interesting to observe the differences in perspective and opinion among those staff members who worked at Dannemora and those who did not. J. Princz and M. St.Germain who did not work at the Center stressed quite strongly the disadvantages of lacking black staff and also the problems raised by the status of the "political prisoner." While acknowledging the importance of this, the McGill staff at Dannemora felt that these issues created more of a clinical challenge than a barrier to efficiency. There is obvious merit to each of these positions.

Cooper: Black inmates don't accept black therapists any more than white inmates accept white therapists when they are confronted with their problems or with their delinquent behavior. Black inmates have come to me at various times and expressed great resentment toward Juanita. They thought she was a sellout to her race and that she catered to white inmates. They called her an "Oreo" which is a chocolate cookie with a white filling. One went so far as to say that she had white blood. Although she was unmistakably black he was sure she had a white ancestor somewhere.

Cormier: Juanita was a very good therapist who was not easily given to nonsensical rationalization. She was certainly treated more severely by some black inmates than a white female therapist confronting them the same way would have been. It is conceivable that we could have achieved more had we had black staff, but simply being black would not necessarily help. It has been demonstrated in ghettoes that for black workers to be effective in organization they have to be exceedingly well trained. Those who were not were less successful than some well-trained white organizers. Black inmates are as resistant to interpretation from blacks as white inmates are from whites, particularly when these interpretations are negative or strike home. We are facing a clinical problem, not a racial one. In my view it would be to the detriment of the black inmate in New York State and probably to all black inmates if we leave unchecked this phrase that we often hear, "You cannot help me because I am black."

St. Germain: I have the feeling that you expect more from a black prisoner. You know that outside a black feels that a white is the persecutor. Why would he not feel the same inside?

Zambrowsky: It's all right with me if he becomes a radical when he leaves prison. We cannot erase the fact that there is a history of oppression. I'm merely stating that in instances where he is using this as a shield, as a defense mechanism to keep from getting to his more specific personality problems, we have to make him aware of it.

St. Germain: What I am implying is that it might be more difficult for a white therapist to do this.

Zambrowsky: I've found that they've known black people, even members of their family who are doing well; they have friends who are not delinquent. If you let them know, "O.K. I acknowledge it, you're black in the United States and have all the problems that go with it. But let's play the game this way — let's go into all the social and individual reasons for your delinquent behavior and not get hung up on just using one of them as an excuse."

St. Germain: Yes, but what I mean is that I would rather play this game with a black therapist.

Zambrowsky: But they would accuse a black therapist of selling out to the white system or else why would he be a therapist? Look, if you're going to play the game all the way, then they have to interpret prisons as being the fortress of the ultimate oppression of black Americans because more of them go to prison percentagewise than whites. So a black person working as a therapist in a prison would, in that framework, be lower than a white therapist. This would be a person oppressing his own kind through the white power structure. That's why the only hope is to get through this defense and show them that beyond a certain point you will not accept that type of rationale, that you will insist on getting to such things as, "What about the fact that you could never form a relationship with a woman? What about the fact that you're an alcoholic? What about the fact that you can't get out of bed in the morning while you're in prison or out on the street? You're talking about revolution and you can't get out of bed in the morning." This kind of thing gets through their defenses. I don't think that you can give therapy and argue about politics at the same time. I think you have to make them aware of the fact that you understand where politics and their own basic personalities separate.

Cormier: Those who usually claim the status of political prisoner are revolutionary terrorists who engage in subversive activities to serve a political cause. We can rightly refer to their crimes as being politically motivated. I think that a person who calls himself a political prisoner by referring to a historical, psychological, or economic background that was discriminatory to his group (and this undoubtedly applies to the blacks of America) is not aware that the term political prisoner does not reflect the clinical reality. There is no clinical contra-indication to recognize all the injustices of the past and present. For me as a Canadian, the way the North American Indians are treated in certain parts of the continent, including Canada, is quite comparable to the treatment of the black in the United States. However, we help neither the blacks nor the Indians by calling them political prisoners. Both blacks and Indians were brought up in a state of social deprivation that fostered delinquency and criminality. That their criminality is influenced by this background should be acknowledged. If a person believes that this background is the sole cause of his criminality, then, unless this defense is broken down, nothing much can be done clinically for this man. Most persistent offenders, black or white, and most clinicians agree that when a persistent offender puts all the responsibilities for his criminality outside himself, the chance of recidivism is very high. I think that because we are not part of the American milieu, we can see this clinical aspect more clearly.

St. Germain: Did I understand well, Ingrid, when you said that blacks are more politicized? Why would that be? I'm asking because I noticed when I visited Dannemora that most of the black inmates have posters in their room about "Black Power" and "Black is Beautiful," and that sort of thing.

Finkler: I think that it is part of this black consciousness which should not necessarily be interpreted as racism or politicization. You know, the whites don't have to put up Wyatt Earp posters for the frontiersman image, the American Dream and all that. The black man is trying to find his rôle in American culture and society, but there's nothing really malicious about it.

Zambrowsky: I think they're reacting to cultural deprivation. As far as the black people in the United States are concerned, it's only in the past ten years or so that a black culture has been allowed to surface at all, in the media, expression, and things of this nature, so I think that right now it's extremely important for them to express their identity.

Cooper: It's something they can feel proud of.

Zambrowsky: I think black consciousness does have certain implications as far as therapy is concerned. Because of what they feel about black consciousness and pride, they will not admit certain things about themselves in public (in public meaning a community meeting) that they will in individual therapy as they might have a few years ago. They find it more difficult to get up in front of their peers and say, "I'm here because I have failed to deal with so many situations." They can say this to their therapist, but they find it more difficult to say in front of their peers than they did even two years ago.

Finkler: Take *Dick S.* as an example. In group therapy, even as small a group as ten, he rants and raves, "Like, you know, man, I'm the product of three hundred years of bullshit — you know. Like, you been slapping it to me . . ." implying that it's all in the environment. Yesterday I talked with him for an hour and a half and not once did this sort of thing come up. He has his problems, sexual problems, but not once did he mention the racial thing. Perhaps he didn't feel threatened with me. He said, "Well, everybody's into their own bag, you know."

Zambrowsky: The Wednesday evening program is a good example of this sort of psychological or unofficial segregation. For some time this program has been basically a black studies program. Different guests come in from the College, mainly black students and some militant black professors. When black studies began last year, there was participation by both white and black inmates. What happened at this year's program is that the white staff psychologically segregated themselves from the inmates taking part in the program because they probably felt threatened by militant black people coming in, or at least by people whom the institution perceived as being militant.

Instead of actively participating in the program, mixing with the visitors and giving them some orientation as to what the behavior of visitors should be as to their limitations of inter-action with inmates, what is appropriate, and so on, they saw these black visitors as a threat. They withdrew from them com-pletely. When the white staff withdrew, the black guests and inmates formed a common front against the white staff, who sat glowering in one corner, sending out all sorts of bad vibra-tions through their stares, but not interacting at all in the process. They pretty well manufactured this common front. White inmates began to attend these Wednesday night events less and less frequently.

I think that the interesting question is whether the white inmates felt threatened by the fact that militant black people were coming in to teach black history and raise black con-sciousness, or whether they were reacting to the passive-aggressive position taken by the correctional officers and staff. My own feeling is that it's the latter and that it caused a psycho-logical segregation. I think that when anything happens at the institution, the impetus comes from the staff.

Cooper: Following on what Josh said about the Wednes-day evening programs, a situation developed where there were black female guests who were being monopolized by one or two of the black inmates. They were building up a relation-ship which was not being controlled and was getting out of hand — kissing, hugging, and stuff like that. The officers were pretty upset about it, but they didn't confront the inmates in question. A staff member came right out in staff meeting and

258

said he wasn't going to ban these women because they were blacks, and he didn't want to be accused of being a bigot. The point is, of course, that he was overreacting because whether they were black or not was irrelevant. The type of behavior they were engaging in should have been dealt with.

Zambrowsky: I think the important thing is that a bad attitude developed among the white inmates. It did not take the form of resentment toward the black inmate, but more toward the staff for allowing differential treatment to exist between white and black inmates. This leaning over backward on the part of the staff, their failure to confront black inmates or visitors for inappropriate behavior also created anxiety among the black inmates. They knew they were getting away with something and delinquents tend to become anxious when they feel that the staff are losing control.

Cooper: At times some of the resident staff did mention in staff meetings that they felt uncomfortable in dealing with the black inmates. However, they seemed to be the minority among both the professional staff and the correctional officers. On the other hand the McGill group, rightly or wrongly, seemed to prefer dealing with the black inmates, possibly because they had fewer problems and were easier to deal with.

Cormier: Yes, I think it would be important to elaborate on this aspect. I think you're the second group of persons in this project to bring up the fact that the black persistent delinquent is less "sick" than his white counterpart. I think we can explain this through the psycho-social condition. In actual fact, blacks have more *real* problems.

In other words, living in a ghetto, being segregated, living in appalling conditions, these are *real* problems. Of course they react. The white man may come from such a milieu but as frequently his problems come from neurotic, rather than social sources. Of course, this is a generalization. We have had many extremely disturbed black persistent offenders. On the other hand, most of our best inmates have been black. We don't negate the role that the environment of the black inmates may have played in producing their delinquency. We simply state that the social and personal pathology which is caused within the individual must be dealt with, because we are powerless to deal with what has happened to them in the past and through their environment. I find it rewarding when a persistent offender, be he white or black in the United States or for that matter in Canada, gains sufficient strength to become an activist and thus to change a society which he has sufficient cause to resent.

PART IV:
EVALUATING IT ALL

1. Treating the Whole Man

*In studying offenders, criminality involves the total
personality and it is this total personality which has
to be considered, not just parts of it.*

The problem of evaluating a treatment program based on
therapeutic relationships presents nearly insurmountable problems of methodology. Individual, group and community therapy, or other variants of milieu therapy, also present problems of
evaluation since relationships are the therapeutic tool.   There
are no exact standards of quality or quantity to measure the
impact of what is given (through interpretation, explanation,
reassurance, non-verbal communication, etc.) nor do scales
exist to measure the impact of what is received.

The results obtained in a therapeutic community for persistent offenders can hardly be compared to those of analytically
oriented therapy given to such offenders. To relate to one
therapist as opposed to being caught up in the many relationships within a community is essentially a different treatment
technique. A center with enough therapists to offer analytically oriented therapy to persistent offenders could serve as a
control group for persistent offenders treated in a therapeutic
community, but we do not know of any such center.   Our
technique was based on social dynamics.

A program based on social dynamics does not preclude
individual or group therapy. It should use individual therapy
as a means of fostering group therapy, with group therapy in
turn fostering community therapy. Following this order, and
when community therapy is working at its best, one result is
that the men become more capable of handling stress in individual relationships from which they learn and derive gratification.

262

Most of our observations were made within the frame of psychoanalytical concepts. This is not to say that therapists were not free to use other concepts, especially those inspired by the fast-developing learning theories. However, the major therapeutic tool was basically the relationship between staff and inmates, between inmates and inmates, and between inmates, staff and administration. Thus an evaluation of the project presents all the difficulties of assessing any treatment based on relationships.

With all the methodological difficulties inherent in the validation of treatment based on the establishment of therapeutic relationships, there is no way of bypassing the many objections, statements and problems centred around Eysenck's study on *The Effects of Psychotherapy*. We are referring here not only to the article, but to the many comments published on it, as well as the author's reply to these comments. These debates that took place in 1965 sum up many opposing views on the effects of psychotherapy. (24, 25, 26)

As a group we attempted to carry on this clinical program, using all the knowledge and competence at our disposal. We have also attempted to evaluate what we were doing, but we certainly recognize that in the final analysis, others may be more objective than we are.

The delinquency of persistent offenders involves the whole personality, and in our clinical experience, dealing with them in and out of prison over many years, we can state that persistent delinquency is only one aspect of a complex pathology. Although delinquency is the most important social symptom against which society rightly wants to be protected, in our endeavour to try to resocialize these individuals, delinquency is often a secondary preoccupation of the clinician. Delinquency is only one aspect of a person who is unable to relate, unable to remain free in society; it is the total basic personality that one must attempt to change, at least to a degree where he may eventually not only refrain from delinquent acting out, but be reintegrated into a society of which he feels part or at least from which he feels less alienated. We were also, of course, concerned with the psychosocial realities that contribute to delinquency as a socially deviant act, as a symptom of a character disorder or psychopathological state. No matter what delinquency is, it is with the persistent delinquent as a whole that we were concerned and in our view the success of the Center cannot be measured by the rate of recidivism, that is, whether the "symptom," delinquency, has decreased or not. We are here at the centre of Eysenck's strong view that certain "symptoms" can be measured or rated very accurately.

We believe that the presence or absence of recidivism is a poor criterion for the evaluation of a treatment program for persistent offenders. Persistent criminality is a chronic problem, and we cannot expect that it will suddenly be reduced to nil. Through a psychotherapeutic program a persistent delinquent may improve in many respects in his personality, habits, thinking, and ability to learn, but he still may recidivate. As clinicians we feel that it would be unsound to take one symptom as a gauge and measure improvement only by change within one type of symptomatology, ignoring the changes in other areas of the personality. This will be illustrated below with clinical examples.

We have no graduated scale to measure how the many symptoms within a pathological personality evolve. Certainly, at the end of the line, in the treatment of the persistent offender, we are left with a clinical judgment. We agree with Eysenck that this is not a desirable state of affairs and that much research is needed to give us tools that would measure what we are doing or think we are doing.

In evaluating a program for the treatment of persistent offenders, we cannot isolate a repetitive pattern of delinquency from the total personality of the offender. This is a very important point in the evaluation of the treatment of an individual or of a treatment program and until such time as we have tools to measure improvement, we will have to evaluate progress or regression of symptoms mainly from clinical judgment. This presents little difficulty when we are facing acute, brief, reactive states, but when we are facing chronic emotional and mental states, with symptoms lasting for many years, such a judgment is often difficult. In the field of clinical criminology, it is not easy to evaluate the progress of a persistent offender in which persistent delinquent acting out is part of a disturbed personality co-existing with other symptoms and other reaction patterns. Persistent criminality is part of an individual and social pathology of long duration, fifteen to twenty years or more in the case of those we were treating in the Clinton Project. The evaluation of a treatment program is not rendered easier by the fact that there is no specific treatment for most of the symptoms enumerated by Eysenck, to say nothing of others that he does not mention. For persistent offenders, not unlike many neurotic patients, we are left in the end with formulating a diagnosis, a prognosis and proceeding with one type of psychotherapy or another, if psychotherapeutic treatment seems the most appropriate, and we are further confronted with the formulation of a clinical criminological diagnosis.

In the end, we are left with evaluating how the diagnosis, treatment and prognosis have withstood the passage of time.

When Eysenck speaks of symptoms, he appears like a man who looks at a patient from a mile away rather than within feeling and hearing distance. When he refers to "hypothetical unconscious inner states," one would like him to have explained what he really meant by this expression. Whether he wanted to put in question the unconscious forces that determine certain symptoms or the inner emotional reality that is partially conscious and partially unconscious, we do not know. As clinicians, one thing we are sure of is that patients (and in our case most of our"patients"are persistent offenders) come with feelings of anxiety and depression that are deep-seated and at times very painful. Many of our persistent offenders are not too much aware where these uncomfortable and painful feelings arise. Persistent offenders, like most patients, do not speak of "hypothetical unconscious inner states" when they describe their symptoms; they simply describe how they feel and often say that they don't know why they feel that way. What is referred to as "inner reality" or "emotional reality" in psychiatry can be as much a symptom as the deviant behavior or psychiatric symptoms mentioned by Eysenck. Persistent offenders do not complain of delinquent acting out, but if a clinical program permits them to do so, they certainly complain of feelings of alienation, disgust, rage, anger, retaliation feelings, fears about their own aggression, and many other symptoms and feelings that are sources of suffering. The delinquency itself is seldom felt as a source of pain. For the clinician and for the persistent offenders themselves, these feelings are more important symptoms than their delinquency; the latter is a by-product of these feelings, emotions and psychological states that can be retraced far back in the life of a persistent offender, as far back as childhood and adolescence.

What many persistent offenders ask to be treated for, especially when they reach a certain age, is not their criminality, but to get rid of depression and paranoid anxiety, to acquire the capacity to relate to people and live among others, to be able to withstand stress and frustration and establish relationships. They do not use these technical terms but this is what they are asking for in their own terms and what they want to be helped for.

To discover whether or not they recidivate is relatively easy; the real problem is to know before their release when and if there is sufficient change in their personality makeup, in the acquisition of controls, in higher tolerance of frustration, etc., to have a fair idea about their capacity to refrain from delinquent acting out after their release. We would like to believe, like Eysenck, that the tools to measure the effects of psychotherapy are, if not readily at hand, at least not an insurmountable problem. The least we can say in many psychiatric entities and certainly in all the psychological and emotional conflict there is behind persistent criminality, we are far from being able to assess scientifically what we are doing in order to reassure society, which would like us to assure them, whether a man will refrain from delinquent acting out or not. In persistent criminality, the major pathology is not delinquency, but all that goes beyond and contributes to many types of social misadaptation and asocial and anti-social behavior, and this includes such complex pathology as constitutional factors, the environment, and the psychological make-up.

From what we have said above, we can state that the treatment or the resocialization process of the persistent delinquent must be directed toward the character and the personality of the offender and the psychosocial and political realities that contribute to make a persistent offender. Our therapeutic tools must use all the knowledge available in order to treat, and what type of treatment is needed must not be put in a position of opposition to other forms of treatment. Eysenck comes to a conclusion very near this statement when, after acknowledging the criticism of his study on the effects of psychotherapy, he concluded as follows:

> Perhaps the whole discussion could be brought to a conclusion if psychoanalytic writers, teachers and therapists were to agree 1) never to claim therapeutic success either retrospective or prospective until there was proper evidence in favor of their claims; 2) never to deny the effectiveness of other types of therapy on a purely *a priori*

266

basis;   3) to consider other methods on their merits and see them practised side by side with psychoanalysis and psychotherapy, being taught in classes, discussed in textbooks, and generally treated as of equal standing until proved superior or inferior by empirical studies.   (p.335)

As the therapeutic tools used in the treatment of the persistent offender in the Clinton Project had been mainly psychotherapeutic, and in fact we know of no other form of treatment for character disorders with delinquent acting out, we agree that we should, as already stated, try to evaluate as much as we can the work we are doing with these men in this therapeutic venture.   In this psychotherapeutic program based on the establishment of many relationships between staff and inmates and inmates among themselves, when it comes to measuring what we are doing and what we think we have achieved, we agree with Hyman and Berger's remarks:

For the present, there is no hint that we have technology or resources to tackle the problem in the manner suggested by Eysenck.   In the meantime, we would counsel against premature attempts to force the issue into a format which is experimental and objective in its appearance but which almost surely will be irrelevant to the underlying problem.   The evaluation of the effects of therapy is not a task we can handle with existing tools.   Let us not, under the impulse of urgency and a misguided sense of the "scientific," pretend we can settle the issue today if only we apply the correct *Methodology* and make crude analogies between successful procedures in science and field studies in therapy.

2. Evaluation of the Program

Society must learn to accept that a delinquent treated by psychotherapeutic techniques may have benefitted from such treatment even though he returns to crime.

Our approach to evaluating the program has followed the medical or psychiatric frame of reference. A brief outline of some representative cases will give a good idea of how the clinical evaluation is made and how each individual must be judged on his own merits. These examples illustrate how difficult it is to speak only in terms of success and failure, as some "successes" are in fact failures, and some "failures" are, to a degree, successes.

In order to arrive at a proper evaluation of each individual, a thorough case history must be taken and considered in a longitudinal perspective from birth to the time the subject was admitted to the Center. The present personality diagnosis entails character traits and symptoms existing at the time the offender was first seen. From the present one must try not only to understand the past itself, but above all the complex present that contains the past. The admission evaluation was followed by the treatment program described earlier. During this treatment, evaluations were constantly reassessed until a final one was formulated before the inmate appeared before the Parole Board. Another evaluation was made after release when parole was granted. In other words we compared three periods in which the individual was his own control: the period preceding admission to the Center, the period spent in the Center, and the period following release on parole.

This evaluation is based on clinical judgment which is by no means easy to formulate. To do so requires a great deal of experience with personality disorders, and above all with treat-

ment in a penal setting. For example, good work adjustment
on the part of an inmate is taken to be a good index of progress,
particularly if there was no such adjustment previously, either
during earlier sentences or short periods of freedom. This
adjustment could easily be a negative index for a persistent
offender who always had good adjustment to prison work but
who could never stand the frustration of working in freedom.
A consistently good work adjustment in prison in a man unable
to adjust to work conditions outside may mean that he is only
able to function well under a quasi-military regime.

Using six case histories, we will attempt to show the method
of individual evaluation.

Some of the abbreviations used are as follows:

I.Q. The standard abbreviation of Intelligence Quotient.

C.I. Coefficient of Incarceration. This is the time spent
in prison after the age of sixteen expressed as a percentage. It
is always a minimum figure since it includes only time spent in
prison after sentencing and does not include detention time
prior to trial.

C.W. Coefficient of Work. This is the amount of time
that the person worked while free expressed as a percentage.
It is a maximum since it includes pretrial detention time, so
that in all cases the actual index of work would be lower, in
some cases significantly lower.

M.E. Maximum date of Expiration, which is the date at
which an inmate's sentence expires regardless of whether or not
he is paroled.

John S. Admitted to the Center in October 1966. Age,
twenty-seven. I.Q., 105. History of delinquency and stays in
institutions prior to age sixteen. C.I., 79 percent. C.W., 56
percent. Present offense, armed robbery. Sentence, three to
six years. One probation violation; two parole violations,
each for a new offense. M.E. date, March 1970.

Born out of wedlock, most of his childhood and adolescence
were spent in institutions and foster homes. His fantasies concerning his mother, whom he met at age eighteen, did not
correspond with reality. She was on welfare and had three
other illegitimate children. Nonetheless he tried to live with
her in the hope of providing her with a home.

There were conflicting reports in the various institution
files as to his I.Q. As a child and as a young adolescent he was

considered to be retarded with an I.Q. varying between 60 and 74. His last testing a year earlier revealed a normal I.Q. We believed him to be of above-average intelligence.

Upon admission *John* talked little, felt persecuted and gave the impression that he was autistic. He asked to be sent back to prison or to be kept in isolation. His only interest was music and it was through this that he involved himself in the program. He spent most of his time playing, listening to and teaching music. He also wrote poems which expressed his loneliness and composed music for some of these poems. It is difficult to describe his progress, but the whole staff agreed that of all the inmates admitted to the Center, none demonstrated so great an improvement. If the psychiatrists questioned whether he was schizophrenic on arrival, the question certainly did not arise when he was released.

A very good résumé of the case was made just prior to his release by a social worker to whom he was quite attached and who represented a maternal figure for him. She too was interested in his music, and wrote to a friend of hers about possibly hiring him: "*John* has tried very hard and made what even to him is such unexpected progress that it would be a pity to let him become depressed and defeated at the beginning. We realize it is not easy to find a job for people like him, what with their past and their imperfect work record; however, *John* gives indication of important changes, and as for motivation, there is no doubt. He feels that he now has a great deal more to live for than before." Thus, in summary, since entering the Center his progress was such that for the first time in his life he emerged from his shell.

He was released on parole in May 1968. We discussed his progress with his parole officer, who also liked music. Their conversation was frequently about music and instrumental techniques rather than about his past criminal career. This seems to have played an important part in *John's* rehabilitation.

In the second year after his release, he got married. We were told that this union represented the end product of the long series of positive steps that he had made — the capacity to establish positive object relationships.

Robert M. Admitted to the Center in October 1966. Age, thirty-one. I.Q., 109. History of delinquency and stays in institutions during childhood and adolescence. C.I., 64 percent. C.W. 60 percent. Present offense — armed robbery and possession of weapons. Sentence, seven to ten years. One violation of probation, new offense. One violation of parole, new offense. M.E. date, October 1974.

One of a large family which broke up as a result of the father's desertion and the mother's death before he was ten, *Robert* was placed in a number of institutions. During his adolescence he had a fight with his foster mother, whom he both loved and feared, and killed her. His delinquency prior to and after the killing of his foster mother was comprised mainly of crimes against property.

During much of his time at the Center he was treated for recurrent reactive depressions related to unresolved mourning over the death of his foster mother. Although he had been delinquent prior to this incident, his adult criminal career was related to and influenced by his pathological reaction.

He was liberated in February 1968 and has been working regularly. He lives in one of the suburbs of New York City and still maintains contact with some of the Center's professional staff. He was married prior to his present offense and is the father of two children. During his stay at the Center, his depressive episodes were noticeable. Since his release, they have diminished both in intensity and frequency. His marriage is going well and the problems are no more than those encountered in a family with two children. In this case, the prognosis was considered to be good.

Alfred E. Admitted to the Center in October 1966. Age, thirty. I.Q., 114. History of juvenile delinquency and stays in institutions prior to age sixteen. C.I., 61 percent. C.W., 63 percent. Present offense – series of fraudulent offenses and crimes against property. Sentence: five to ten years. One probation violation. One parole violation. M.E. date, September 1974.

Alfred is one of five siblings whose father deserted shortly after he was born. Thereafter his mother lived in a common-law relationship. She gave birth to two more children. He was raised in dire poverty and four of the five siblings became delinquent. He described himself as being aggressive and always fighting during his childhood and adolescence. His criminal activities as an adult were almost always property crimes. Study of his criminal career showed this to be related to sociological factors. He grew up and lived according to the customs of the ghetto.

271

His involvement at the Center was in two phases. Initially he was very active and participated in all the therapeutic, recreational and sporting activities. However, he soon gathered a group of friends around him and tried to form a clique. Unpredictable and easily provoked by this group, he became the Center's rebel and gained prestige by busying himself with other people's problems. Because of his negative influence the staff felt that he should be sent back to prison with the understanding that he could be readmitted later, if he so wished. He returned to the Center after two months in prison and was greeted enthusiastically by both inmates and staff. Despite his poorly controlled aggressiveness, he had a likeable personality.

Following readmission, his participation was far greater than before. This time he did not try to form any cliques. He was paroled in March 1968. He still had to face the inevitable frustrations that are part of trying to reintegrate oneself into society. Again, he tried to solve his problems by aggressiveness. He also started to drink. However, the moment he saw that things were going badly for him, he telephoned the Center and asked for help. The conversation proved helpful to him and a staff member with whom he had a good relationship visited him periodically when in New York.

Alfred is now married and living outside the ghetto where he grew up. His wife, who was also raised in a poor area, though not delinquent, knows about his past. She seems to be a very stabilizing factor and one who offers him considerable security.

Frank G. Admitted to the Center in October 1966. Age, twenty-six. I.Q., 110. History of juvenile delinquency and stays in institutions prior to age sixteen. C.I., 76 percent. C.W., 2.2 percent. Present offense, robbery with assault. Sentence, five to seven years, six months. One parole violation, new offense. M.E. date, July 1970.

Frank was from a multi-delinquent, multi-problem family. He came to the Center with a double reputation, one for the many disciplinary reports incurred during previous sentences and the other for being an expert B. & E. man (breaking and entering). The latter earned him the title "cat burglar." From the time he arrived at the Center, the guards complained about him: he was "demanding". . "arrogant". . "puffed up with his own importance". . "a chronic bitcher". . . etc. By the end of his third month, he was able to talk to at least two officers and

asked one of them point blank: "Do you dislike me? " The
officer answered "yes" directly. This was followed by a ninety-
minute discussion of *Frank's* personality and behavior which
had antagonized both staff and inmates. This interview was
the turning point in developing new attitudes where he
accepted confrontation — be it individual or group therapy —
with the professional staff and with his peers. As a result of
this interview, the guards saw a very favorable change in his
general behavior.

During the first three months at the Center, his therapist
had noticed an absence of anxiety, depression and feelings of
guilt. After this confrontation, this changed and *Frank*
became anxious and depressed. He would become preoccupied
and distressed when he saw children abused on a television
program or in movies. Using this knowledge, *Frank's* therapist
was able to elicit similar memories of his own childhood which
resulted in an intense therapeutic alliance. We also noticed
that he was very preoccupied with sex, which led to his
obtaining erotic literature by devious means. However,
examination of this facet did not reveal any sexual perversion.
We noted that he kept his cell and belongings impeccably
clean and neat.

Frank was paroled in August 1967. He returned to New
York and found work with the help of his therapist. It is
important to note that his C.W. was very low for since the age
of sixteen he had spent a total of only two years in freedom
during which he had only one job lasting about one month.
Following his release he worked steadily for fifteen to eighteen
months.

His therapist visited him on two occasions while in New
York. The improvement noted at the Center was being maintained despite the many obstacles and frustrations. In
March 1969, however, he was arrested for armed robbery. We
received no information as to what may have caused the crime,
the most serious one of his criminal career.

Mel W. Admitted to the Center in October 1966. Age,
twenty-nine. I.Q., 114. History of juvenile delinquency and
stays in institutions prior to age sixteen. C.I., 58 percent.
C.W., 3.7 percent. Present offense, robbery and assault.
Sentence, five to ten years. One probation violation and six
parole violations — all on technical grounds. M.E. date,
September 1971.

273

Mel was not yet three when his parents were accused of neglecting their family. When the family broke up two years later the children were placed in foster homes or in institutions.

It is difficult to give a brief outline of *Mel's* past. His therapist said that he was his own worst enemy. His crimes were generally against property, except for his present offense, which was a sexual one in conjunction with robbery and possession of a weapon. Two of six parole violations were committed after his release from the Center. His first release lasted less than twenty-four hours; he had not gone where he was supposed to go, and he was returned to prison and thence to the Center. He was released again in January 1969. The six months he was on parole could be broken down into two phases: during the first three months he worked compulsively and his boss thought very highly of him; during the second three months he continued to work, but by this time he was drinking excessively, and because of this his parole was revoked. He was returned to prison and then to the Center for a third time. He was paroled again in March 1971.

Prior to his last discharge, one of his therapists noted that, "*Mel* is probably the most lucid therapist in the Center, including the professional staff. He is articulate, positive, constantly aware of the defenses, evasions and deeper problems of others, though he still remains incapable of dealing with his own problems. However, his behavior or level of functioning has improved with each successive release on parole — despite the fact that he has violated each time — and still leaves the possibility that he has improved just enough to make it all the way this time." Though *Mel* was at the Center for a total of thirty months, it was only in the last three months of this admission that he could apply some of his insights to himself. He was also able to recognize for the first time the flagrant failures for which he was responsible. If the expression "failure neurosis" could be used, it might apply to *Mel's* case. Of all his failures, the most severe would be if the Center were to refuse him readmission should he violate for a fourth time. It would be naive to hope that delinquents of his type could reintegrate themselves successfully into society without first having some reeducation. In this type of case, the failure and the reasons for failure must be further researched if treatment is to be effective. For the moment, we see an individual whose criminal tendencies are reduced, who is unable to live in prison but as yet is incapable of living in freedom.

Herman T. Admitted to the Center in October 1966.
Age, thirty-two. I.Q., 110-114. History of juvenile delinquency
and stays in institutions prior to age sixteen. C.I., 69 percent.
Unstable and vagrant, he lived and worked in many parts of the
country. Present offense, armed robbery. Sentence, seven to
fifteen years. M.E. date, 1977.

Herman's adult criminal offenses were three major ones
similar to his present crime, plus two minor charges. His record
is not very different from that of other persistent offenders
although psychiatric evaluation revealed that he had had
several depressive episodes and that he had attempted suicide.
He has been unable to form good object relationships or to
assume any form of responsibility. This inability is seen in his
three marriages; all ended in divorce, each coinciding with his
major offenses. He was very dependent on his wives but these
were no longer necessary when he was imprisoned. Consequently
when they asked for a divorce he did not oppose it. However,
after 1966 he became more and more concerned with his son
by his third marriage. He was frightened by the possibility
that the boy might grow up to be like him. From our first
contact with him, he was treated more like a patient than a
delinquent. After eighteen months in the Center, he was
paroled in March 1968. Three weeks later he became very
anxious and depressed. He started drinking to alleviate his
symptoms, but with the help of his therapist and parole officer
he overcame this crisis. Further similar crises, including
attempted suicide, occurred. After this latter incident he
accepted voluntary admission to hospital. After discharge he
remained in society for a further four months, following which
he was returned to the Center in May 1969 for parole violation.
During his second stay, treatment centered around his neurotic
symptoms.

Prior to his release in February 1970, one of the staff who
had known him for several years said, "It is to be noted that
although he has many aspects which require considerable improvement, he seems stronger now than at any previous time."
Arrangements were made for him to be followed up by one of
our former colleagues who had treated him during his first stay
in the Center. During a period of fifteen months after his
release he was quite dependent on his therapist. Despite this
dependency, he was actively involved in his treatment. As a
result, his crises were dealt with much more quickly and
effectively. Two years have passed since his release. He was

275

once in danger of losing his parole on technical grounds but it was arranged between his clinic and the parole board that he remain on parole. He recently married for the fourth time. We were told that his approach to this marriage seemed to be more realistic than it was to the others.

* *

Persistent delinquency covers "symptoms" or behavior that is condemned by law. Understandably, society wants these "symptoms" treated promptly and to be assured of a permanent "cure." Society must learn to accept that a delinquent treated by psychotherapeutic techniques may have benefitted from such treatment even though he returns to crime. The cases described illustrate how favorable changes can take place despite recidivism.

Evaluating psychotherapeutic treatment of persistent offenders presents difficulties that are particular to this group of men. As stated earlier, persistent criminality abates with time. This abatement, quite noticeable in the thirties, but spectacular after the age of forty, makes us wonder how many of those with a favorable outcome after treatment at the Center would have had the same result even if they had served their sentence in a regular penitentiary. For example, *Robert M.* might have worked out his prolonged mourning reaction by himself. We can even state that he was in the process of working it out by himself prior to admission to the Center. However, we felt that we helped him considerably toward solving what became for him a chronic problem. In the same way, with *John S.*, we can only point to his intense need to be involved in a relationship; he had used the constructive relationship at the Center to come out of what was seemingly a schizophrenic world. This certainly contributed to his good adjustment after release. In these two cases, which so far have shown spectacular results, we cannot claim that psychotherapeutic treatment alone was responsible. Success was achieved at a critical moment in the lives of these men who were chronically "disabled" both in their individual and social adjustments. *Alfred E.* also seemed to reach a turning point during his stay at the Center.

In the case of failures — failures being defined as the commission of another crime or breach of parole after discharge

276

from the Center — we deliberately selected those which would illustrate how difficult it is to assess failure. *Frank C.*, *Mel W.* and *Herman T.* demonstrate both success and failure. *Herman T.'s* case illustrates that it would have been illusory to treat his delinquency rather than the obvious depressive states which at times justified a diagnosis of agitated depression. His history shows that treating a persistent offender at the age of twenty is a problem. Treating this same man ten years later is quite another matter for although the physical man is much the same his mentality has changed. Thus the emphasis on the area of treatment has to be altered as he grows older.

The major problem of evaluating a program for the treatment of persistent offenders is that most such offenders do not return to the penal system after the age of forty. What happens to offenders with age is a complex problem.

In looking at a criminal career, Glaser enumerates the many pathways in the abatement of criminality as follows: "Late Reformation after long Crime Careers, Early Reformation after Extensive Crime, Crime-Facilitated Reformations, Reformations after Brief Criminality, Reformations after One Extreme Crime, Crime-Interrupted Non-Criminal Lives, Retreats from Crime and Non-Crime, Crime-Contacting Ex-Criminals. Pseudo-Reformations, Marginal Failures, Eventual Recidivists, Immediate Recidivists, The Zig Zag Path." (28)

Like Glaser, we must remain very conscious that success and failure cannot be measured only by the presence or absence of recidivism. The Center could only look for late reformation since all the inmates were selected on the basis of their early start in delinquency and their persistent adult criminality. Therefore our aim was to speed up reformation that would possibly have come with time. Since the program was geared to the total personality, we hope that some persistent offenders will, after their stay in the Center, be fully reintegrated into society. However, we are aware that the recidivism of others will call for further intensive treatment, as in the last three cases.

We have carefully evaluated the first fifty individuals in the same way we did the above six cases. This was the first time we were working with fifty cases at once in a given program, and it was pleasing to find that in it most of them became aware for the first time, or at least became *more* aware, of their feelings of anxiety and depression along with the underlying cause for these feelings. For many, it was a new experience to be able to tolerate these painful feelings, so accustomed were they to act out in order to prevent their emergence. In many of the offenders these feelings became a sign of alarm in the predelictual state (the state of mind preceding an offense), so much so that it had not been an unusual experience for this first fifty (and the many who came afterward) to recognize the state of mind in which they were prior to the commission of an offense and feel the anxiety and depression as a warning bell. In fact, quite a number of them rang up either the Center or the Clinic in Montreal to ask for help. One of the concepts we adopted from the beginning was to try to discover as much as we could about their feelings before, during and after an offense (predelictual, delictual and postdelictual state). This taught us more about their way of life and it is our impression that we could pass this knowledge back to them. When an inmate became aware of painful anxiety prior to committing an offense and rang one of us before acting, it was an emotional experience for both sides.

3. Group Evaluation

With the exception of those whose exposure to the therapeutic community technique was brief, delinquent behavior even in those who recidivated had diminished considerably.

The treatment of persistent offenders is not a venture that can be entered upon blindly. Consequently we sought views and criticisms of the Clinton Project right from its beginning. The originality of the program, our views on the evolution and abatement of criminal careers and our assumption that such careers can be shortened were all factors that aided the acceptance of the program. However, soon after the Center opened, the problem of evaluation was sharply and clearly raised.

Well-known authorities in program treatment for offenders have stated unreservedly that a given type of program could not be considered valid unless a control group of comparable offenders were treated by a different type of program or technique. Theoretically it may be possible to match a group of patients or offenders against another. In fact, however, this is difficult if not almost impossible to achieve. Many valid studies based on group controls have contributed greatly to the clinical practice of psychiatry (or clinical treatment in general), but these have usually been based on known drugs in psychopharmacology in treating well-defined diagnoses or symptoms. Studies based on such controls are now subtle tools in psychopharmacology.

Psychotherapy or therapeutic relationships used in a program cannot be compared to psychopharmacological drugs. It is difficult to measure intervention in a therapeutic relationship. The very fact that what is "given" and what is "received" may have different meanings for the therapist and the patient is a serious hindrance to the measurement of what takes place. This does not, however, altogether preclude attempts at evaluating psychotherapeutic programs.

In evaluating the Clinton Project we did have one control group that consisted of an equal number of persistent offenders who were eligible for admittance to the Center. This was by no means a "guinea pig" group inasmuch as treatment was not withheld. They were simply not admitted because the program was initially restricted to fifty inmates. It is important to state this since at the start a number of inmates who had previous acquaintance with research projects wondered whether they had a "double" somewhere. The thought that they would receive treatment while someone else was deprived of it in order to serve as a guinea pig made them feel uncomfortable. We were able to reassure them on this score.

In a correctional system as large as that of New York State, there was no problem in finding fifty inmates to make up a control group. These inmates followed the different programs of the prisons in which they happened to be. Everyone in the two groups was eligible both for admission to the Center and for parole within eighteen months. This method of selecting a control group can be criticized, but as clinicians and researchers we felt that the only logical selection of the two groups was on clinical grounds. A control group aimed at matching subject to subject according to factors such as age, background, type of criminal record, race, color, mental state, character diagnosis, criminological diagnosis, and others, presents as many if not more possibilities of error than the proposed control group which was concerned only with the two factors mentioned. When forming matching groups with many precise data that are assumed to be the same, it is easy to forget that men are basically not alike. It is as difficult to match two twenty-five-year-old persistent offenders as it is to match two twenty-five-year-old healthy, law-abiding citizens when points such as character, symptoms or absence of them, individual and social backgrounds, and personal and social elements are taken into account. In studying offenders, criminality involves the total personality and it is this total personality which has to be considered, not just parts of it.

Information on the experimental group of the first fifty inmates at the Center in October-November 1966 is, of course, more complete and detailed than on the control group.   For that information we had to depend entirely on data obtained from files without personal interviews.   Matching all items was therefore not possible; so our comparison rests mainly on the number of types of crimes committed and the criminological diagnosis of the individuals, including post-release behavior.

Most of the first fifty inmates at the Center came from broken (12 per cent) or unstable (54 percent) homes, and 64 percent of them came from multi-problem and multi-delinquent families   (Table II).   In 18 percent of the cases the pathology was confined to the inmate, that is, they were the black sheep of the family   (Table III).   Half the inmates were single at the time of admission, the remainder were either separated (20 percent), divorced (14 percent), or living in common-law relationships (10 percent), while only three men were still married (Table IV).

In 58 percent of the cases, there was a history of delinquency in one or more members of the family of origin, those most frequently involved being the inmates' fathers and/or collaterals such as uncles, cousins, etc.   Over 50 percent of the inmate population had a juvenile record and, in keeping with our criteria for admission, 74 percent had a high coefficient of incarceration with a correspondingly low coefficient of work while out of prison   (Table IV).   According to the McGill classification the majority of inmates was classified as either primary (36 percent) or secondary (56 percent) delinquents (Table VI).   In regard to the types of offenses committed there were more property offenses committed per inmate than crimes against person, this being in line with studies carried out by others.

The inmates were also rated for their overall participation in the program as well as for their performance in the shop. Regarding the latter, the inmates appeared to make better adjustment in the shop, despite some marked individual differences, than they did in their work while free.   Almost 60 percent were regular in attendance and their work was productive.   A further 30 percent attended the shop regularly, but were not productive.   Shop performance was not concerned primarily with production, but with their ability to remain at their machines and to deal with problems arising in the work area.   Although no one was forced to go to work, they were expected to do so since this was an integral part of the program

281

and poor or non-performance was handled by means of confrontation.

As to their overall participation in the program, they were rated on a five point scale (0 to 5), the majority being rated as "favorable" or "good" performance. This was obviously a gross means of behavioral measurement since it did not take into account the fluctuations that occurred during their stay at the Center.

Of the fifty admitted, forty-two completed the program and were released on parole from the Center. The remaining eight inmates were returned to prison at their own request or for poor participation in the program. The mean length of stay at the Center was just over sixteen months.

One of the major functions of the clinicians was to furnish an evaluation report on each inmate when he met the parole board. Included in these reports were relevant background data, the inmate's participation in the program, advisability of release, prognosis and recommendations regarding management of his case if he were released on parole. It should be borne in mind that the decision of the board is final. However, in most cases, the recommendations made by the staff as to whether or not the inmate was suitable for release were taken into consideration.

Each evaluation report was rated as to the clinician's prognosis of the inmate's performance while on parole and this was compared with the inmate's actual performance on parole. In only 30 percent of the cases did the actual performance tally with the staff's prediction; in 40 percent, the parolee's performance was *better* than predicted; and in the remaining 24 percent, performance was *worse* than predicted.

Follow-ups on the first fifty men were carried out in two parts. The first part of the study was carried out on March 31st, 1970. At this time, forty-two months after the project's start, twenty-eight men (36 percent) had not violated parole after an average of twenty-three months; nineteen men (38 percent) had recidivated and three men had not yet been released. The latter were three of the eight inmates who had been transferred from the Center.

The type of violations these men committed after their release from the Center is significant. In the nineteen cases that had recidivated, ten had violated their conditions of parole; seven had committed offenses similar to those on their previous record; only two men were arrested for new offenses and these were two of the eight men who had not completed the program. The average length of time (twelve months) spent on parole by these nineteen men was less than the time spent by those who had not recidivated.

The second part of the follow-up continued from April 1970 to January 1972, twenty-two months in all. During this second phase there was a noticeable improvement: only thirteen men had violated. The remaining thirty-seven (74 percent) were on parole or their sentences had expired and they were still functioning well in the community. It is interesting to note that, except for five men from the group who had been transferred, the recidivism was for technical violations of parole. In the case of the five men, all had been convicted for new offenses.

The first fifty men were observed from the time of their admission to the Center in October 1966 to January 1972, that is for sixty-four months. Twenty-five, or 50 percent, had no violation whatsoever following their release. They lived an average of forty-three months in their respective communities (Table VII). Thus, when comparing the first phase with the second, there is an overall improvement in their behavioral adjustment. With the exception of those whose exposure to the therapeutic community technique was brief, delinquent behavior even in those who recidivated had diminished considerably.

4. The Control Group

If the men seem happier with their lot, less alienated, and succeed in maintaining themselves in freedom, either permanently or for longer periods of time than before, this in itself could be a better indication of success than the legal criterion of whether they recidivated or not.

As already mentioned, all the data gathered on the Control Group was obtained from the prison files. None was interviewed by our staff. Thus, accuracy of past history, both family and personal, was not as detailed and complete as that of the experimental group. Had this been possible there might have been far less discrepancy.

One interesting fact was that the control group was slightly older. The majority were in the age range of twenty-five to thirty-nine. In the experimental group the majority were in the twenty-five to thirty-five-year age group. It is important to bear this in mind for although delinquency abates with age, the rate of recidivism in the control group remained high on release from prison in comparison with the experimental group at the Center. However, when it comes to the number and types of crimes committed and the criminological diagnosis of the individuals, the two groups are more comparable.

Between October 1966 and January 1972, all the men in the control group had been released from prison on parole. During this period seventeen had recidivated once, and six had recidivated twice. Comparison of the type of recidivism in the two groups, showed that twelve control cases were convicted for new offenses compared with eight cases from the experimental group (all the latter save two were committed by the group that had been transferred out) (Table VIII).

As of January 1972, the control group had twenty-six men (52 percent) on parole or who were considered non-delinquent because their sentences had expired. The authorities had heard

284

nothing further from their respective field officers. Of the balance, four men (8 percent) had died, one while committing a crime; eight men (16 percent) were in prison; three men (6 percent) had absconded; and the whereabouts of the remaining nine men (18 percent) was unknown   (Table IX). Some explanation regarding these nine men can be put forward. Some or all have served their sentences and are adjusting satisfactorily. Others may have left the state and may or may not be doing well with the result that the Central Parole Office in Albany had no up-to-date information when this follow-up was carried out in January 1972.

Given that all the men are functioning well, whether a few or all have recidivated, the experimental group had a better, albeit slight, edge over the control group in terms of satisfactory adjustment following release from prison. It should be stressed that detailed information on the control group was not available as to their whereabouts and performance on parole any more than it was on their histories. A bias in favor of the experimental groups was therefore inevitable since it was more accessible. Also follow-up was easier, since the men themselves frequently wrote or telephoned, or even met with clinicians.

Since crime abates with age irrespective of treatment intervention, did we effect any change in these fifty men?

The effects of milieu therapy on these men and those who followed (over 300 in all) have been profound. Some found the setting difficult to adjust to and returned where they came from, as evidenced by the group of eight men who were transferred. Most have admitted to serving "hard time" at the Center. The beneficial impact on them has lasted for varying lengths of time following their release on parole. With a few exceptions, using the individuals as their *own* control, they had adjusted to freedom in a much better way than when previously on parole.

During the first phase of our follow-up, a questionnaire was sent to inmates on parole. Not all of the first fifty received it because some were in prison or their address was not known. Hence, only twenty-three replies were received. The questions dealt mainly with their social adjustment vis-à-vis their work, family and parole. Further questions dealt with health, personal problems and relationships as well as their opinions of the Center and whether they felt the need for follow-up over and above parole supervision. With regard to the three last questions, over 80 percent of those who replied said they were now doing better than at any previous time following release. However, 70 percent stated that on release from the Center, they had to contend with many problems including anxiety, tension, insecurity and depression. They strongly urged some form of follow-up, especially soon after discharge when the anxiety symptoms were at their zenith. Thus, a few violations might have been prevented had such a service been available to them.

The results of the follow-up study showed that although the rate of recidivism was comparable in the two groups, there were differences in quality both in personal adjustment and in the types of violation. For example, the experimental group violated more frequently on technical grounds, whereas the control group had a higher incidence of new arrests. To re-iterate, success or failure cannot be measured only by the presence or absence of recidivism. If the men seem happier with their lot, less alienated, and succeed in maintaining them-selves in freedom, either permanently or for longer periods of time than before, this in itself could be a better indication of success than the legal criterion of whether they recidivated or not.

Mention has been made regarding the problems of evaluating and comparing a therapeutic group with a control group. Since the aim of the therapeutic community technique is to make each individual aware of his behavior, thus gaining insight and motivation to seek help, we believe that each in-dividual should act as his own control.

Among the many comments on Eysenck's study on "The Effects of Psychotherapy," there is one in particular that has special interest for those of us who work in penal institutions. Beyond the problem of evaluating the actual effects of psycho-therapy, if treatment based on the establishment of therapeutic relationships had only the effect of humanizing psychiatric hospitals and the prison milieu, this effect alone should not be considered as minimal. We recognize that the humanization of mental hospitals did not start with the technique of psycho-therapy as we practice it today; what was referred to as the "moral treatment" of the psychiatrically ill had already con-siderably changed in a number of hospitals prior to the Freudian era. Any statement or empirical judgment that severely re-stricts the effect of therapeutic relationships to the point that it is virtually an invitation to put aside such techniques amounts to

286

returning to the type of asylum described by Goffman (29) and to institutional symptoms and syndromes described by Vail (58). Certain symptoms, certain types of behavior are no longer observable in progressive mental hospitals because therapeutic relationships exist where hitherto custody prevailed.

Following changes that took place in some mental hospitals, prisons have also come a long way. From regimes of silence and solitary confinement, prisoners can now communicate among themselves and are generally in good contact with society through various media like radio and television. Other privileges, such as visits and correspondence permit relationships which were previously forbidden. This alone does not make good prisons, but it does bring about the creation of a milieu that previously generated its own psychopathological states, such as prison psychosis, Ganzer syndrome, and a high rate of suicide in solitary confinement.

In prisons or penitentiaries that encourage therapeutic relationships between staff and inmates, a new climate is created where we can truly study the many etiologies involved in the commission of crime with a minimum of secondary pathology in adapting to the deprivation of liberty. (39, 40, 3)

Undoubtedly, setting up therapeutic relationships and creating a therapeutic milieu present special problems in prisons where deprivation of liberty is a punishment, but it is nevertheless possible. Under a program such as the Center's it was no small achievement that men who were living within a walled maximum security institution lived according to a minimum security regime. Security and treatment were both based on the relationship of inmates and staff.

Under these conditions, we feel that we have achieved results which could be observed in the attitudes, feelings and behavior of most of the men from the time they entered the Center to the moment they were discharged. These changes are not as measurable as we would like them to be and do not necessarily result in a non-delinquent social adjustment. The difference between living in a therapeutic milieu and a conventional prison is that, while living with these inmates, we are not studying a prison but are treating prisoners.

We reach a point at which the watcher and the watched equally learn about each other, and how to live better in society and with themselves.

287

AFTERMATH

1. Dannemora Revisited

*(Dannemora alumni) seem to perceive the Center as
the positive"core": it is almost as if there were a tacit
agreement among them that if any of them did go
back into crime, he would not drag his former
colleagues with him.*

Three of us in the McGill group recently returned to visit
Dannemora after a year and a half away. Because of the nature
of the program, the Center had demanded an intense emotional
involvement from all of us who had worked there and we had
felt very sad to leave. We returned as rather strange observers,
on the one hand sensitive to all the memories revived, and on
the other struggling to be objective about changes that had
been made in the program after we left.

The initial physical impressions created an almost surrealistic
feeling of being in a place which was familiar and at the same time
foreign. On the front lawn a large imposing sign informed us that
we were approaching the Adirondack Correctional Treatment and
Evaluation Center (ACTEC). It was no longer the Dannemora
State Hospital and the Clinton Diagnostic and Treatment Center.
The state hospital had at long last been closed and its patients
transferred to other institutions in New York State. The Center
was no longer a distinct entity, but was only one of several programs under ACTEC.

On entering the Administration Buildings, we found plenty
of new signs but few personnel.   The closing of the state hospital had reduced the inmate population and therefore the staff
— though a number of new functions seemed to have been
created. One such was the "Co-ordinator of Volunteers," which
had previously been merely an informal sideline of someone's
job. All this lent a much more official and formal atmosphere.
Names and titles of staff members were proudly and prominently
displayed and, if one judged by the number of wooden plaques,

administrators abounded. One prominent sign designated an obviously important room, the "Concatenation Room." Its purpose remained a mystery but these overt transformations led us to wonder what more subtle changes had taken place.

To enter the area where the Center is housed, it was necessary to pass through a series of locked gates operated by a security officer. Previously we had passed through this series of gates with ease; but this time we had to go through a metal detector, after first depositing our jewelry, lighters, watches and any other metal objects on a table. It was difficult to decide who was more uncomfortable, ourselves or the officer on duty, with whom we had over the years exchanged pleasantries. Although he knew us well, he was scrupulous about checking our visitors' passes and ensuring that all technicalities concerning the metal detector were rigidly enforced. Contributing to the strained and formal atmosphere was the automatic rifle on the wall above his head. This was to prevent prison escapes.

This was our introduction into what we soon discovered was an overall change of policy about security and it affected everything at the Center. Two years earlier, one of the senior officers at the Center had pointed out that where a good treatment program exists, security looks after itself. The security aspect now played a far greater role than we would have imagined it ever would. There are several possible reasons for this, the most important being that the Center is no longer a separate and somewhat autonomous body. It has become part of a system which is under the New York State Correctional Services which do not distinguish between its various institutions when it comes to security and administrative regulations. Such strict adherence to state regulations fundamentally changes the orientation of the whole program.

The state-wide "tightening up" of institutions, undoubtedly in reaction to the Attica situation, began after we left the Center. Inmates now have to wear prison uniforms during working hours rather than the previously acceptable "appropriate" clothing. There is also much less latitude and flexibility about inmates' choice of room decoration than had previously been the case. Instead of styles ranging from the ornate to the spartan to the near-pornographic, we now had something like traditional prison decor. The former latitude in room decoration allowed the inmate not only to express his personality, but helped the staff understand his values and tastes.

291

Inmates' visiting privileges had also been reorganized significantly. Previously these had been allowed in an atmosphere of almost complete privacy. This was another area where the inmate's own sense of responsibility toward himself and the Center was relied on, and during McGill's six-year involvement this faith was not abused. Now, because of state regulations, inmates and their visitors both undergo a thorough search before and after the visit. There are two procedures: newer inmates undergo a "full frisk," that is, they are stripped and completely searched; inmates who have been at the Center for a longer time undergo a partial frisk. The visits now take place in two large rooms which can accommodate as many as twenty visits at one time. (Our visiting facilities were geared to one visit at a time.) Visits are now under continual officer observation and are structured as to time and format.

The new formality even stretched to our meeting with our former colleagues, many of whom had become good friends during our close association. The staff had set aside an hour to answer our questions and this in itself lent a formal air since on previous visits we had more or less blended in with the daily program. There was definitely an air of staginess to the whole affair, the three of us asking questions, and the director providing the answers. It was as if we were acting out a set piece with none of the spontaneous give-and-take that had existed in our other meetings with them, although admittedly our stated and official reason for being there was to determine what changes had taken place. There were prepared answers to our prepared questions, yet we had the impression that the officers, particularly those who had been with the program from the beginning, wanted to speak but were afraid to do so. Their silence reflected a remark that was made: "We are all afraid to talk here now." The implication was that some "higher power" might be listening.

The officers seemed very uncertain about the new scheme and so they remained silent during the meeting, seemingly embarrassed, uncomfortable and unable to resolve the dilemma of inevitably breaching a loyalty, no matter which position they took. On the other hand, the staff was strongly defensive.

If the staff were afraid to talk openly, the inmates typically were not. They expressed themselves directly and with a lot of feeling at this particular community meeting. When various staff members asked, "What's wrong with this community?"

"There's no life — no talking," one inmate said very succinctly, "We won't talk about drinking because we may be shipped." This response, which seemed to reflect the general fear in the whole community, was ignored by the staff members. In the staff meeting which followed the community meeting, one of us asked whether the inmates' fear was valid. The staff admitted that they didn't answer the question because they themselves were unsure as to what punishment would be imposed. They were unclear about the policy apparently laid down by the administration which had resulted in some men being shipped back to prison when their drinking was discovered. However, this had never been clearly stated; as a result the whole community avoided pertinent issues. A new officer said that he didn't know what to do when he found a man drinking but since he did not want to have him "shipped" for it, he didn't make out a report on him. Nor would he put the man on the floor for fear that this might happen.

Thus, the whole community, officers, professional staff and inmates, seemed to be involved in a web of subterfuge and silence, dealing with delinquent behavior individually rather than on a community level with the focus on changing behavior.

This lack of a clear and integrated approach permeated the whole therapeutic program; there was no consistent method of dealing with delinquent behavior. Two absolutely essential ingredients in our concept of a therapeutic community had been 1) to allow an inmate to act out his symptoms so they could be better understood and ultimately treated, and 2) to transform the officer's role into one where he would join the inmate in therapeutic and social relationships. To a great extent these prerequisites are no longer possible under the new system. The present rules dictate that acting out behavior and breaches of regulations be handled by an Adjustment Committee. Since there are prescribed penalties, community floor and group therapy sessions are no longer the prime instruments in dealing with either acting out behavior or with conflicts which exist within the community itself.

The flow-of-treatment process which had been the policy before, (individual—group—community) appeared to have stopped. In fact it was reported in the meeting arranged for our benefit that the main source of therapy at the Center was now individual and group: according to the director it was better than ever. He admitted, however, that there were fewer clinical workers than before as most of their staff had backgrounds in educational psychology and tended to deal more with behavior rather than feelings. The Center now had less staff for individual counseling since the clinical coordinators of the two units no longer took cases. This meant that there was one caseworker for every twenty-five men as compared to a ratio of one to ten men which existed previously.

Treatment policy appeared to be in a state of flux. On another visit several months later, it was noted that the focus of treatment had apparently changed again. Individual sessions with an inmate were used in times of crisis rather than as a regular and integrated part of his treatment.

While McGill was involved with the Center we were often accused of creating difficulties because we were not permanent and full-time workers there. It seemed to us, however, that the program was more chaotic and confused than when we had been there. A major factor might have been the poor communication between members who worked side by side. Each therapist and officer seemed to be "doing his own thing," because of a lack of any clear policy and a fear of punitive and repressive measures by the authorities.

It was only at a local restaurant over cheeseburgers and draft beer that artificial barriers between ourselves and our former colleagues disappeared, and some of the real feelings emerged. Officers who had been with the old program were discouraged and bewildered as to where exactly the present regime was going. New professional therapists we'd known for several months before our departure stated that it was very important to have outside consultants like ourselves who were not involved day to day with the program. They seemed to think there was a real advantage to having "semi-outsiders" who could give a more objective analysis and thereby offer different or more constructive solutions. Some officers who had been with us from the start of the Center said they wanted to get out. One mentioned the idea of early retirement, and another considered working part time. This was a line of thought we had never heard before even when there had been days of disappointment and difficulty.

Inmates and staff related how all breaches must be written up and dealt with by the Adjustment Committee. As a result, rather than trying to determine the nature of the conflicts and the causes behind the acting out, the inmates do their utmost

294

to conceal any such incidents in order to avoid punishment.
Problems such as drinking, stealing and fighting, so symptomatic of individual or group disturbances, are no longer the subject for therapeutic resolution. Consequently, the inmates
have begun to develop a mentality much more akin to that
found in the traditional prison code.

Another form of punishment implemented at the Center
since our departure was the so-called "special housing units,"
of which there were seven or eight. These, in simple terms,
are isolation cells where an inmate is taken to cool off at the
very crucial moment when an attempt should be made to determine the reasons for his anxiety. The inmates' jargon referred
to these cells as the "bing." This special detention wing also
provided an out for inmates who wanted to avoid personal
problems since they could so easily get isolated from the
community population. It struck us that a setup where open
discussion did not occur was more prone to favoritism: that
is, whether an officer made a report or not depended on his
relationship with the particular man.

One can easily see how these new measures changed the
officer-inmate relationship. The stereotyped roles of the
watcher and the watched become much more evident as the
officer resumes his policing and security-maintaining role. He
relinquishes the potential of becoming a trusted confidant to
the inmate. The therapeutic community is largely based on
the removal of the stereotyped inmate-officer relationship,
for it was only this measure which could transform the overall
milieu. Group therapy and community meetings in themselves cannot overcome an atmosphere in which most of the
staff are concerned with security.

Some officers find it difficult to be shunted back to a more
mechanized, less human role. Others have found it hard to
understand why the inmates began drawing away from them
until the inmates themselves explained that they felt much less
comfortable with persons who observed and reported rather
than joined in the therapeutic task. In the therapeutic role
officers had felt that they contributed something to rehabilitat-
ing inmates when they confronted them during community
meetings. Now that the writing of reports can lead to possible
punishment, they are uncertain about what to do with information which comes their way. Many officers have become inconsistent not only about writing reports but also about which

inmates they will report on. This results in rather haphazard discipline, varying with the aggressiveness or passivity of the officer and the inmate involved. Previously, confrontation was a two-way process — inmates could put officers and professional staff on the floor as well as be confronted themselves.

Besides the Adjustment Committee, mentioned earlier, other structures have emerged to reduce confrontation in both directions as well as the extent of the average inmate's community activity. One is the "Inmate Liaison Committee," which is made up of inmates who are appointed to deal with problems and grievances about the administration of the Center. Instead of giving each inmate the chance to air his feelings regarding staff or administration on the community floor, complaints are now funneled through a few inmates who, in a closed setting, work out these problems with a few members of the administration. On another visit to the Center, one of our group attended a community meeting where an inmate member of the Liaison Committee was questioned about certain complaints. This inmate, an ex-mental patient, became very excited and defensive in answering the inmates' questions but the community did not attempt to focus on the way he had handled himself on the committee or with the inmates' questions.

This predominance of committees runs counter to our philosophy that it is beneficial for the individual to learn to air his own grievances and to try to resolve disagreements and conflicts without having an intermediary to do his work. At one time the inmates themselves had sole control of the Wednesday night program, an evening activity originally geared to reflect their interests and needs. Now staff and a volunteer committee, along with an inmate committee, organize this program with considerably more input from the non-inmate population than previously. Apparently the inmates' former emphasis on Black Nationalism seemed to perturb the administration and state employees. The issue boils down to whether it is preferable to run a program in which one gets to know the inmate by allowing him great latitude in terms of self-expression or to try and shape his behavior to coincide with previously defined guidelines.

We are happy to be able to report an improvement since our time in the pay scale for the work program. Inmates who had previously been paid 30 cents a day now receive between 6 1/4 cents and 28 3/4 cents per hour on a graduated scale. Poor shop attendance is no longer dealt with by confrontation

by staff or officers whose goal is to correct the problem.   Under
the new system, payment is simply withheld for non-attendance.

Another area of fundamental change is the transition from
a shop program to that of an academic college preparatory program.   This has broad implications regarding other aspects of
the treatment program.   Essentially, such a move suggests that
inmates require a better education and better qualifications in
order to compete successfully for adequate employment on the
street.   While this is certainly valid to some extent, our
experience and observation suggested that a barrier to successful employment among inmates was due more to their inability
to develop sufficiently positive work attitudes and habits than
to a lack of academic or vocational training.   On this premise
we emphasized developing better work habits and exploring
the failure to function at work.

Another facet of the new approach is its orientation toward younger offenders, a trend that means that fewer and fewer
persistent offenders will be admitted to the Center.   In reply to
our questions, the director stated quite clearly that the program
was operating on the belief that persistent offenders could not
be helped; thus the focus must be on the younger offender.
This statement reverses our original premise that persistent
offenders are amenable to treatment as they get older and criminality abates with age.   In dealing with younger offenders one
avoids the real challenge encountered in the treatment of the
persistent offender on the road to abatement.

One member of our trio had revisited the Center on a
number of occasions when accompanying students and consequently had extra opportunities to observe the prevailing state
of affairs.   She got the impression that there was more personal
dissension and outright disagreement between staff members.
Disagreement had often occurred previously, of course, particularly over various ideas about how to handle an inmate problem,
but these were now being expressed on a very personal and
vindictive level.   In one quarrel she observed between an officer
and a therapist, each hurled insults at the other for not carrying
his work load.   This was possibly due to the extra strain on the
staff members because of the high number of inmates per
therapist.

Another impression was that each inmate concentrated on
his own particular plans for the future, e.g. whether or not he
could get his furlough, and when and whether he was eligible to

go to the other programs related to the Center, including that of the university. There was no attempt in community meetings to focus these inmates on present frustrations or past delinquency. She was taken aback at one staff meeting when one of the officers asked whether she felt what was happening at the Center was "O.K." and whether the program was serving a real purpose. She was inclined to answer yes, but had to admit that she was confused as to just where the program was going at that point.

* *

The changes in the program reflect self-destructive mechanisms in the therapeutic community. Fundamentally, a program alters when the staff and inmates alike are unable to tolerate the taxing and frustrating approach of accenting symptomatic behavior and engaging in continuous confrontation within the milieu. The reaction is to fall back to the less demanding, more traditional approaches of individual therapy and increased dependence on rules, where role definition is clear cut, to create a more comfortable climate for staff and inmates. Often these are not consciously planned changes but rather a retreat from an approach which is more emotionally demanding and anxiety provoking.

Thus, while the program retains the characteristics of a therapeutic milieu with community meetings, there is no longer any insistence on the consistent integration of techniques and policies in order to implement therapeutic community aims. This is not in any way to derogate the qualifications or aims of the current professional staff. They are trying to run a humane treatment program within a prison and the result is certainly better than that found in standard prisons. It is simply that it is no longer a therapeutic community program as we know it — a place where offenders were allowed to act out and at the same time be dealt with therapeutically.

The three of us felt sad after our visit, though we were not exactly clear as to why we felt that way. It seemed to us that with all the dissension and confusion among the staff, it was the inmate, the person for whom the program had been built, who was suffering. When they complained about the system while we were at the Center, a strictly defensive measure to get the heat off themselves, we had been able to relate it back to their own personality.   But because of the difficulties that the staff were now having with the new unclear policies, most of the community meetings we witnessed seemed to focus on administrative measures and away from the inmates' personal problems. Inmates and staff no longer felt free to disagree with the system and among themselves in open discussions that had been aggressive, elating and stimulating.   The day was near when the watchers and the watched would no longer speak the same language.   What was significant to us was that already they could not understand their silences.

Perhaps most depressing of all, though, was the long silent ride home as compared to the noisy, 'cathartic' type of trips we were used to.   The silence went with the final realization that separation was complete, and, for better or for worse, the offspring was irrevocably on its own.

2.   In Their Own Backyard: Reunion in New York City

We, as therapists, have developed strong, enduring relation-ships with many of them.   All the difficulties, hassles and crises entailed in therapeutic community work seemed worth the trouble.

When we learned that the American Society of Criminology would be holding its annual meeting in New York City in October 1973, those of us at the McGill Clinic who had worked at Danne-mora planned our trip so that we could look up some of the Center's former inmates and see how they were doing in their own backyard.

We started by telephoning Father Walsh at Dannemora. Father Walsh, one of the chaplains at the Adirondack Center, makes frequent visits to New York City and is better informed of the whereabouts and activities of former Center inmates than almost anyone else.   He was delighted to help and called *Billy M.* in New York, one of the men with whom we had had close con-tact.   *Billy* was so enthused about the prospect of our visit that he tried to call us long distance to set up a schedule of activities. Due to a mix-up of telephone numbers he failed to reach us in Montreal, but all was straightened out when we reached New York.

Often when we worked with the men at Dannemora, we re-gretted there was no follow-up service for those who returned to the city.   Individual therapists might see some they had treated but seldom more than once or twice.   Generally, the men left the Center to try out what we had been discussing for months and we never knew whether our joint efforts — theirs and ours — had any positive effect.   Even the sporadic letters from some telling us how they were doing petered out over the months

As we now looked forward to seeing some of them, we felt anxious as well as happy.   We had known these men within the protective walls and structure of a prison and a therapeutic program; our relationship had been that of therapist-inmate or therapist-patient. How would we interact now? We need not have worried. The rule which we had followed in our relationships within the Center, that of being ourselves, worked on the outside as well.

Billy had been in touch with a few other fellows from the Center and he and *Thad W.* met us at our hotel to plan the evening. They arrived shortly after nine and it was a joyous reunion, replete with backslapping, hugging, and the wordless exchange of broad grins. We sat in the hotel lounge for a bit and reminisced about old times. They brought us up to date on the recent activities and projects of our friends and ex-members. Particularly striking was the pride they took in their achievements since leaving the Center and their desire to impress on us how much they felt they had gained from their experiences there. They were so emphatic that at one point we wondered if they felt this was an expected gesture on their part, but we were soon convinced that it was genuine appreciation.

Contrasted to the pride and happiness over what they and some of their *confrères* had achieved was their extreme disappointment in others who they could see were backsliding. One in particular, with whom they had been quite close at the Center, had recently begun to do poorly. They had tried unsuccessfully to get in touch with him when they heard we were arriving in the hope that perhaps a little more contact with us might be beneficial. During the evening they reiterated their obviously real concern about this man who they seemed to feel was "letting down the side" and, in a way, giving the Center a bad name. Their efforts to reach him seemed mainly inspired by the confidence they felt in our "healing" powers.

As *Billy* and *Thad* seemed very anxious to show us the town and entertain us, they took full charge of the agenda, the main item being a visit to the Greenwich Village coffeehouse where *Don M.*, another alumnus, was appearing as featured vocalist with a fairly big-name pop music group. Our companions had the good grace not to remind us of how the staff at the Center had constantly urged *Don* not to rely too heavily on his musical talents but to put his energies to better use in the shop.

We piled into *Billy's* car for the ride down to the Village, and it proved to be a hair-raising experience. *Billy* drives a car with the same gusto and disregard for minor rules that he had demonstrated in the therapeutic community. We narrowly missed hitting a cab and for the next four blocks *Billy* drove while peering over his shoulder and explaining to those in the back seat that it had been the taxi driver's fault. When we reached the club, he tried to get us all in for a reduced price on the strength of his friendship with the featured vocalist. When his request was spurned he sulked and refused to enter with the rest of us. He eventually joined us about an hour later, having finally succeeded in conning the management into letting him in for nothing and refunding our admittance fee. Later, bored with the show because they were not playing "his kind of music" and *Don* had not yet made his appearance, he began to insist in a loud stage whisper that we should all leave. This was the same boisterous, larger-than-life *Billy* whom we had often heard vehemently expressing his ideas on the community floor and who was listened to because of the force of his personality, which was matched only by his huge frame.

What impressed us most forcefully during the evening was that the behavior and personality of our friends had not really altered substantially except for the exclusion of delinquent behavior. This was evident from both their actions that evening and their descriptions of the lifestyles they had adopted. There was *Billy*, manifesting the same expansive friendliness, impulsive and impatient, still a "hustler" except that his hustles were now legal and to a large extent constructive. *Thad* was also essentially the same. While at the Center he had kept himself very busy with extra-curricular activities such as leather-craft and being editor of the prison newspaper. His lifestyle continued to revolve around an almost unbelievably heavy work load. He was holding down three jobs, the result of which was readily evident when he fell asleep at the table; his snores provided an obbligato to the musical entertainment. His total pre-occupation with work provided him with the escape from depression and from the demanding personal relationships which he sought.

Outside their regular jobs, the two of them were starting a newspaper for an underprivileged black community on the out-skirts of New York City, *Billy* as editor and *Thad* as photographer. They were very busy as the first edition was in the throes of production.

Don joined us after his performance and we found him least changed of all. He had always maintained at the Center that the only thing he wanted to do when he was released was to develop his musical talents. After his release it was touch and go, apparently, until the breaks began to come through in his musical career. His prognosis on leaving the Center was probably the least favorable and now he seemed the most comfortable, the most at peace with himself, the one who had the least need to impress us with his accomplishments. Perhaps this was because he had found a way of functioning in a career which imposes fewer demands of conformity and a stable life-style than the paths *Billy* and *Thad* chose to follow.

All three seemed to have gained a greater ability to cope with frustration and to let things fall into place on their own rather than panic at the first sign of a setback. They seemed to have left the Center with greater confidence in their own ability to resolve problems. This confidence saw them through many a difficult period. *Billy* and *Thad* had maintained contact with several other ex-inmates from the program and they seemed to spend time helping one another; but others we saw had maintained no similar contacts.

The next day we met with *George H.* and *Morry F.* Both of them told us they had had some shaky moments just after their release. They had felt extremely alienated and seriously contemplated criminal activities before they were able to settle down. Ultimately, they seemed to have made a positive adjustment and both were now working at steady jobs.

We managed to get hold of another alumnus, and he came down to the Congress with his common-law wife, expressing disappointment that we had not been able to reach him earlier. A very intelligent black man of thirty-five, he had spent fifteen years of his life in prison before finally being released; he had been a real leader at the Center and one of the most promising prospects for rehabilitation. This was how both staff and inmates had viewed him even though we knew full well the difficulties he had undergone, his long imprisonment and his lack of self-esteem which had always hindered him previously.

He arrived with his wife, both very smartly dressed, and repaired to a restaurant-bar for a drink. He seemed very elated at the fact that we had gotten in touch with him and with little prodding recounted what had happened in the year since his release from prison. He said that he left the Center uncertain about whether or not he would go straight (although he had always maintained to us there that he was going to get a legitimate job). The job to which he had been released did not pan out and for several months he apparently went back to his old ways, smalltime hustling on the streets of New York.

303

However, it came as a great surprise to him that his old ways no longer had the same satisfaction and he was astonished that the way of living he had been taught at Dannemora, going straight, had actually "taken." He said it was almost as if he had to try out his old ways before he could really believe that the new one would work. He gave up hustling after several months and got a job in one of the big department stores, a job much beneath his capacity. It was obvious that, like the other men that we saw, he was struggling with the same personality hang-ups as the others. His lack of self-confidence prevented him from going back to school and trying to get a higher level of education which would enable him to take a more interesting job. He complained of being bored most of the time, a recurrent problem, but he had been able to work out a satisfactory relationship with the woman who was his common-law wife and this provided him with some comfort.

Another evening we called *Jack C.* and told him where we were having supper, in case he wanted to see us. He came and spent about an hour telling us of his experiences since his release. Here was another person who, though working, was lonely, confused, seeking anonymous homosexual contacts on the streets of New York. Something he said brought home to us the extreme difficulties these men have in reintegrating into society. He was living in a hotel where you can rent a room on a long-term basis. He said he had chosen this because it made him feel "at home" again because the long corridors with doors opening onto them reminded him of prison.

In speaking with all of these men we came to realize just how fragile the early adjustment period is. We were well acquainted with prerelease anxiety which we had witnessed so often at Dannemora — insecurity, doubts and fears. We heard how these are intensified on actual release. Everyone stated that a stabilizing factor during this precarious period of adjustment was the contact and support of friends they had made at the Center. They would get in touch with men who had been released earlier and these were able to offer advice and encouragement during this crucial period.

The type of contact we witnessed and heard about among Dannemora alumni seemed uniformly positive. From no source did we ever hear of these men forming alliances for illegal or destructive behavior. They seemed to perceive the Center as the positive "core," almost as if they had made a tacit agreement that if any of them did go back to crime, he would not drag his former colleagues with him.

One of our long-term frustrations at the Center had been the lack of a related after-care program for released men, a deficiency related mainly to the distance between the Center and New York City. Our visit only confirmed our belief in the need for such a program. It also convinced us of the therapeutic value that ex-inmates can have on one another, particularly when they emerge from an institution whose orientation was consistently aimed at reintegration into society. We feel more strongly than ever that these men should be given more support in organizing their efforts to assist one another. However, this should be done in such a way as to leave initiative and strategy in their hands. The most beneficial method would be to provide persons who could help solve technical, administrative and legal problems which pose difficulties for ex-inmates.

What gave us great satisfaction was the fact that the concern for one another which we tried to instill in the men has seemingly become well entrenched. They had a feeling of "family" which, if anything, seemed stronger now than when they were at the Center. A second great satisfaction was the realization that we, as therapists, have developed strong, enduring relationships with many of them. All the difficulties, hassles and crises entailed in therapeutic community work seemed worth the trouble. Seeing our former inmates or friends in the tough environment in which they had to make it or break, was both rewarding and educational. It was like seeing the end of a process of which we had been a part at an earlier stage. Now we were seeing the most important part — the end result. It brought home to us the difficulties they encounter when they return to the street and have to cope with their old environment.

3. Epilogue

The realization that prison not only changes prisoners but —
possibly more deeply — changes their keepers was one of the
major ideas behind the Clinton project.

Twenty years have now gone by since the day in 1955
when I first entered the Canadian Penitentiary Service as a
psychiatrist, and the Clinton Project took place within these
twenty years. It is out of an emotional need that I want to
close this book with some personal notes. My colleagues at
the McGill Clinic in Forensic Psychiatry, particularly those
who were associated with the project, as well as the students
at the Clinic, will understand my need to use the same style
that we so often employed as a group in our conversations, in
case conferences or in seminars.

So central was it to our work that the question of freedom
and the deprivation of liberty was a recurring theme in these
informal conversations. At times we would get lost in
philosophical and social discussions on liberty and freedom and
how we arrived where we are in our civilization, but in fact
liberty was a down-to-earth reality for us, not a concept.
Sooner or later one of us would take the initiative of getting
back to the subject, and we would take the plunge from the
high level of philosophical discussion down to the perimeter of
the prison and to our basic daily problem. What does it mean
to be incarcerated, to be guarded, to be geographically contained,
and above all, what did it mean to us that, want it or not, we
were watchers of men as much as the guards with whom we
were working?

It seldom occurs to those who are always on the right side
of the gates, or who have never entered them to wonder what
it is like to live inside the walls, but for those who enter the

306

gates prison ceases to be an abstract. Twenty years is quite a length of time and it is tempting to count it day by day, like the hero in Solzhenitsyn's *A Day in the Life of Ivan Denisovitch*. In my case, mathematically it amounts to 365 multiplied by 20 and divided by two. The fact that I have to divide by two means a great deal, for I was not a prisoner, I was someone going in and out of the prison.

I was a psychiatrist in a penitentiary on a half-time basis, and the other half I was a professor at the McGill Clinic in Forensic Psychiatry engaged in research and clinical criminology. This explains why I did not have an emotional need to count every day of my life in prison, though it does not mean that the days I spent there did not have a profound impact on both my emotional and professional life. I quite understand that Denisovitch was counting his time day by day; for him freedom and liberty had social and political meanings and each day should have been a free day, not a prison day. My prison days were simply part of my work. It is sufficient for me to know that it represents the major part of my professional life. I never felt deprived of time, like Denisovitch, nor was I "doing time" or "making time," expressions that common-law prisoners use to designate the days, weeks or years that they spend in prison. People in prison have their own ways of counting or living their time. During these twenty years I have seen many offenders, in and out of prison, and I became used to their ways of counting time. Most of us don't really count time — we usually subtract it. We may not do so consciously, but when I say that I have worked twenty years in prisons I don't need to go far into my consciousness to realize that I have twenty years less of time at my disposal. We don't always think this way, but sometimes the reality is inescapable.

When listening to persistent prisoners, I could well understand the expressions "doing hard time," "doing rough time" and others to designate time according to the mood of the moment. They were clear enough. It is not unusual to hear one of them say, "I did two 2's, one 3, two 5's" and so on, somewhat like a cashier counting out dollar bills. I often had to point out that they were counting years of their life, the majority of their adult life in fact. No matter how it came about, through their ways of perceiving time or other emotional perceptions, I soon became aware that life in prison changes prisoners in many ways and that their way of counting time was only one manifestation of these deep changes.

My own most crucial emotional experience was the realization, early on, that prison was changing me. This did not come out of a deep analysis of my feelings but, as a clinician and researcher, it was in many ways reassuring. Like it or not, in deprivation of liberty staff and inmates are both condemned to be watchers and watched. Most are not aware of the extent of their involvement in these opposing roles. The realization that prison not only changes prisoners but — possibly more deeply — changes their keepers was one of the major ideas behind the Clinton project.

This project is now terminated but we are grateful to the New York State Department of Correctional Services for sharing many, though by no means all, of our views on persistent criminality, sufficiently at any rate to have established the project with the McGill Clinic in Forensic Psychiatry. During these six years the guardians and prisoners lived most of the time in the light of this consciousness, an inescapable reality that the watchers and the watched usually suppress in prisons. An umbrella only succeeds in keeping your head dry; at Clinton the watchers and the watched were wet from head to toe. This is the story we have told in this book.

The Clinton program as described in this book no longer exists. It would be presumptuous of us to believe that this is because of our departure. When we left it was not just a few professionals who took leave of Clinton, it was an independent strong symbolic force within a penitentiary system. We sincerely hoped that the program would carry on and that the Center would evolve into a teaching, treatment and research center as was first envisaged, but this did not happen. We feel that we achieved something during these six years that was worth reporting. This is not to say that the Clinton Project created a model prison. It did not. Nor did we have such an aim in mind.

Whenever individual human beings are deprived of liberty, independent voices should always speak loud enough to be heard. At Clinton we were the necessary voice in deprivation of liberty. It was quite an experience to have been allowed to be this voice in a small sector of the New York correctional system and we are pleased that during those six years the Commissioner's office showed no fear, even when we were oftentimes not singing what was considered to be the right hymn.

Four years have passed since we left, and we would like to think that perhaps Albany will one day remember that academics who had nothing in common with armchair criminologists made Dannemora their part-time habitat. We would also like to think that somebody in the system may feel that ours was a necessary voice that should be recalled.

A university presence in prison would be just another academic exercise if the professors and the pupils involved are not deeply concerned with the individual and social problems at the root of criminality. As independent workers in the system they will undoubtedly discover that it is easy to ask a prisoner to change if you believe that he alone is responsible for his criminality, but they should question not only the prisoner but the society from which he comes, and in the end question themselves. They must attempt to help a prisoner to seek solutions to his problems other than delinquency, and it would be even more important for them to query why society does not look for other solutions than prison for most of the criminals it incarcerates.

It is now currently held that prisons are a mirror of society, a view which we share. We look forward to the day when society will recognize its own reflection in these mirrors and accept that asking prisoners to change is unrealistic when society has nothing to offer to people who, though they be criminal, have just cause to be angry. Delinquency is no more a solution to their anger than imprisonment is.

The urgent call to close the prisons is certainly utopian, but belief in utopia has some advantages. Man can come near enough to his utopias. In the meantime, I believe that as long as prisons exist, independent voices must be heard, not outside the walls but inside.

B.M.C.

1. Statistical Tables

Table I General Data on Sample

INMATE - NUMBER	AGE (at 12/66)	EDUCATION	I.Q.	BEHAVIOR DISORDER (before age 16)	INSTITUTIONALIZATION (before age 16)	INCARCERATION INDEX (after 16, at 12/66)	MONTHS OUTSIDE (after age 16)	MONTHS WORKED		WORK INDEX		CIVIL JOBS (Number)	LONGEST TIME IN JOB (months)	TIME IN FORCES (months)	SKILLS (number)	PRISON SKILLS USED OUTSIDE
								Incl. Forces	Excl. Forces.	Incl. Forces	Excl. Forces					
114	28	jhs	107	9	yes	13	128	111	64	87	79	8	57	47	1	no
137	30	gs	110	-	-	36	115	98.5	56.5	86	48	12	12	42	3	-
134	30	jhs	113	9	-	43	101	87.5	32.5	86.5	71	9	16	55	1	no
128	34	gs	110	9	yes	88	28	-	25	-	89	15	3	-	2	no
118	27	gs	112	11	yes	66	41	-	38.5	-	90	4	33	-	3	no
147	27	gs	105	6	yes	69	44	-	24.5	-	56	9	9	-	2	no
143	24	hs	102	5	-	21	78.5	-	53	-	66	3	50	-	-	-
135	33	jhs	102	10	. -	48	110	-	27.5	-	25	4	*	-	2	yes
112	31	jhs	109	6	yes	64	78.5	-	48	-	60	8	25	-	4	no
126	26	jhs	121	14	yes	34	85.5	-	58.5	-	68.5	7	29	-	1	yes
113	32	jhs	105	3	yes	69	63	36	24	57	38	9	5	12	1	no
141	27	jhs	99	8	yes	53	62	44	34	71	55	14	6	10	1	no
146	25	gs	109	15	-	35	73	-	19	-	26	10*	4	-	1	no
104	31	gs	117	9	yes	82	32	-	9.5	-	27	5	4	-	2	yes
124	26	jhs	117	10	-	55	59	-	59	-	100	1	*	-	1	no
132	34	gs	91	12	yes	65	80	-	*	-	90	32	36	-	3	no
144	27	gs	108	9	-	52	66.5	-	46	-	69	15	9	-	3	yes
130	26	gs	110	10	yes	76	30	-	0.75	-	2.5	1	0.75	-	2	no
122	29	gs	114	3	yes	58	68	-	2.5	-	3.7	4	6	-	2	no
111	29	jhs	116	12	-	77	36	-	1.5	-	4	2	1	-	2	no
145	26	gs	106	10	yes	67	39	-	5	-	12	3	2	-	1	no
138	32	gs	105	6	yes	51	108	-	26	-	24	9	6	-	1	yes
150	29	gs	117	15	-	63	68.5	23.5	15.5	33	23	9	6	8	-	-
151	29	jhs	113	12	-	36	171.5	60	45	36	36	14	14	15	1	no
105	35	jhs	102	11	yes	42	137.5	-	49	-	36	12	12	-	1	yes
139	24	jhs	-	16	yes	20	109.5	-	36	-	39	3	24	-	1	no
131	38	gs	98	7	yes	47	140.5	56	35	40	34	8	6	21	2	no
140	26	gs	101	-	-	29	85	-	36.5	-	42	15	6	-	1	no
117	27	jhs	122	12	-	58	57	24	17	42	34	5	12	7	-	-
121	31	gs	106	7	yes	78	40.5	-	17	-	42	5	6	-	2	yes
119	32	jhs	97	12	-	41	116.5	-	53	-	45	6	32	-	1	no
106	28	gs	96	14	-	72	43	-	20	-	46	6	6	-	4	no
108	24	gs	101	9	yes	64	37	-	19	-	51	7	4	-	2	no
133	27	jhs	100	8	yes	63	51	29	26	57	54	9	2	3	2	no
110	35	jhs	110	10	yes	31	163	110	83	63	61	11	13	27	2	no
129	30	gs	115	11	-	40	103	72	64	70	67	36	7	8	1	no
125	25	hs	91	12	-	67	37	-	28.5	-	77.5	10	8	-	2	no
148	29	jhs	90	7	yes	60	62.5	-	32	-	51	8	9	-	2	yes
149	33	jhs	117	-	-	81	71	67	66	94	93	18	10	1	1	no
115	25	gs	126	9	yes	78	23.5	-	20	-	85.5	8	6	-	-	-
116	30	jhs	114	11	yes	61	69	45.5	43.5	66	63	11	9	2	1	no
153	35	jhs	90	16	-	36*	151	-	151	-	100*	2	84	-	3	no
154	30	jhs	102	6	-	82	31	-	12.5	-	42	8	3	-	5	no
159	38	jhs	112	14	-	12.5	235.5	235.5	205.5	100	85.5	*	*	30	-	-
158	25	jhs	101	9	-	47	61	-	60	-	98.5	7	1.25	-	1	yes
157	34	jhs	117	10	yes	78.5	47	-	38	-	81	*	6	-	2	yes
109	26	jhs	117	13	-	32	87	-	46.75	-	54.5	9	24	-	2	yes
162	47	gs	90	5	yes	21	265	-	60*	-	23	9*	18	-	6	yes
161	24	jhs	102	11	-	24	65	35	12	54	18.5	3	6	23	1	no
160	33	jhs	104	-	-	32	129	127	79	98.5	62	7	24	48	5	no

* Unable to assess

APPENDICES

Table 2.		Age of Sample at December 1966			
20-24 yrs	25-29 yrs.	30-34 yrs.	35-40 yrs.	40-plus	Total
4	23	17	5	1	50

Table 3.	Level of Education		
Grammar School	Junior High School	High School	Total
21	27	2	50

Table 4.	Behavior Disorder		
Before age 11	12-16 years	17 years plus	Total
32	13	5	50

Table 5.	Institutionalization Before Age 16	
Yes	No	Total
26	24	50

Table 6.		Coefficient of Incarceration			
0-25 o/o	26-40 o/o	41-60 o/o	61-80 o/o	81-100 o/o	Total
6	10	13	17	4	50

Table 7.		Coefficient of Work			
0-25 o/o	26-40 o/o	41-60 o/o	61-80 o/o	81-100 o/o	Total
9	8	13	12	8	50

Table 8		Number of Civilian Jobs				
1-4	5-9	10-14	15-19	25 plus	Not Known	Total
12	22	8	4	2	2	50

Table 9			Longest Time on Job (months)					
-1	1-4	5-9	10-14	15-19	20-24	25 plus	Not Known	Total
1	9	19	6	1	1	7	6	50

Table 10	Time in Armed Forces (months)			
Nil	1-12	13-24	24 plus	Total
33	8	3	6	50

Table 11	Prison Skills Used Outside		
Yes	No	Not Known	Total
12	32	6	50

314

Table 12   Workshop Attendance - September, October, November 1967

No.	Time at Center in months (as at 1.9.67)	Half Days Absent						Sick Call			Late		
		Without Excuse			With Excuse								
		Sept.	Oct.	Nov.	Sept.	Oct.	Nov.	Sept.	Oct.	Nov.	Sept.	Oct.	Nov.
101	10	2	1	-	2	1	-	4	3	3	1	-	1
102	11	10	2	4	10	2	4	8	4	7	1	3	1
104	11	7	1	1	7	1	-	3	9	2	-	3	2
105	11	2	-	-	2	-	-	-	-	-	-	-	-
106	11	2	1	-	2	-	-	-	-	1	-	-	-
107	11	5	13	6	4	11	4	-	9	13	1	1	7
108	11	5	3	1	5	3	1	4	4	-	1	2	-
109	11	2	1	1	2	-	-	2	4	4	3	1	-
110	11	8	3	2	8	3	2	3	2	2	-	1	-
111	11	2	8	3	2	8	-	-	-	4	-	-	-
112	11	4	7	-	4	7	-	-	-	1	-	-	-
113	11	3	-	-	3	-	-	2	2	4	-	-	2
115	11	3	2	-	3	2	-	1	4	-	-	3	?
116	11	2	1	-	2	1	-	1	-	-	-	-	-
117	11	5	-	-	5	-	-	1	1	2	-	1	-
121	10	3	-	-	3	-	-	-	-	-	-	-	1
125	10	3	-	-	3	-	-	9	10	1	1	1	1
126	Par.24 Oct. 10	1	-	-	1	-	-	2	-	-	2	-	-
127	10	5	1	-	3	1	-	-	-	-	-	-	-
128	10	3	1	-	3	1	-	-	1	-	-	-	-
129	10	16	8	-	6	4	-	2	3	-	-	1	-
132	10	13	4	2	12	-	-	-	2	3	-	2	-
133	10	6	3	4	4	3	2	2	5	3	1	5	-
134	10	5	4	2	5	4	2	-	2	-	-	-	-
137	10	3	2	-	3	2	-	-	-	-	-	-	-
138	10	14	14	25	11	-	16	4	2	7	2	-	-
139	10	2	-	-	2	-	-	-	-	1	-	1	-
141	10	5	4	18	5	4	-	4	4	4	-	1	1
143	10	2	2	16	2	2	-	5	6	-	2	-	-
145	10	5	2	-	5	1	-	-	-	-	1	1	-
146	10	8	1	3	7	1	-	1	2	3	-	1	1
147	10	4	-	-	4	-	-	-	-	-	5	11	1
148	9	12	-	-	12	-	-	6	6	2	1	5	2
149	9	3	1	-	3	1	-	-	-	3	-	-	-
151	Par.16 Oct. 9	12	-	-	12	-	-	8	-	-	1	-	-
152	7	12	7	11	10	4	2	4	2	2	1	-	-
153	6	11	3	9	11	3	2	10	4	5	-	-	-
154	6	5	-	4	5	-	4	1	-	3	-	-	-
155	3	4	1	2	4	1	-	1	-	2	-	-	-
156	2	2	8	10	2	3	-	3	2	2	-	2	1
157	2	-	2	2	-	2	2	1	-	-	-	-	-
158	1	-	-	-	-	-	-	-	-	-	-	-	-
159	2	2	2	2	2	2	-	2	3	1	-	-	-
160	Arr.30 Aug. -	3	1	6	3	1	-	-	-	1	1	-	-
161	Arr.15 Sept. -	2	1	-	2	-	-	1	3	7	-	6	6
162	Arr.15 Sept. -	4	4	3	4	4	2	-	-	3	-	-	-
183	Arr.17 Oct. -	-	9	-	-	9	-	-	-	-	-	1	-
184	Arr. 17 Oct. -	-	8	-	-	8	-	-	-	-	-	-	-
185	Arr. 17 Oct. -	-	9	-	-	9	-	-	-	3	-	-	-
186	Arr. 24 Oct. -	-	2	4	-	2	-	-	-	2	-	-	-
188	Arr. 31 Oct. -	-	-	-	-	-	-	-	-	-	-	-	1
190	Arr. 31 Oct. -	-	-	2	-	-	-	-	-	1	-	-	-
192	Arr. 2 Nov. -	-	-	-	-	-	-	-	-	1	-	-	5

Table 13   Workshop Attendance - Compilation of 10 Best and 10 Worst. (September - November 1967)

Inst. No.	Half-days Absent	Half-days Excused	Sick Call	Late
		10 Best		
101	3	3	10	2
105	2	2	-	-
106	3	2	1	-
109	4	2	10	4
113	3	3	8	2
116	1	3	1	-
121	3	3	-	1
128	4	4	1	-
139	2	2	1	1
147	4	4	-	17
TOTALS	29	28	32	27
		10 Worst		
102	16	16	19	5
107	24	19	22	9
129	24	10	5	1
132	19	12	5	2
138	53	27	13	2
141	27	9	12	2
143	20	4	11	2
146	12	8	6	2
152	30	16	8	1
153	23	16	19	-
TOTALS	248	137	120	26

2. The Professional Staff

Bruno M. Cormier, M.D.

Associate Professor,
Department of Psychiatry,
McGill University.

Director,
McGill Clinic in Forensic
Psychiatry.

Colin C.J. Angliker, M.D.

Director,
Miriam Kennedy Child and
Family Clinic.

Formerly: Assistant Director,
McGill Clinic in Forensic
Psychiatry.

Paul Boulanger, M.S.W.

Probation Officer,
Quebec Probation Service.

Formerly: Research Associate,
McGill Clinic in Forensic
Psychiatry.

Ingrid Cooper, M.S.W.

Lecturer,
School of Social Work,
McGill University.

Research Associate,
McGill Clinic in Forensic
Psychiatry.

317

Abraham Ferstman, M.S.W.

Private practice — marriage counselling.

Formerly: Research Associate, McGill Clinic in Forensic Psychiatry.

Harold Finkler, M.Sc.

Department of Indian and Northern Affairs

Formerly: Field placement student from Ecole de Criminologie, University of Montreal, McGill Clinic in Forensic Psychiatry.

John T. Goldthwait

Professor of Philosophy and Coordinator of College Evening Program. State University of New York College of Arts and Science, Plattsburgh, N.Y.

Lydia Keitner, M.S.W.

Director, Forensic Psychiatry Service, Erie County Department of Mental Health, Buffalo, N.Y.

Formerly: Research Associate, McGill Clinic in Forensic Psychiatry.

Miriam Kennedy, P.S.W.

Deceased.

Research Associate, McGill Clinic in Forensic Psychiatry.

Susan M. (Waters) McCondichie

Lecturer, Birmingham Polytechnic, England.

Formerly: Research Associate, McGill Clinic in Forensic Psychiatry.

Betty Malamud, M.S.W.

Group Social Worker,
Regional Psychiatric Centre,
Canadian Penitentiary Service.

Formerly: Research Associate,
McGill Clinic in Forensic
Psychiatry.

Guyon Mersereau, M.D.

Assistant Clinical Professor,
State University of Buffalo.

Staff Psychiatrist,
Hamilton Psychiatric Hospital,
Forensic Services.

Lecturer,
McMaster University.

Psychiatrist,
Niagara Regional Detention Centre,
Correctional Services of Ontario.

Formerly: Director,
Forensic Psychiatry Service,
Erie County Department of
Mental Health, Buffalo, N.Y.

Research Associate,
McGill Clinic in Forensic
Psychiatry.

Paul J. Williams, M.A.
(Psychology)

Deputy Director,
Correctional Development Centre,
Canadian Penitentiary Service.

Formerly: Psychologist and Unit
Coordinator,
Diagnostic and Treatment Center,
Clinton Prison, New York Department of Corrections.

Research Associate,
McGill Clinic in Forensic
Psychiatry.

Joshua Zambrowsky, LL.B.,
M.A.

Freelance Writer

Formerly: Research associate,
McGill Clinic in Forensic
Psychiatry.

3. Source Material

"Deprivation of Liberty — Institutional Treatment and the
   Persistent Offender."
   Bruno M. Cormier, unpublished.

"The Clinton Project — Theoretical Basis."
   Bruno M. Cormier, unpublished.

"An outline of the Criteria for the Selection of Inmates."
   Bruno M. Cormier, unpublished.

"Therapeutic Community in a Prison Setting."
   Bruno M. Cormier.   Proceedings of a series sponsored
   jointly by the Allan Memorial Institute and the McGill
   School of Social Work, Montreal, March 1968.
   International Annals of Criminology. 1970, Vol. 9,
   No. 2, 419-441.

"The Training of Personnel in a Therapeutic Community."
   Abraham Ferstman, Paul J. Williams. Proceedings of the
   Fifth Research Conference on Delinquency and
   Criminology, Montreal, 1967.

"The Watcher and the Watched."
   Bruno M. Cormier, Paul J. Williams. *Canadian Psychiatric
   Association Journal,* Vol. 16, No. 1, February 1971.

"Officer-Inmate Interaction in a Prison Therapeutic Community."
   J. Zambrowsky, C.C.J. Angliker, B.M. Cormier, unpublished.

"Women as Therapists in a Prison Therapeutic Community."
Colin C.J. Angliker. Paper presented at the Annual Meeting
of the Canadian Psychiatric Association, Halifax, June 1971.

"The Therapeutic Community — Whom are we Treating? "
Colin C.J. Angliker, *Laval Médical*, Vol. 42, January 1971.
International Annals of Criminology, Vol. 9, No. 2, 1970.

"Work Program in a Therapeutic Community" Part I
Miriam Kennedy, Bruno M. Cormier. Proceedings of the
Fifth Research Conference on Delinquency and
Criminology, Montreal, 1967.

"Work Program in a Therapeutic Community"Part II
"Comparison of Work Adaptation in Prison and Freedom."
Bruno M. Cormier, Susan M. Waters, unpublished.

"Work Program in a Therapeutic Community" Part III
"Attitudes and Patterns."
Bruno M. Cormier, Susan M. Waters, unpublished.

"Acting out in a Therapeutic Community."
J. Zambrowsky, unpublished.

Race Relations, Part I.
"Individual and Group Interaction."
Bruno M. Cormier, Ingrid Cooper, Harold Finkler, unpublished.

Race Relations, Part II.
"Staff Discussion."
Bruno M. Cormier, J. Zambrowsky, unpublished.

"Attica 1971 — A Ripple Effect."
Colin C.J. Angliker, unpublished.

"A University Goes to Prison."
John T. Goldthwait, unpublished.

"Clinical Assessment of Individual Cases."
Bruno M. Cormier, Colin C.J. Angliker, unpublished.

"An Evaluation and Follow-up Study on the First Fifty Cases."
C.C.J. Angliker, B.M. Cormier, P. Boulanger, L. Keitner,
G. Mersereau, B. Malamud, unpublished.

"Women in a Man's World."
Bruno M. Cormier, Lydia Keitner, Ingrid Cooper, Betty
Malamud, unpublished.

Bibliography

1.   ANGLIKER, Colin C.J. "Object Relations in Penal
      Institutions."   Paper presented at the Vth World
      Congress of Psychiatry, Mexico, 1971. (Unpublished)

2.   *Attica. The Official Report of the New York State
      Special Commission on Attica.*
            New York: A Bantam Book, 1972.

3.   BARNES, Harry Elmer and Negley K. Teeters.
            *New Horizons in Criminology: The American Crime
            Problem.* New York: Prentice-Hall, 1944.

4.   BETTELHEIM, Bruno. *Love is Not Enough.*
            Glencoe: The Free Press, 1950.

5.   BETTELHEIM, Bruno. *Truants from Life.*
            Glencoe: The Free Press, 1955.

6.   BUFFARD, Simonne. *Le Froid Pénitentiaire.*
            Paris: Editions du Seuil, 1973.

7.   CAUDILL, W. *The Psychiatric Hospital as a Small
      Society.* Cambridge, Mass.:   Harvard University
      Press, 1958.

8.   CLEMMER, Donald. *The Prison Community.*
            New York: Rinehart and Company, 1958.

324

9.   CORMIER, Bruno M. "A Criminological Classification of Criminal Processes." Chapter in *Crime, Law and Corrections* (Editor Ralph J. Slovenko). Springfield: Charles C. Thomas, 1966, pp. 165-190.

10.   CORMIER, Bruno M. "Depression and Persistent Criminality." *Canadian Psychiatric Association Journal*, Special Supplement, Vol. 2, 1966. pp. S.208-220.

11.   CORMIER, Bruno M. "The Psychological Effects of the Deprivation of Liberty on the Offender." *Proceedings of the Canadian Congress of Corrections*, Montreal, 1957, pp. 137-149.

12.   CORMIER, B.M., R. Boyer, A.T. Galardo, M. Kennedy, A. Obert, J.M. Sangowicz, A.L. Thiffault, R.A. Washbrook. "The Persistent Offender and his Sentences — A problem for Law and Psychiatry." *Proceedings of the Fourth Research Conference on Delinquency and Criminology.* Montreal, November 1964, pp. 462-480.

13.   CORMIER, B.M., A.T. Galardo, J.M. Sangowicz, M. Kennedy, R.A. Washbrook, P.J. Williams. "Episodic Recidivism." *Proceedings of the Fourth Research Conference on Delinquency and Criminology*, Montreal, November 1964, pp. 171-193.

14.   CORMIER, Bruno M., Lydia Keitner, Miriam Kennedy. "The Persistent Offender and His Family." *Proceedings of the Fifth Research Conference on Delinquency and Criminology.* Montreal, 1967. pp. 21-37. Also: *McGill Law Journal*, Vol. 13, No. 4, 1967.

15.   CORMIER, B.M., M. Kennedy, J.M. Sangowicz, M. Trottier. "Presentation of a Basic Classification for Clinical Work and Research in Criminology." *Proceedings of the Canadian Congress of Corrections*, Montreal, 1957, pp. 21-34.

16. CORMIER, B.M., M. Kennedy, J.M. Sangowicz, M. Trottier. "The Natural History of Criminality and Some Tentative Hypotheses on Its Abatement." *Proceedings of the Canadian Congress of Corrections*, Montreal, 1957, pp. 35-49.

17. CORMIER, B.M., M. Kennedy, J.M. Sangowicz, M. Trottier. "The Latecomer to Crime." *Canadian Journal of Corrections*, Vol. 3, No. 1. January 1961, pp. 2-17.

18. CORMIER, B.M., M. Kennedy, J.M. Sangowicz, R. Boyer, A.L. Thiffault, A. Obert. "Criminal Process and Emotional Growth." *International Psychiatry Clinics*, (Editor D. Ewen Cameron). Boston: Little, Brown & Co., Vol. 2, No. 1.

19. CORMIER, B.M., M. Kennedy, J.M. Sendbuehler. "Cell Breakage and Gate Fever: A Study of Two Syndromes Found in the Deprivation of Liberty." *British Journal of Criminology*, July 1967, pp. 317-324.

20. CORMIER, B.M., R.A. Washbrook, M. Kennedy, A. Obert. "A Study of Fifty Young Penitentiary Delinquents from Age 15 to 25." *Proceedings of the Fourth Research Conference on Delinquency and Criminology*. Montreal, November 1964, pp. 77-113.

21. CORMIER, Bruno M. and Paul J. Williams. "La Privation excessive de la Liberté." *Canadian Psychiatric Association Journal*, Vol. ll, No. 6, December 1966, pp. 470-484.

22. CUMMING, John and Elaine Cumming. *Ego and Milieu.* New York: Atherton Press, 1962.

23. DEUTSCH, Albert. *The Mentally Ill in America.* New York: Doubleday, Doran and Company, 1937.

24. EYSENCK, H.J. "The Effects of Psychotherapy."
    International Journal of Psychiatry, Vol. 1,
    No. 1, January 1965, pp. 99-142.

25. Discussion on Eysenck's article, "The Effects of Psycho-
    therapy." *International Journal of Psychiatry*,
    Vol. l, No. 1, pp. 144-178 and Vol. 1, No. 2,
    April 1965, pp. 317-328.

26. EYSENCK, H.J. Reply to Discussion on article,
    "The Effects of Psychotherapy," *op. cit.*,
    International Journal of Psychiatry, Vol. 1,
    No. 2, April 1965, pp. 328-335.

27. FISHMAN, J. *Sex in Prison*. New York: Padell, 1934.
    (Reissued in 1951).

28. GLASER, Daniel. *The Effectiveness of a Prison and
    Parole System*. New York: The Bobbs-Merrill
    Company, Inc., 1969.

29. GOFFMAN, Erving. *Asylums*. Garden City:
    Doubleday, 1961.

30. HOPPER, Columbus B. *Sex in Prison: The Mississippi
    Experiment with Conjugal Visiting*. Baton Rouge:
    Louisiana State University Press, 1969.

31. HUNT, R.C., and E.D. Wiley: "Operation Baxstrom
    After One Year." *American Journal of
    Psychiatry*, Vol. 124, 1968, pp. 974-978.

32. IBRAHIM, Azmy Ishak. "Deviant Sexual Behavior in
    Men's Prisons." National Council on Crime and
    Delinquency: *Crime and Delinquency*, Vol. 20,
    No. 1, January 1974, pp. 38-44.

33. JACOBSEN, Edith. "Observations on the Psychological
    Effect of Imprisonment on Female Prisoners."
    Searchlights on Delinquency. (Editor K.R. Eissler).
    New York: International Universities Press, Inc.,
    1949. pp. 341-368

327

34.   JONES, Maxwell. *The Therapeutic Community.*
       New York: Basic Books, Inc., 1953.

35.   JONES, Maxwell. *Social Psychiatry in Practice. The
       Idea of the Therapeutic Community.*
       Harmondsworth: Penguin Books, 1968.

36.   JONES, Maxwell. *Beyond the Therapeutic Community.
       Social Learning and Social Psychiatry.* New Haven:
       Yale University Press, 1968.

37.   LANE, W.D. "Democracy of Law Breakers." *New
       Republic*, Vol. 18, 8 March 1919, p. 173.
       (Quoted in Sutherland, *Principles of Crime.*)

38.   LAPOINTE, Guy. "The Re-education of Disturbed
       Adolescents." *The Therapeutic Community.*
       Papers with Discussion. Proceedings of a Series
       jointly sponsored by the Allan Memorial Institute
       and the McGill University School of Social Work,
       presented in Montreal March-April 1968, pp. 67-76.

39.   LEWIS, Orlando F. *The Development of American
       Prisons and Prison Customs, 1776-1845.* (With
       special reference to early institutions in the State
       of New York). Montclair, N.J.: Patterson Smith,
       1967.

40.   LEWIS, W. David. *From Newgate to Dannemora - The
       Rise of the Penitentiary in New York, 1796-1848.*
       Ithaca, N.Y.: Cornell University Press, 1965.

41.   McELWEE, Thomas B. *A Concise History of the
       Eastern Penitentiary of Pennsylvania, 1835.*
       (Known as McElwee's Report). Cited in Barnes
       and Teeter, *op. cit.*, p. 515.

42.   MIKES, George (ed.) *Prison* (A Symposium).
       London: Routledge and Kegan Paul, 1963.

43.   NOVICK, Louis J. "Therapeutic Community Program
       in a Chronic Hospital for the Aged." *The Thera-*

peutic Community. Papers with Discussion.
Proceedings of a Series jointly sponsored by the
Allan Memorial Institute and the McGill
University School of Social Work, Montreal, 1968,
pp. 67-76.

44. OSBORNE, Thomas Mott. *Society and Prisons.*
New Haven: Yale University Press, 1916.

45. RAPOPORT, Robert N. *Community as Doctor. New
Perspectives on a Therapeutic Community.*
London: Tavistock Publications, 1960.

46. REDL, Fritz and David Wineman. *The Aggressive
Child.* Glencoe: The Free Press, 1957.

47. *Report of the Royal Commission to Investigate the
Penal System of Canada.* Ottawa, H.M.S.O., 1938.
(Known as the Archambault Report).

48. *Report on Sexual Assaults in the Philadelphia Prison
System and Sheriff's Vans.* Philadelphia: Philadelphia
District Attorney's Office and Police Department,
1968.

49. ROBERTS, Ron E. *The New Communes.* Englewood
Cliffs, N.J.: Prentice-Hall Inc., A Spectrum Book,
1971, p. 111.

50. SIMONS, Siebert P. and Bruno M. Cormier.
"Delinquent Acting Out and Ego Structure."
Laval Médical, vol. 40, no 9, novembre, 1969,
pp. 933-935.

51. STANTON, A.H. and M.S. Schwartz. *The Mental
Hospital.* New York: Basic Books, Inc., 1954.

52. STEADMAN, Henry J. "Follow-up on Baxstrom Patients
returned to Hospitals for the Criminally Insane."
American Journal of Psychiatry, Vol. 130, No. 3,
March 1973, pp.317-319.

329

53.   STEADMAN, Henry J. and A. Halfon. "The Baxstrom
        Patients: Backgrounds and Outcomes."
        Seminars in Psychiatry, 3: 387-387, 1971.

54.   STEADMAN, Henry J. and G. Keveles. "The Community
        Adjustment and Criminal Activity of the Baxstrom
        Patients: 1966-1970." *American Journal of
        Psychiatry*, Vol. 129, No. 3, September 1972,
        pp. 304-310.

55.   STURUP, Georg K. *Treating the "Untreatable" Chronic
        Criminals.* (Herstedvester). Isaac Rey Lectures.
        Baltimore: Johns Hopkins University Press, 1968.

56.   SUTHERLAND, Edwin H. *Principles of Criminology.*
        Chicago: J. B. Lippincott Company, 1934.

57.   SYKES, Gresham M. *The Society of Captives: A Study
        of a Maximum Security Prison.* Princeton, N.J.:
        Princeton University Press, 1958.

58.   VAIL, David J. *Dehumanization and the Institutional
        Career.* Springfield: Charles C. Thomas, 1966.

59.   VEDDER, Clyde B. and Patricia G. King. *Problems of
        Homosexuality in Corrections.* Springfield:
        Charles C. Thomas, 1967.